GEORGES BALANDIER was born in 1920. A trained ethnologist, he has traveled widely in Africa, and is the founder of the Sorbonne's African Studies Center, where he was the guiding spirit of the Institut d'Etudes Politiques' inquiry into the emergent African nations which was published under the title THE THIRD WORLD. He is also the author of DAILY LIFE IN THE KINGDOM OF THE KONGO, POLITICAL ANTHROPOLOGY, and THE SOCIOLOGY OF BLACK AFRICA.

AMBIGUOUS AFRICA

CULTURES IN COLLISION

GEORGES BALANDIER

Translated from the French by
HELEN WEAVER

DISCUS BOOKS / PUBLISHED BY AVON

AVON BOOKS
A division of
The Hearst Corporation
959 Eighth Avenue
New York, New York 10019

ISBN: 0-380-00560-3
First Discus Printing, January, 1976

Printed in the U.S.A.

Contents

Acknowledgments

▼▼▼▼▼▼▼▼▼▼▼▼▼▼▼▼▼▼▼▼▼▼▼▼▼▼▼▼▼▼▼▼▼▼▼▼

Thanks are due to the following for permission to reproduce illustrations:

Figures 10 and 42 are reproduced from *L'Homme noir d'Afrique* by B. Holas, Ifan Initiations Collections, Dakar; figures 12, 13, 24, 25, 26, 38, 45 from *Arts de l'Afrique Noire* by Marcel Griaule, pub. du Chêne; figures 19 and 20 from *Mission dans l'Est libérien* by B. Holas and P. Dekeyser, Ifan Reports, Dakar; figures 27, 28 and 30 from *Les Masques Kono* by B. Holas, pub. P. Geuthner. Figure 18 is reproduced from the Guinea Archives and figure 43 from the Libreville Archives. Figure 46 is taken from a sketch by R. Lecoq.

Introduction

▼▼▼

BEYOND an Africa whose ambiguity is apparent, a new Africa is being born. Technical innovations, social and cultural upheavals, political crises and violent controversies are so many ordeals preparing the way for this renaissance. In the face of such decisive changes, landmarks indicating the general direction must be found. A preliminary question therefore arises: how does African thought reflect this evolution? This consideration constitutes the first stage of any thoroughgoing analysis.

To consider fully an area as vast as African thought requires as much modesty as presumption. This is all the more true since African thought lacks neither variety nor fluidity. On the contrary, it expresses the diversity of Negro civilizations; it attests to a history as rich in event and enterprise as it is in affliction; it seeks, according to Léopold Sédar Senghor, to help in the construction of a "universal civilization."

To analyze and interpret this highly complex system of thought one must have presumption. Without this quality, it would be impossible to find synthetic formulas which would explain common characteristics without denying the diversity which decrees that the Bantu thought of Central Africa differs, for example, from the Bambara thought of Mali. But this work of elucidation also requires modesty. If African thought demands a complex initiation on the part of the Africans who wish to study it thoroughly, it demands even more of the "foreigner" who dares to discover it: a sympathy which entails the renunciation of all intellectual pride.

In spite of the risks involved, exploration of this field must be conducted from the outside, if there is to be any real communication between African civilizations and "foreign" civilizations. Such exploration is divided into three phases: definition of the traditional heritage, evaluation of foreign influences and of their effects, and location of changes in progress. Three stages in the course of a troubled history, leading up to a future largely determined by the African nations and the various world powers.

When one mentions the element of heritage in connection with African thought, one alludes automatically to the role of tradition. What we find is not so much a body of thought progressing by way of contradiction and controversy as one preserved and transmitted on behalf of the entire community. It bears the weight of authority, of a collective achievement necessary to the protection of all. Ethnologists and sociologists who have specialized in Africa are familiar with the phenomenon: in the last analysis everything is attributed to the will of God or the ancestors. As a consequence such a view is deeply concerned with the sacred and any criticism of its fundamental principles is necessarily regarded as a sacrilege. Its tenets are called into doubt only in very exceptional circumstances: when the old state is emerging under a hero regarded as conqueror, founder and civilizer, as with the "kingships" of East and Central Africa, or when the very foundations of the sacred are shaken, as with the successive stages of Islamization which caused a genuine transformation of the culture and of the society.

A second characteristic is immediately apparent: traditional African thought makes use of symbolic rather than discursive means of expression. Negro civilizations are often richer in symbols than in material productions. They seem to have been so arranged that the order of society, the order of thought and the order of the universe are in close correlation. The studies of certain French Africanists, especially those of Marcel Griaule, have demonstrated this aspect of African society in connection with the Dogon and Bambara of Mali. Among these people every object and every social event has a symbolic as well as a utilitarian function: it serves and signifies at the same time. Griaule's demonstration was based on fabrics, especially those blankets whose weaving and decoration constitute a "book," a system of signs which anyone in possession of the key knows how to interpret. Many material creations—houses and granaries, household objects, chairs—receive the impress of symbolic thought, so that the latter is called to mind at all times and in all places. Traditional African societies have not recorded their knowledge in libraries and on monuments; they have registered it in the objects which form the material framework of existence. Griaule has compiled a painstaking inventory of the figures, signs and characters which provide this transcription; his list is extraordinarily full, containing several thousand elements even in the case of the modest civilization of the Dogon.

The role accorded to the symbol explains certain fundamental characteristics of African thought, which seems to be as dramatic as it is contemplative. In various collective manifestations—funerals, royal rituals, initiations—in which the entire community is involved, it finds symbolic expression in all its richness. To give only one illustration among many, John Beattie, an ethnologist who studied the Nyoro of East Africa, was able to reconstruct their political theory by means of a thorough study of the rituals and procedures pertaining to kingship. Attitudes and objects, just as much as words—that is, political vocabulary—are the medium of this theory. But a second consequence should not be overlooked: in traditional Africa symbolic action is linked with utilitarian action; the rite is still associated with the tool. This is true whether we are speaking of agricultural techniques and the practices pertaining to fertility, or preindustrial techniques like the art of the forge or the quarrying of gold which assign an important role to ritual. This association of the symbolic and the utilitarian, which in a sense keeps the tool subordinate, determines the basic orientation of traditional African civilizations. These are civilizations of consent rather than civilizations of mastery and power. They are more concerned with respecting the profound meaning assigned to the world than with attempting to possess it.

These general ideas are inadequate, for they fail to suggest the modalities of African thought. Even in a simplified analysis, however, it is possible to differentiate the principal modes of this thought by the order of experience to which it is applied. On the highest level there is the order of the *invisible*, which is the subject of both mythical and mystical thought. Mythical thought is the source of all so-called "profound" understanding; an illustration would be the fine Peul initiatory text published by Amadou Hampaté Ba under the esoteric title *Koumen*. Mythical thought also serves as an ideological instrument for sanctifying and justifying the status quo. Mystical thought, on the other hand, is open to personal revelation. It may innovate and often gives rise to radical changes, especially in the case of mystics appearing in the wake of Islam or "religions" born of opposition to Christianity. In second place should be ranked the order of *transmitted knowledge*. To this category belong the general instructions communicated during initiations and above all the ideas disseminated by oral literature and the arts. The latter constitute an education because they are a collective product, because in a sense they are made by the community and for the community. In regions like Bamileke country in Cameroon where the plastic arts flourish, these products form a veritable encyclopedia of basic information. Last but not least we must mention the order of *action*. This order governs utilitarian thought, including technology, military art, pharmacology and medicine. It also orients political thought, which reflects all the richness of the political experiences Negro peoples have known in the course of their long history.

The undeniable and still vital influence of the past threatens to conceal more modern aspects. African thought was not permitted to discover itself until the last decades of the nineteenth century. It was subject to external influences well before the mass invasion of the Europeans. Its ties with the Mediterranean world are very ancient. Islam left its mark on the African Middle Ages—as one need only remember Timbuctu, active center of intellectual life, to realize. Relations established with the Europeans from the fifteenth century affected the social and cultural order as well as the political equilibrium, as was the case in the old Kingdom of the Congo. But it is the influence of the colonial nations in the last hundred years that has been most disturbing, and for reasons which are often fundamental.

For civilizations and cultures in which the sacred plays an important role, any modification of the relation to the sacred is necessarily a disruptive factor. The introduction of Christianity produced a rupture with African religious tradition; it imposed a unitary vision which contradicted the old religious pluralism; it substituted a "dramatic" history for an often repetitive history in which each generation tried to abide by the will of the ancestors.

Changes which have taken place in the manipulation of knowledge are equally important. Generally speaking it may be said that European civilization has expressed itself as a civilization of the *book*. The old chronicles all reveal the prestige attached to written knowledge, which indeed is regarded as the chief cause of European material power. The current "hunger for education" is only an extension of this tendency. The ever-increasing role accorded to the knowledge transmitted by schools and libraries has created and is still creating an authentic intellectual revolution. This is a knowledge which is no longer imposed by tradition, but by reason; a knowledge which gives rise to criticism and dissent; a knowledge which conveys foreign ideas requiring a certain "translation;" a knowledge which is becoming the privilege of a minority, whereas traditional knowledge was widely disseminated. The difference is obvious.

There is a third factor, for with the European invasion the technical dynamism begins to operate and material values gradually emerge. The quest for the "European secret," which was denounced by Paul Valéry and which appears in the earliest records of missionaries and explorers, leads finally to a discovery of the power based on applied sciences and technical expertise. This search for power and progress has seen many vicissitudes before arriving at its goal. It has sometimes led to despair and to a sense of irrevocable damnation. It has frequently employed methods of a magical and religious nature before attaining a rational level.

Finally, and this is not the least effective of these factors of transformation, we must not overlook the trying experience of alienation during the colonial period. This is responsible for the numerous movements aimed at liberation of individuals (including those utilizing mystical possession) and of collectivities (first through sacred nationalisms, later through political nationalisms). It has also brought about a liberation of minds, which leads us to consider recent intellectual changes and the outlook for African thought.

The shocks and upheavals of the last fifty years have caused Africans to turn back to their own culture and their own past. This impulse has stimulated the African renaissance and has served to revive and intensify both national and historical awareness: a first generation of Negro historians is contributing energetically to this all-important task. This renewed self-awareness has also given rise to a glorification of African civilizations, an insistence on their riches; this, at the instigation of revered elders like Jomo Kenyatta and of impassioned young historians like Cheikh Anta Diop. Carried to its logical conclusion, this movement is leading to a new appreciation of the value of traditions and of old systems of thought. On the one hand there are the radicals who are energetic critics of the old Africa, and on the other the neo-conservatives who compare African values with the cult of technology—as, for example, Cheikh Hamidou Kane in his remarkable essay, *Ambiguous Adventure.*

Located at the crossroads of very diverse influences, modern Africa has moreover produced a syncretic thought rich in varied contributions. It was Abdoulaye Ly, the forceful Senegalese essayist, who justly extolled the virtues of this legacy, which is liberating for two reasons: first, because it results from the combining of different traditions, and second, because it opposed colonial alienation. This syncretism is also expressed on the level of doctrines and political ideologies; African socialism constitutes a unique version of socialist theory and practice.

A third change that should be noted is the new desire to acquire in a conscious and voluntary way an African personality. This ambition, which is related to the foregoing trends, expresses itself on various levels of complexity. Sometimes it takes the form of a political and ethical imperative to decolonize and, in the words of Sékou Touré, to "reconstruct the African personality;" more rarely, it appears as an actual theory, as in the case of the philosophy of negritude developed by Aimé Césaire and Léopold Senghor, or the "pan-Africanism" underlying the political thought of Kwame Nkrumah.

In conclusion it may be observed that contemporary African thought is naturally orientated toward a free exchange of ideas. Senghor expresses this when he invites the men of this age to enrich one another through their "mutual differences," to all attend a great "meeting of minds." His last book, *Liberté I,* plots the itinerary of this noble undertaking. In adopting this attitude of give and take, African thought wishes to contribute to the humanization of a world which is becoming standardized and mechanized at an accelerating rate. It is trying to help maintain differences which are no longer an obstacle to understanding, but the necessary condition of any civilization professing to be alive and to serve mankind. Herein lies its greatness. The present work attempts to show this by presenting the results of a long interrogation of Negro societies which is also a passionate interrogation of our time.

1

The Play Of Memory

▼▼▼▼▼▼▼▼▼▼▼▼▼▼▼▼▼▼▼▼▼▼▼▼▼▼▼▼▼▼▼

I REJECT my childhood memories because I loved them too much. Only one of them finds favor with me today, one which is at the source of my first dreams of Africa. Vincent, a classmate, had passed a note asking me to meet him in the schoolyard at recess. There, with mysterious precautions, he handed me a snapshot he had received that very morning in a letter from his uncle, a woodcutter in Gabon. The picture showed a powerful man with unruly hair, his shirt unbuttoned to the waist, a gun over his shoulder; beside him, disjointed and grotesque, its head held like a toy in the hands of a Negro hunter, was a gorilla which had been shot in the forehead. This hunting scene fascinated us. We swore to run away, eventually, and join forces with this invincible uncle, the symbol of male power and adventure.

Was it the memory of this childhood scene which led me to this very spot in Gabon, on the Ogooué River, where the imaginary line of the Equator runs through a high forest permeated with the odor of driver ants? I ask this question as if its answer could of itself account for my career, my travels, my passion for out-of-the-way experiences. I know, however, that the question will hound me, and I shall evade it by a trick or a paradox. This has always been my reaction when a friend or relative questions me about my "vocation;" I had no choice in the matter. Everything changes, though, when I remember the Africans who were as much the companions of my meditation as my informants.

To explain foreign peoples with whom one has lived and whom one has loved is, inevitably, to explain oneself. The analysis of such accounts, even when they preserve a scientific character, affords the revelation of a personal adventure. I believe that by consulting the works of ethnologists one can trace the principal stages of their own lives. When they extend their inquiry, they necessarily enrich this autobiography, which develops contrapuntally along with their studies. Such a result does not always remain hidden, but only exceptionally is it overt, as in *Afrique Fantôme,* the book with which Michel Leiris launched his career as an Africanist, or again, in *Tristes Tropiques,* with which Claude Lévi-Strauss, reviving the tradition of the philosophical voyage, defined himself in relation to his profession.

Is not this alienation to which modern ethnology introduces us actually the heir of traditional procedures? Time and again the best minds have submitted their reflection to what might be called the "test of savages." Montaigne's curiosity had already been whetted by Villegaignon's discoveries in Brazil. In his essay "Of Cannibals," he voiced his reservations concerning reports by "clever people," for according to him the latter "observe more things and more curiously, but they interpret them." Yet it is precisely these "interpretations" which give them away. They cannot confine themselves to the evidence; they place and reveal themselves with respect to what they have seen.

Few ethnologists have clearly indicated the reasons for their choice, for their adoption of a profession which leads them to uproot themselves from their own civilization in order to confront others very different from it. Still, their eclecticism and their cultural exile always put them in the position of critic with regard to their own society. There is at the basis of such a vocation a dissatisfaction, a need to become involved in radically different modes of existence. If the practice of the profession reveals the illusory nature of such an undertaking, it is also quick to sharpen the critical faculty. This explains official hesitation when faced with the recommendations of specialists who began by placing themselves outside the system in order to evaluate it more accurately.

Montaigne himself extolled the "perfection" of "cannibal" customs as a means of denouncing certain weaknesses of his own society and evoking the laws of "great and powerful mother nature." In idealizing natural man, he was using a method Diderot was to adopt in his critique of manners and customs, a method Rousseau was to enrich by seeking beyond known evils for the foundations of all human societies. Down through the centuries an amazing continuity appears: the appeal to the example of the "savage" or the "primitive" most often appears in the arguments of reformers and even revolutionaries. The author of a book of no importance has shown that such men, despite the apparent paradox, were obsessed by the "myth of origins," whatever their passion for building a future society.

Hence the danger of seeking lessons in civilizations which are different and more "primitive" because they are less encumbered by a complex material production. Comparison, never entirely innocent, has nonetheless a test value. But let us remember that this test is experienced in a very direct way by the ethnologist in action. I have no intention of describing here, in the style peculiar to professional explorers, the dangers and discomforts of an undertaking pursued off the beaten path. My point is rather to show that access to a foreign civilization and the confidence which is earned by a patient understanding are more the result of a discipline than of a superior skill or a scientific technique. Everything is a problem. For instance, I cannot forget a certain Negro child in the vicinity of Dakar who for several hours was the most demanding of taskmasters. This example will scarcely be convincing, I know, although it remains precious to me. I should have to describe the renunciations enforced, the initiations undergone, as well as the fears—those that literally paralyzed me one evening in January 1949 when I had to participate in an important ceremony with the votaries of a Gabonese cult. There is always some secret, the product of these tests and these fears, unknown even to the most well-informed colleagues, that is hidden in an ethnologist's experience.

No social experience or commitment can be so complete. One might reply that exoticism is on the wane, and with it all these rigors and ordeals. Towns are springing up where fifty years earlier there were only the dwellings of petty native sovereigns; highways, railroads and airports have shattered that isolation which protects particularism; factories have enclosed within their walls these "primitives" who are more at home

3

with rites than with complex machinery; churches have driven underground the fragile abodes of savage gods, and modern assemblies have replaced the ancient parlays. Are we any less alienated among so many familiar objects; have we standardized the world to the point where we feel at home anywhere on its surface? The illusion is quickly dispelled. These towns, these trains, these factories have undergone a change by virtue of their exportation; the landscape they compose is still not the one to which we are accustomed. Nor should we allow the modern facade of traditional societies to deceive us; in no case does it excuse us from that comprehensive approach which is the basis of the ethnologist's least questionable method.

I was speaking a moment ago of discipline; we must understand the term in its proper sense. I think of a foreign colleague of mine, a distinguished Indianist who in his habitual setting seems like a sophisticated man, one of almost Byzantine refinement. If, however, you come across him during his on-the-spot investigations, he seems quite the reverse: stripped to essentials, simple and unpolished. This example illustrates the elation which attends the temporary return to a more rudimentary form of existence; but there is much more to it than that. The abandonment of artifice is also a way of renouncing those attributes, material for the most part, which characterize our civilization. It is difficult to imagine how an ethnologist who was anxious to establish the best possible rapport could carry out his research with an equipment that classified and isolated him. On the contrary, he must obliterate his origins by a veritable feat of mimicry. Only in this way can he mitigate his foreignness and enter into the indigenous system. In the course of the investigation, as of the theoretical elaboration, all difficulties are reduced to a "problem of communication."

Once this communication has been established, it proves to be compelling. It is not with impunity that the ethnologist installs himself in an exotic society. He hopes to carry out his discovery ever further, and conducts an experiment which transforms him in an insidious manner; he arrives at categories of thought which infect him with a certain bias. I cannot help thinking of that lamented master Maurice Leenhardt, who acquired such a profound and subtle understanding of Melanesian thought that his detractors reproached him for "thinking like a Kanaka" instead of according to our norms. It is very easy to criticize. Has not one of our colleagues been condemned for an openness to Confucian thought which makes

4

him difficult to follow; and another, for a long association with Sudanese peoples which has resulted in a commitment of the mind as well as the heart?

This continuous impregnation is implicit in the ethnological activity, and can result in a real marriage between the investigator and the civilization he is courting, a marriage which may take material form: a friend of mine is so passionately devoted to a certain Negro cult he discovered first in Brazil and then in Dahomey that he is never without the collar which signifies his initiation. It is clear, then, that the ethnologist may command respect as an eloquent witness. He is an interpreter; he attacks common ignorance and preconceived ideas; his work, in its least questionable aspect, has a militant quality. Isolated from the start by the very object of his study—these so-called "peripheral" peoples—he remains so by his rejection of conformism and his critical intervention.

I thought it necessary to make these preliminary remarks. They show the complexity of the relationship which is established between the ethnologist and his research, and the peculiar position he occupies in his own society. He has an unconscious influence, difficult to assess, upon the facts to which he addresses himself, and he finds himself affected in turn by the discoveries to which his study leads him. He must make an effort of immediate comprehension as well as one of scientific analysis. Nor should he be surprised if some people regard what he does as more of an art than a science, thus emphasizing the subjective element, that "personal equation" which in this case stands for the whole man with his preferences, his commitments and his choices.

Under the circumstances a kind of self-criticism, based on an elementary intellectual honesty, becomes necessary. It is such an undertaking that I should like to attempt, not forgetting the problems raised by the transition from traditional to modern Africa.

This shift from one face of Africa to the other was the center of my scientific curiosity. When I left Europe in May 1946 to conduct my first on-the-spot investigation, I was leaving a society in ruins, a society whose collapse seemed to justify condemnation of a civilization which nonetheless chose to regard itself as "missionary." I longed for Africa as I longed for a break with the past, for a cruder, more authentic existence. By an obvious paradox, I was eager to discover the most universal and least deceptive aspects of human nature under the most primitively Negro garments. I yearned toward old Africa with a passion fed by Conradian reminiscences, with the illusion that the celebrated *Heart of Darkness* was still a guide. Since my first stopover was in the town of Dakar, I was rapidly to lose such naive expectations. Having started out armed with a technique for expatriation, I felt cheated on finding myself so much at home. Very soon familiarized with the outward forms of exoticism—and particularly with the spectacle of the Dakarese, who were often magnificently dressed—I found myself confronted by a town and a landscape which had been made commonplace, whose human originality seemed to have been obscured by a screen of materialism. I was wrong, the victim of my own impatience, but I did not discover my mistake until much later.

I may as well admit that my disappointment provoked me to a genuine infidelity. No sooner had I arrived in that Negro world I had so passionately longed to discover than I wanted to leave. The opportunity presented itself: it remains the source of a friendship which I can never recall without emotion. One morning there came to see me in my office at the African Institute one Mokhtar Ould Hamidoun, a scholarly Moor who wished to offer me his services. He was one of those men who, once encountered, are never forgotten. Tall and slender, with a face which was fine and proud without being arrogant, he was lost in a long white garment, trailing over one shoulder one of those strips of blue cloth with which the Moors wrap their heads. He carried in a dishcloth the manuscripts in which his erudition was contained. Mokhtar revived that attraction to Mauritania which I had once felt for reasons not free from a kind of childishness, since they owed a great deal to Ernest Psichari's confession, *Les Voix qui crient dans le désert*. To these inducements was added the Saharan glamor surrounding Théodore Monod, the learned director of the African Institute. And so, the victim of an imperious inner necessity, I had to cross the Senegal River. At Rosso, I arrived at the Cercle du Trarza, where I lived for several weeks.

In Mauritania it is the landscape that is mobile, at the mercy of the sand and the wind. The nomadism of men and flocks cannot conceal the extraordinary stability of the society and the civilization. Here there is a languor of pastoral life, a social system in which the hierarchy, fixed in its decorum, is based upon a religion of scholiasts. While the latter are not without their charm, it did seem to me that these Moors, who had been

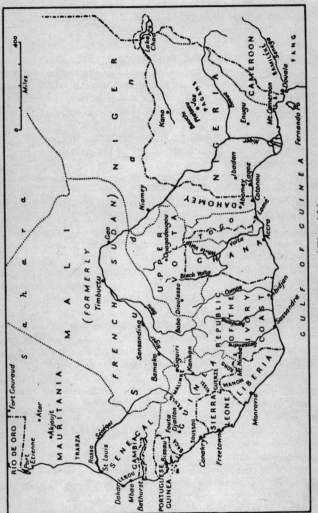

Fig. 1 A map of West Africa

retired conquerors for several decades, were engaged in pastoral and rhetorical games which were too divorced from the modern world. However, I let myself be seduced by these learned diversions and devoted myself to a study of musical theory which led to a complex philosophy and arithmetic. My curiosity subsided; I had the feeling that, under the pretext of erudition, I was avoiding more pressing obligations. I did not suspect that technology and its demands were shortly to disrupt this calm. The iron of Fort Gouraud and the copper of Akjoujt were discovered in rich deposits available to societies ill-prepared to exploit them. The industrial zones of the Saharan complex were soon to superimpose their pattern upon the cultural circles and tribal maps traced by the ethnologists of the previous century.

Back at Dakar, I tasted that exhilaration which attends the launching of a new investigation. This one was being conducted right outside the town among an ethnic group that had the charm of all fishing communities, the Lebou of the Cape Verde peninsula. I could scarcely have had the illusion of exploration, but I felt that, in the domain of culture at least, I was crossing boundaries more real than the barriers erected by states or natural accidents. I took this opportunity to try to weigh the respective chances of particularism, tradition and modernism; this, at any rate, was the subtitle I gave to the report I wrote with my friend Paul Mercier, based on the material we collected. The attention it accorded to the play of new forces seems significant today of an intellectual transformation which was only beginning. I had caught a glimpse of the second face of Africa, but I was hoping that in the struggle of forces the ancient civilization would prevail. I belonged, for a time, to that group of ethnologists who cannot allow history to rob them of their "primitives."

Later on I was asked to take over the direction of the local office of the African Institute at Conakry. Here again I preceded those material—and resulting social or political—upheavals which were about to occur. The islands of Los with their carapace of bauxite still stood intact against that strange and leaden sky. The peninsula of Kaloum, which carries the town to its tip, showed its monotonous rust color, the crust of iron soon to be entrusted to the tools of miners. Conakry, under its coconut palms and mango trees, retained that old-fashioned look and decadence which give old colonial towns their charm. There I rediscovered some of those adulterated impressions I had already received during my short visits to Saint-Louis in Senegal.

Revisiting Conakry in October 1954, I recalled my exotic enthusiasm of 1947 with surprise. Now I saw mines and miners, an expanded and busier port, buildings that did not belong, a less artificial economic and political life: hard realities and the difficult construction of a modern society. I had the conviction of having witnessed the end of an era, the real falling of a curtain. It is true that the physical setting of my work at the time lent itself to a distortion of judgment, for it seemed to rest entirely on artifice. Whenever I glanced out to sea, where the native fishing port appeared framed by the town's two cemeteries, I was inevitably reminded of Valéry's magnificent poem. Here was the *cimetière marin*, an artful and unreal creation. In this same Boulbinet, among rocks battered by the sea and protected from its onslaughts, rose the then wretched buildings of the African Institue or, more accurately, the premises it shared with the Department of Health, which maintained a quarantine station there. My neighborhood was frightful, made up of lepers and victims of sleeping sickness and smallpox—an Africa consumed by disease and resigned to the point of unconsciousness. It is impossible to imagine such a combination of circumstances: the inhuman grandeur of the natural setting, and the constant presence of death and the worst physical deterioration; one must have experienced it. Such extremes breed anxiety, and few of my European friends had the courage to venture as far as the first gate, the one to the botanical garden.

In presenting these recollections, I am not trying to dramatize but rather to suggest to what extent such a situation can influence one's thinking. Any detailed or scholarly research would then have seemed pointless; my first reaction was to ask these Guinean civilizations to teach me their profoundest lessons. On my first mission, I was to devote myself to the Peul groups of Fouta Djallon. Once again, chance confronted me with an Islamized society of feudal structure where prestige was based on the number of herds and men at one's command, and where the erudition of the *karamoko* imposed a hierarchy of scholars.

This investigation referred me back to my Mauritanian experience and ill equipped me to grasp the specific nature of the Negro world. My difficulty was intensified by the fact that during the colonial period, evolution had contributed to the advance of Moslem law by the decline of customs. This ambiguous contact could not be entirely satisfactory, but it did provide

9

an unforgettable encounter: through his work, which is entirely devoted to the Peul, I discovered Gilbert Vieillard. I still remember the deep respect inspired in me by the discovery of his manuscripts, which were collected at the Institute of Dakar shortly after his death. A legend was growing up around the memory of this scholarly administrator who was so passionately devoted to his subject that in the end he became one with the civilization he was studying. In the villages of Fouta Djallon, people were always fervently recalling his fine use of the language; one sensed that he was loved and missed. Some of the Europeans who had known him used to say somewhat disapprovingly that he was "a man lost to the West."

By an amazing coincidence I discovered at this same time, and not merely through their books, two great Africanists who had disappeared during the last war. Bernard Maupoil had devoted himself to the archives of Guinea, and I came upon his personal imprint in a thousand places. In Dahomey he had had an authentic revelation: while studying geomancy at the school of the old *bokonon,* or fortunetellers, in the kingdom of Abomey, he had touched on a conception of the world and of existence which he found peculiarly convincing. Once again Africa had claimed one of our best minds, by which I do not mean that she destroyed him the better to retain her hold over him: Bernard Maupoil was to die tragically, for resisting the German occupation. The same struggle claimed Charles Le Coeur, author of a too little known book, *Le Rite et l'outil,* and the foremost authority on the Teda of the Tibesti. Here too, Guinea afforded me several opportunites for personal contact, not to mention that critique of rationalism, so forcefully led by Le Coeur, to which I subscribed at the time. When I remember these scholars, who were such impressive models for the young ethnologist I was in 1947, I cannot help imagining their disappointment were they to confront the Africa of today. For is not the price of progress the breakdown of traditional civilizations and the spread of a certain monotony throughout the world? Naturally they would feel out of their element, but this would be because of the disappearance of what they loved most.

In the space of a few years, love of Africa resulted in the brutal deaths of several enthusiastic and hard-working investigators. As I begin this book, it is my duty to evoke these men who had disappeared by the time I first set foot on African soil. They guided me and showed me what devotion to research can be, what physical and intellectual risks it requires. First, there was the geographer Jacques Weulersse, still a young professor, courageous in mind as in body, who died of exhaustion on his return from a long trip to French Sudan. There was Jean-Charles Leclerc, also a geographer, struck by lightning in his camp at Kissidougou and abandoned by the Kissi, who regarded such a death as a manifestation of divine will. And then my friend Jacques Richard-Molard, a third geographer, who died of a fractured skull on Mount Nimba in Portuguese Guinea: a man of great learning, but above all a generous man, whom the periodical *Présence Africaine* chose to honor with a special volume of his collected works. In this terrible death also the natives saw the hand of the divinities who haunt the mountain and defend themselves fiercely against all human approach. The mind remains paralyzed before these tragic strokes of chance.

It was in this Mount Nimba region, among a people who are little concerned with boundaries since they sprawl over Guinea, Ivory Coast and Liberia, that I was to conduct my final investigations. I was confronted by a civilization in which traditional religious life still dominated the landscape and the rhythm of work. Even when they emigrated to distant towns, the young men took with them small replicas of the masks they wore in the fraternal society. Profoundly impressed and attracted by this choreography of sacred personages, I undertook with passionate thoroughness to discover its intellectual and emotional context. However, the decline of the institution was evidenced by certain unmistakable signs: the inferior execution of the newer masks and their commercialization; the sensational and mercenary use of the stilt mask, the *Nyomo Kwouya*, even in fairs and markets; the indifference of a minority which had become critical of ancient rituals. Even in this forest region far from the great centers, I again found myself confronted by the problems of Africa in transition. At varying rates of speed, analogous movements were stirring Negro societies which, through force of habit, were still considered immutable and delightfully exotic.

It is true that my connections in Conakry, which were regarded as somewhat unorthodox by the administration, inspired me with more up-to-date ideas. My collaborator, Madera Keita, a man of quality in the true sense of the phrase, and the local force behind the African Democratic Assembly, introduced me to various representatives of Guinean political groups. I endeavored to understand their anxieties and their

11

hopes, to grasp their problems behind an eloquence that was sometimes revolutionary. They forced me to a subtler and more dangerous awareness. A similar influence was exerted by another Negro friend, the Guadeloupan poet Guy Tirolien, then administrator at Conakry, who was carrying on an obsessive quest: a search for "the soul of the black land where our ancestors sleep." This was the period when young Negro intellectuals were advancing the myth of negritude as a message of unity and power.

It was somewhat later, however, on the occasion of a trip to Nigeria, that I was to discover the Africa of contrasts in all its distinctness, and to observe that gap which makes it possible for civilizations to exist side by side without being able to communicate. I was in that mining region, dominated by the town of Jos, in which one finds provincial villas transplanted from England and wealthy Moslem homes. This center, whose economic life rests on the mining of tin and factories for the processing of rare ores, is located at the conjunction of Islamized conquering peoples and ancient indigenous populations which retain their pagan and peasant character. Thus, not far from a landscape revolutionized by the European's industry, crawling with tractors, giant cranes and work camps, the representatives of a semifeudal Islam and of a very old Africa—those "half-naked pagans"—remain firmly established. Can elements as separate as these maintain any but circumstantial relations? By way of answer, I recall this scene, which resembles a photographic montage: beside a long tarred road which owes its life to faraway tin speculation, surrounded by cranes and piles of loose soil, a handful of these "pagans" walk with hesitant steps, carrying meager burdens and clad only in rings of colored straw which slap against their buttocks. I am reminded of something Paul Mus wrote recently: "The difference in levels of civilization which now tears mankind asunder will increase every year"—if we do not decide what to do about it at once.

I am lingering over my memories of these first approaches and hesitations because they reveal a shift to problems which were eventually to take their place at the center of my studies. I had learned that a new life animated the body of Negro societies, that the clash of civilizations could not with impunity continue to play into the hands of the most favored. It was still a confused impression, but my next missions were to give me a clearer picture of the African future.

In southern Cameroon, where wide paths lined with cacao

trees offer a perspective of a better life, I was able to weigh the strength of modernism and those forces operating against the old colonial spirit. In Gabon, along the Ogooué River which is so bound up with our historical memories and the legend of Brazza, I discovered a more elementary protest in the face of poverty and the destruction of traditional cultures. I encountered a sinister resignation to this poverty: I can still see the miserable villages of the Ndjolé region on shores abandoned by hope. Devastation of forests, societies and men; too heavy a burden had weighed down a land already exhausted by the slave trade.

Here I should like to describe one of my Gabonese informants, a Fang villager of about forty who was distinguished only by a greater facility in expressing himself. This man felt that "nothing worked any more." According to him, everything that can give existence a full and joyous meaning had been lost. After itemizing all the current miseries of Fang society, he concluded our series of conversations with the cryptic moral, "Blame it on civilization!" One civilization accuses another; we are judged by a simple peasant of a very humble village. What a reversal of roles this is, in which we are cast as formentors of social disorder! I decided to help these people by placing my studies at their service: a modest, limited program of agricultural equipment was the result, a gesture in itself inadequate to resolve problems of such magnitude which, moreover, are not merely of a material nature.

Next, the Congo, that Zaïre River of the first discoverers of Central Africa: I attacked it impatiently, bursting with memories and references. Here was one of the few regions about which African history does not remain silent. One has the sense of a brilliant past. The kingdom of the Congo aroused the enthusiasm of the German ethnologist Frobenius and wrung from him the admiring cry, "Civilized to the very marrow of their bones!" It led André Breton to imagine "all the grandeur of lost Africa." Here was the river, symbol of African rebirth, which Léopold Sédar Senghor glorified in his sumptuous *Éthiopiques: "Oho! Congo couchée dans ton lit de forêts, reine sur l'Afrique domptée. . . ."**

The water rushes powerfully out of Stanley Pool, but a hydroelectric plant now dominates the right bank. Exoticism is disappearing, and no one has the right to complain. The theme

---

* "O Congo lying in your bed of forests, queen of vanquished Africa. . . ."

Fig. 2 A map of Central Africa

of glorification must be changed without regret. I had little
time to dwell on the toll of shattered illusions; here, problems
have the dimensions of the river itself. They have invaded the
cities, Brazzaville and Leopoldville, where new social forms
are being drafted. They have penetrated every Congolese village, where the shade of the palm trees has lost its former
sweetness. They are peculiar to each people, despite slight su-

14

perficial resemblances, because each reacts according to its own character. The Bateke, isolated on the plateaus that bear their name, use their traditions as a shield. The Bakongo, seekers of progress and daring innovators with respect to the Christianity they have embraced, want to impose their initiative and are disturbing others in the process. Between the two there are many small Babinga groups which, though mobile, are still subject to a very ancient servitude. What a distance there is between the problems imposed by the urban proletariat and the problems of these Negrillos, who are exploited by their Negro masters! And yet Africa in the making contains them all, knotted and tangled like the strands of a skein in the hands of an inexperienced seamstress.

One memory has summoned another in these pages with an amazing necessity. Obnoxious though the first person may be, one must make an exception in the case of the ethnologist. He must provide the context for his testimony which, even more than a scientific technique, proceeds by multiple and complex interventions between the observer and the civilization observed. What he does requires an extreme sensitivity, a continual effort of adjustment. And he must "discover" himself even as he studies the results of his research. As in his scientific work, he can succeed in such an attempt only if he pursues it in all its ramifications, and somehow reveals what goes on behind the scenes.

2
Young Africa

▾▾▾▾▾▾▾▾▾▾▾▾▾▾▾▾▾▾▾▾▾▾▾▾▾▾▾▾▾▾▾▾▾▾▾▾▾▾

A CHILD begins to learn a civilization from the first days of his life. A kind of psychological montage is formed during childhood, and it is through this that common attitudes are constructed and the relative permanence of societies is maintained. "Who does not see," Montaigne has already insisted, "that in a State everything depends upon this education and nature?" Psychologists and pedagogues have discovered this ancient truth. But it was in the work of American ethnologists, particularly Margaret Mead, that the method of observing how personality is organized in the context of a culture was defined. It was not long before anything seemed permissible in this new field which promised such spectacular results. We are familiar with some of those it has produced. An Englishman named Geoffrey Gorer goes so far as to deduce Russian national character from the method of diapering babies in that country; he maintains, apparently without batting an eye, that the very tight swaddling of infants conditions adult attitudes toward authority. I shall not follow this example; the position of the Negro child clinging to his mother's back in a loincloth which holds him tightly does not determine his reaction to dependency in general nor toward African nationalism in particular!

With all due caution, however, I believe I should take a lesson from these examples. In a certain sense the ethnologist finds himself in the position of a child with regard to the culture he undertakes to study. He has everything to learn in order to understand better, from the inside, how this culture functions; he must go through all the phases of the initiation. And he can discover a great deal by tracing the steps by which his homologue, the child, assimilates the instructions or teachings imposed on him and gradually takes his place in the society. By this I do not mean a "game" which would consist of retracing all the child's emotions and reactions, from the moment the mother puts him on her back for the first time to the moment when, by initiation, he becomes an adolescent united with the male community. We may cover all these stages adequately and more rapidly by observing the different strata of the infant population. In this way, behind an outward appearance of acceleration, the ethnologist can reconstruct the whole sequence of Negro childhood, and pass through the front door of this society which in the early days of his investigation seemed so impregnable.

My first investigation conformed almost instinctively to these requirements. I had decided to study the civilization of the Lebou, a small tribe of fishermen living around and to the south of Dakar in a region where a stretch of sandy palm groves is being worn away by the sea. These two elements of the landscape, besides determining the dualism of human activities, provide the backdrop for an unusual history. Anxious to retain its individuality in spite of its nearness to the capital, a contagious center of modernism, this Senegalese society remains proud of its past. In the late eighteenth century it established a republic in opposition to the surrounding feudalities. Such an area of study attracts the ethnologist by virtue of its neatness, its narrow limits and the diversity of forces at work. I was to change my tune quickly, for resistance to the indiscretions of a foreign investigator whose objectives were something of a mystery immobilized me for a time. The Lebou villagers had good reasons for being instinctively suspicious: my position as a nonbeliever with respect to Islam, my presumed association with the administrative machine, and finally, the unusual nature of my approach in the eyes of people accustomed primarily to official visits or to soldiers who had come from neighboring camps in search of women. I would have encountered a complete inertia—that cheerful feigned innocence which the African can play to perfection—had it not been for the children and young people.

A few at a time, they came forward. I whetted their curiosity; I offered them the spectacle of my menage and my routine. In an ironic reversal of roles, I became the "exotic" subject for dozens of amateur ethnographers.

But there was much more to it than this, and above all the lure of the wealth which they assumed to be mine, the gifts which each of my observers expected from me. My modest equipment, my meals, my clothing: I saw them all with a fresh eye because they excited so much envy. One must have been a center of longing in this way for the multitude of the deprived, to know how odious the most commonplace of our conveniences can become. As this scene inevitably repeated itself wherever my investigations took me, I discovered what a Tantalus-like torment Europe had imposed on the African masses who had become hungry for its goods. All the learned and ingenious ex-

Fig. 3 A Lebou canoe

planations in the world, including those that justify the gift as a source of cordial relations, will in no way change this state of things. However, among the preoccupations of my observers, one in particular was very intense. In the eyes of these young people who were worried about the future of the villages and especially about their own future, I was the image of "modern" man. Each hoped to question me to discover whether this impulse toward modernism which provoked the opposition of the elders was really worth the trouble. From the first my presence established complex relations the observance of which was more vital to the success of my research than my own plans. That objectivity so dear to the laboratory technician would give way under the weight of obligations like these.

A minor episode may open a new avenue of approach to the eager curiosity of the ethnologist. Two young informants are arguing heatedly about some fact relating to the "age group" to which they belong, and end by quarreling and exchanging insults.

"Your mother's vagina!" says one.

"I fornicate with your mother!" replies the other, and the blows begin to fall.

This outburst, this gravity of insults took me by surprise. In a series of observations collected in the early nineteenth century, Baron Roger, beginning with a similar amazement, offers some remarks which echo my questions: "Among the natural sentiments which these people faithfully preserve, we must distinguish the respect, obedience and affection which they always show toward their mothers. ... The greatest insult one can utter is the all too familiar *sahr sa ndei* (by the genitalia of your mother). This oath has frequently been drowned in blood." This illustrates how a seemingly unimportant incident led me to examine the image the young Lebou child forms of the mother, as well as the image the man has of the woman.

The boy spends a large part of his childhood, a period much longer than the time required by mere biological dependence, with his mother and in the intimate company of women. He takes his meals with women, and from them he acquires fundamental disciplines and common attitudes. He helps them by performing little chores which constitute an early training for work. He is admitted as a spectator to rituals which feminine conservatism has retained, but which remain forbidden to the eyes of men. He participates in the little secrets and gossip which circulate among the "squares" into which the dwellings are divided. For six or seven years the mother's loincloth dominates the young Lebou's horizon, which is at first limited to the feminine aspects of society. As a result he becomes more affectionate and forms an idealized image of woman. The child who is pampered in this way—to the indignation of neighboring tribes, who see it only as weakness—will be a man who is reserved toward girls, even in his most urgent proposals.

Let us build no utopias or monuments in praise of an amazing purity of customs; the proximity of the urban centers of Dakar and Rufisque has ended by altering this formerly widespread reserve. In the alleys after dark a few artlessly made-up girls wheedle the young men in order to obtain a few pennies. They play on the attractions of exotic love, games learned from European soldiers who come to the villages for lack of other victims. They are ridiculed and scorned, not for their sexual freedom, but for the commercial use to which they put it, in songs which the children repeat for the sake of amusement:

> Labu Ngar, Fall Ndyay, they are there.
> Labu Ngar, Fall Ndyay, they are there.
> During the night, you earn hundreds of francs.
> During the day, you earn another thousand francs.
> It's too much to spend! It's too much work for you!

There is no mistaking the decline of customs, even when ritual preoccupations place an effective restraint on it. The dances of sexual provocation known as *grimbe* are, for the most part, losing their traditional meaning, which associated them with fertility techniques, and exalting the erotic aspect. This choreography features movements simulating the sexual act and the gesture of sexual discovery, to the accompaniment of a chanting whose meaning is unmistakable. If the evolution continues, it will stop only with a daring spectacle that will shock even "civilized" dealers in theatrical eroticism. At these dances boys and girls mingle and enjoy pantomimes and pleasantries while the adults laugh. This public eroticism has unquestionably lowered the prestige of women and placed sexuality in an unaccustomed context.

The child does not discover the act of love by a kind of accident which corresponds to his curiosity. From a very early age he witnesses the visits which the father pays to each of his wives; they do not surprise him in the least, although an underlying jealously reduces even further the weak authority which tradition allows the sire over his descendants. Up until the moment of initiation, he will retain a bewildering freedom of word and gesture. The multitude of insults of a sexual nature which boys hurl at one another in the course of their quarrels is the most striking illustration of this. Until his eighth or ninth year, then, the child's sexuality encounters almost no restrictions; it will only become intensified at puberty, to be domesticated immediately by the ordeal of circumcision. Until recently, however, this freedom excluded any erotic obsession or ostentatious obscenity; it has been corrupted only to the extent that the sexual relation has been degraded as a result of outside influences.

A freedom of this kind, which is uncontested throughout the period when sexuality is unfixed, contrasts with the reserve of "initiated" young men. For the latter the fact of circumcision, although it provides access to women, also imposes a severe discipline. Clothing, gestures and conversation may now be judged according to the criterion of decency, which is infallibly invoked, to the acute shame of the guilty party. Public relations between boys and girls, men and women, follow a formalism against which no one would consider rebelling. Allusions of a sexual nature in mixed company are absolutely forbidden, not to mention sexual overtures, which, moreover, are conveyed only by conventional signs. Even engaged couples are constrained publicly to codified attitudes and plan their assignations by using formulas with secret meanings. Spontaneity is at all times repressed. A young man, whatever the violence of his feelings, cannot reveal his affection to a girl. To do so would be a breach of etiquette; indeed, an emissary is responsible for going to her and reciting the few stereotyped phrases of the declaration:

> You are the woman I have chosen. I love you.
> And love does not kill!
> We would have children, we would be
>   father and mother.
> I would be proud as a master.
> Today I tell you that I love you.
> If you love me, you must tell me too.

Saint Jerome's formula "Love knows no order," which Montaigne adopted, has no universal significance. There is hardly a Negro tribe living according to tradition in which this sequence of apparent license and severe restraint is not revealed. Even in societies once considered "anarchic," like that of the Gabonese Fang described by Adolphe Cureau in his study of the "primitive populations" of Central Africa, I have had occasion to observe to what an extent the freedom of the young people, who were encouraged to "celebrate youth," was succeeded by the strictness of relations governing the couple. The Fang proverb states, "Woman is an ear of dry corn—anyone with teeth may bite her;" this is an incitement to a misleading laxity, and one which should not be heeded without discretion.

Today the adulterous wife is merely ridiculed and chastised. The Lebou designate her in public with the words *ndyaro kat,* "a woman who goes after men." But this was not the case when tradition still carried its full weight. Then the Lebou reacted collectively, a phenomenon to which the Fang added violence. A whole scale of physical punishments were enforced: exhibition of the guilty wife, naked before the assembled villagers; a punishment which consisted of tying her to a tree containing an ants' nest; or, worse still, removal of the clitoris, causing a wound which was exacerbated with ground pepper. This was a very serious matter, and created conflict between clans. It is difficult to imagine that a gifted storyteller could then have conceived a work worthy of a village Feydeau on the theme of the inconstant wife. Now it is less unlikely, so profoundly have times changed and so deeply has our "Aphrodisian" civilization left its mark.

Let us be careful not to see these punishments merely as savage cruelty, or credit our influence with a mitigation of suffering. In these African societies the relations created by marriage obey imperatives which are less of a moral than of a social nature; this only makes them the more intolerant, since the disorder is greater or more apparent when it affects the life of the whole group than when it primarily concerns the couple. This is because of the position of women in societies where interpersonal relations are more direct than they are in our European countries. In these societies, relations are not so much mediated by things, because techniques of production are still elementary. The circulation of persons, rather than of goods, forms the fabric of human intercourse. In this sense, the role of the woman within a simple or complex system of matrimonial exchanges becomes fundamental, as Claude Lévi-Strauss demonstrated in a work *(Les Structures élémentaires de la parenté)* which has become a classic. Once in the system, the woman is strictly subject to the rules that govern it, whatever degree of sexual freedom she enjoyed up to then. The adulteress inevitably creates not only a disorder of the emotions but an "affair of state."

Let us return to our two examples. Among the Lebou, there is more to it than the intimate and affectionate relationship between mother and child. The mother, of whom it is said that "milk is the source of kinship," enrolls her child in a direct way in the basic social unit—the group of individuals born of the same maternal line. She chooses for her descendants the man with whom they will maintain the most intense relations on the level of affectivity as on that of everyday life: the maternal uncle. Indeed, this uncle supervises the child and protects him, if necessary, from the ill-treatment of the father. The boy of twelve or so takes his meals with this uncle and looks forward to living with him permanently as soon as the retreat of circum-

22

cision is over. It is between these two "parents," so close and so intimately related, that goods and power circulate. But in addition to this, the Lebou wife is a link between the two tribal groups united by her marriage. She appears as one of the elements that help to preserve the social structure—for tradition has oriented her choice, sometimes against her affections—and as an instrument of clan politics. In such a context, freedom of heart and hand must necessarily disappear.

The Gabonese Fang, who have already been cited to illustrate this point, offer an example which is less disturbing to the Western mind, but the lesson it affords is analogous. Their society accords the dominant role to the father and to the paternal line; however, this in no way changes the position of the woman. Naturally, she acts as an agent of production and reproduction, and in this sense lays the foundations of prestige and power, but she also appears as an instrument of alliance and pacification. It is through her that the fabric of cordial and co-operative relations between clans, so important in societies like this one, where power is diffuse, is woven. Her marriage requires of her future husband the payment of a dowry which immediately passes to her eldest brother, who uses it to take a wife of his own; so that a double movement of women and dowries reinforces or extends the sphere of alliance. Hence a fundamental ambiguity decrees that the wife be both the element which is least free—so that she can say, with the proverb, "I am nothing before a man, I am as stupid as a chicken"—and the element of which most is required. Here again freedom is curtailed without possibility of appeal.

In civilizations where social planning operates with such precision and necessity, a relaxation of control and of morals has repercussions whose scope we can scarcely imagine. In our societies we feel that adultery jeopardizes the normal existence of the family group; here it does more, because it tears the fabric of society. It is no longer a question of morality or puritanism; a civilization itself is at stake. Obedience to the movements of the heart, the romanticism of infidelity, the complications of the game of love are so many refinements reserved for societies whose material foundations are sufficiently resilient to withstand their consequences. Elsewhere it can only be a case of the privilege of princes, of exceptional wealth.

The emancipation of the African woman, which involves consideration of her emotional life and causes elderly critics to declare that "she has gotten out of hand;" versatility in relations between the sexes; the affirmation of "libidinal sexuality," to borrow Roger Bastide's phrase, at the expense of "socialized sexuality"—these are so many moral revolutions which society cannot assimilate without serious disturbance. And the trouble remains all the more pronounced in that the moral framework has deteriorated in the absence of an adequate movement toward reconstruction.

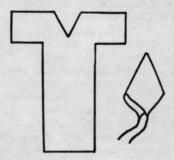

Fig. 4 A Lebou circumcision dress and hat

It is important to understand that the causes of this revolution in relations between the sexes are complex and often indirect. The contagious influence of our values cannot be denied. Our civilization impresses an outsider with the importance it accords to eroticism and with the activities and commercialism to which this eroticism gives rise. I still remember the astonishment of one of my Negro friends, the essayist Alioune Diop, at the widespread eroticism he encountered whenever he returned to Europe. Advertising excites by means of representations of the female in London as well as in Paris; I remember noticing sometime or other a poster extolling some feminine undergarment which had not hesitated to use a model who bore an embarrassingly close resemblance to Queen Elizabeth. Let us also remember the way prostitution parades itself, the women "on display" in the red-light districts of Amsterdam, and those collective forms of release which North American puritanism tolerates as "strip-tease shows." The empire of Eros is more secure in our societies than it is among the naked Coniagui of Guinea. We have exported this ambiance, to adopt a fashionable word which nobody really understands, along with our machines, our laws and our monotheism.

But beyond this, a whole series of indirect effects may be observed. First of all, there is the more or less marked decline in the old rituals of initiation. Among the Lebou, practices relating to circumcision are dying out under the influence of a stricter Islam and of our methods of education. The operation is sometimes performed in a dispensary during the first few months of the young boy's life. The consequences are easy to foresee. Ritualized circumcision afforded access to normal sexual life at a precise moment; it involved restraints which domesticated the force of the young male, who then joined the group of the men. The ceremonies celebrated his newly acquired plenitude, as the occasional songs indicate:

It is I who strike the lion with my hand!

Or this passage, more revealing of sexuality:

O bull, behold the heifer of the house of the circumcised,
It is you who overcome the heifer of the house of the circumcised.

Meanwhile the obligations imposed channeled this force and placed it at the disposal of the whole society. Let us also remember that the initiatory retreat provided strict rules and an instruction—the equivalent of a course in civics—which glorified the history and individuality of the Lebou people. The whole edifice of these positive effects collapses as the ritual declines. There tends to be a steady increase in the state of detachment of the individual and of emptiness at the heart of institutions, for no substitute rule is yet in force. Such a decline, accelerated by the influence of missionary Christianity, has already begun in Central Africa, as I have had occasion to observe in Gabon and southern Cameroon. I have no intention of defending Negro conservatism; I simply want to show the dangers to societies characterized by a primitive form of "planned economy" of this weakening of traditional structures, which provides only a temporary and illusory personal liberation.

To return to our subject, there are other causes which contribute to this revolution in relations between the sexes. Greater ease of communication permits a life of more intense relationships and limits the effectiveness of control: the markets, the holidays of neighboring groups, the opening of villages to passing "foreigners" seem like so many excuses for infidelity.

The men complain, not without exaggeration, that the women offer little resistance to the solicitations they provoke; they are beginning to miss the old restrictions. All those forces which have severed the individual from his traditional context, whether we mean the physical separation imposed by emigration to places of salaried employment or the "cultural" separation created by modern influences, have first contributed to the disturbing of fundamental balances.

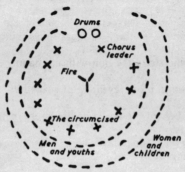

Fig. 5 Lebou circumcision songs

In the old social context, relations between men and women were always governed by the groups to which each belonged. That direct encounter which is the result of inclinations and physical affinities—those "appetites" which, as Montaigne put it, "proceed from the body and the soul"—scarcely existed. In the Lebou village it was the "age clubs," associations bringing together all boys or girls having approximately the same age, that determined initial adjustments between the sexes. Every year, toward the end of the dry season, a mixed gathering allowed the formation of couples for whom a kind of game which did not always remain Platonic constituted an apprenticeship in the co-operative relations prevailing between the sexes.

Consequently, when these boys and girls attained marriageable age, considerations of clannic situation, of position within the familial groups and of the status of these groups dominated the possibilities of choice. So much so that Abdoulaye Sadji, a novelist of Lebou origin, shows that traditional marriage partook of "heroism and sacrifice" to a degree that made it "very different from a real celebration." Neither spontaneity of

26

choice nor improvisation in the rules governing the couple's common existence was tolerated. Moreover, when the effectiveness of social ties declines, when the restricted family begins to find greater autonomy, when the elements of the couple are forced to establish relations in a more free and improvised manner, myriad uncertainties and impossibilities arise. It is difficult to manage relations which no longer observe the strict controls of tradition, but on the contrary allow personal exigencies to prevail over collective ones.

In a certain sense marriage, when associated with a definite system for the distribution of wives as in the traditional society, is an economic phenomenon; it involves the circulation and consumption of wealth, an exchange of services eliciting widespread co-operation. But this situation has been altered through the influence of the monetary economy, creating an imbalance between a conception of marriage which still conforms to traditional models and an economic life which has become totally alien to these models. This lag is easily understood. The traditional dowry was composed of symbolic objects and monetary tokens which governed only matrimonial exchanges; the rarity of these objects and tokens, like the strict control exercised over the flow of exchange, permitted the system to function relatively smoothly. Everything is distorted as soon as modern currency is introduced into the makeup of dowries and concern for profit, for speculation, makes its appearance.

We are only beginning to appreciate how far the mercantile spirit and the laws of our economy have succeeded in debasing personal relations in societies which are unprepared to accommodate them. The dowry offered as compensation changes its meaning in the new context; like prices, it varies in rate and permits actual bargaining. The same is true of the "gifts" required between in-laws and the festivities accompanying the marriage ceremony, which may constitute a second economic barrier for young men of less well-to-do families. Where once there was what might be called a "planned" distribution of wives and marriages, there now appears a competition in which wealth is all that matters.

In 1946 among the Lebou this competition was so intense that men twenty-five to thirty years old were still bachelors, and embittered by the impossibility of raising the sums necessary for marriage. To what a sad parody of our stock exchange this nevertheless proud people had fallen! Actual prices—

monetary compensations of several thousand francs for a divorced woman, higher for a widow, up to and often exceeding twelve thousand francs for a young girl—had been substituted for the old valuations, which were respectful of tradition, of course, but also of the individual, who was less neglected than she is today by this matrimonial bookkeeping. In addition to these requirements there is the cost of the festivities: a certain wedding on the outskirts of Dakar cost over a hundred thousand francs at this time, which shows how powerful the ability to capitalize can be. It is no longer enough to laugh at rich old men who buy up young, beautiful and coveted women:

> Do not put them together,
> Grey hairs and firm breasts,
> It's not nice,
> Do not put them together.

This compensation by ridicule is hardly adequate today. The young Lebou, particularly those in Dakar, have tried to organize their protest in the form of a struggle to obtain a "matrimonial agreement"—a modern regulation in which the necessity for wealth is not so crudely stated. The Lebou still have those values which Islam once superimposed upon their overthrown traditions. The situation seems more serious in regions where Christianity has spread sufficiently to weaken traditional controls but too superficially to impose its own system of values. The phenomenon seems all the more pronounced in that the areas of Christianization often coincide with those of greatest economic development. Such is the case in Central Africa. Sister Marie-André du Sacré-Coeur, who is devoted to the cause of the African woman, was scandalized at the traffic in marriages which she observed in 1951 in several regions of Cameroon. She quotes the list of accounts of the leading dowries with horrified fascination: "One amounting to 500,000 francs, ten oxen, and a case of apéritifs; another, 100,000 francs, a new wagon, two oxen, twenty kids; a third, in a village, 200,000 francs, two oxen, ten sheep, five pigs, clothing, kitchen utensils, cases of liquor." This sort of thing is not a common occurrence among the people, but these examples indicate precisely what margins of profit certain "wife-givers" reserve for themselves.

Around the same time in that region of Cameroon where the cacao tree dominates all activity, I noted the frequency of dowries in the neighborhood of 100,000 francs. Gabon, on a less spectacular level because of its relative poverty, reveals comparable trends. Everywhere, the flow of currency tends to govern the distribution of wives; each accelerates at the same rate, each encourages speculation. It is easy to push people into divorce in order to speculate on an increase in dowries, to encourage adultery in order to collect the compensation provided; so that the wife finds herself "placed" according to the hazards of inflation or lowered to the role of prostitute in residence. It is tempting to anticipate the future by marrying off young girls who for several years, until they are old enough to join their husbands, will justify blackmail by gifts. We cannot doubt the power of the underlying economic motives. In the absence of more exhaustive proof, I offer this example: a well-to-do planter, provided with wives who were still young, lured several bachelors to his estate; he is no fool—his wives enjoy lovemaking more to their tastes and he has manpower at his disposal which costs him next to nothing.

All this does not proceed without serious conflicts. The women rebel—or adjust too well, so that in regions where there are camps of laborers some of them buy their freedom and become sole mistresses of their profits. This adds to the indignation of an administrator who, in one of his annual reports to the governor, stated that "the men live off the women and the women live off their bodies." In young people the desire to overcome the substantial obstacles to marriage sometimes assumes the quality of an obsession. This reaction does not seem to be determined by the ordeal of sexual frustration, since the relaxation of morals and sexual mercantilism create myriad opportunities, but rather by the threat to prestige. What actually matters in Negro societies, and not merely in the Cameroonese-Gabonese group I have just mentioned, is the reproductive capacity offered by the legally acquired wife. She alone enables the man to prove himself as a progenitor—in his capacity as *esa,* founder of a line, to use Fang terminology—and consequently to achieve a more complete social status, a position of greater influence.

In the present situation the African man may be afraid to see ever receding, not the time when he will have sexual access to women, but the time when he will create progeny. A young Gabonese Fang whom I met in the vicinity of Oyem kept a detailed journal of his anxieties, in which he expressed his constant desire to assure himself an issue before he died. In the pages of this notebook, whose reflections were all fixed on the same theme, there appeared a real anguish: "I will look for a way to end my life unless I leave a child. . . . I will do what I must to marry a woman who will give·me children. . . ." This obsessive litany was repeated throughout.

Daniel Ngema Ondo, educated and Christianized, is therefore reduced to hoping that some powerful magic will solve his problem overnight. He consults his dreams, and finds formulas: "The devil recommends three herbs to make a barren wife give birth. . . ." He has centered his whole existence around a single question: how legally to àcquire a wife capable of producing offspring—or, in effect how to acquire social existence in all its fullness.

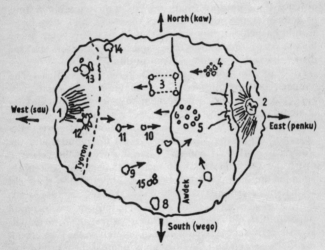

Fig. 6 A map of the sky by the sixteen-year-old Asisse

1 Moon (*wu*)	6 *Awa*	11 *Asan*
2 Sun (*Dyanta*)	7 *Arot*	12 *Dapran*
3 *Bunte Karu Mak*	8 *Bidoyu gedi*	13 *Marot*
4 *Delon*	9 *Adama*	14 *Marakot*
5 *Dyangu*	10 *Useinu*	15 *Amrot*

Cases like this show that the child is closer to the heart of African society than we would be inclined to think. Camara Laye's book, appropriately entitled *Dark Child,* offers more than images of exotic charm; it reflects this reality. We are only too happy to remain the dupes of our pedagogical knowledge, our techniques and our behavior toward the child; like our beliefs, we export these with that stubborn conviction that once led the French to impose "our ancestors, the Gauls" upon young students in African schools. It would have been more generous to pay some attention to those institutions which account for the fact that the Negro child is by no means "savage." It is only in situations of profound social degradation that he appears to be the victim of a purposeless freedom.

I should like to return to the Lebou boy who was the enthusiastic guide of my first on-the-spot investigation. In his apparent freedom and the servitude imposed on him by the familial economy, he is rather like our young country boys. He soon comes to know the bush where he spends his time picking, trapping, and hunting small animals with the *mbaha* sling made from the bark of the baobab. Every place offers him a familiar landscape in which he can interpret social signs which are invisible to the stranger—from sacred trees to subtle traces of local history. Everywhere he can instantly calculate the resources and weigh the dangers. He knows which boundaries he must not transgress, and the land they enclose is to him a primer in which the past is still written, in which he dares to decipher that cosmic order which he will soon be taught. I asked several of my informants to draw maps representing the countries and localities with which they were familiar. The results were revealing. If a few could extend the world to include the major European nations, the majority confined themselves to the familiar limits drawn by sea, rivers, village territory; they gave greatest prominence to those localities most highly developed or most sacred. Hence the maps traced that concrete space, so early explored by the child, which formed an accurate replica of Lebou society and was impregnated with the civilization elaborated by the ancestors.

Such an education, which might be called natural, obviously has its disciplinary aspect. The child is put to work watching the fields, protecting the harvest from the depredations of birds like the ravenous *mange-mil* and various pests, or taking the field workers their day's food. As soon as he reaches twelve or so, he participates actively in the work of weeding and harvesting. But it is above all the sea around which he likes to orient his activities: he knows how to control the brute force of the breakers on the river bank, and he delights in the excitement created by large catches. And when the *yaboy*, that common fish which is the veritable manna of the Lebou, is reported to be passing, one should see how eagerly he abandons his classes

31

in the village squares to run to the fishing spots. He mingles his cries with those of the women and the rhythmically working paddlers. He helps to draw in the nets. He works amid the silvery wriggling of the fish, helping to collect them in large baskets or loading the carrying nets. Once calm has been restored, the time for accounting will come, and some of the fish will then be allotted to him. The captains of the canoes do not fail to treat him as a responsible and competent fellow fisherman.

The entire education of the young Lebou is not measured by the discipline of work and the free apprenticeship of the natural environment. He knows other obligations which make him at the same time more familiar and more foreign in our eyes. Although this society was not definitively converted to Islam until the late nineteenth century, religious exigencies have nevertheless rapidly become powerful. The Koranic school, which is represented in every district of the village, constitutes a center of reunification, education and discipline. The "masters of the Koran," who possess a knowledge which is often elementary, inflict tedious classes in the reading and writing of Arabic and the recitation of *suras* (divisions of the Koran). On the secondary level, in a competition with the schoolteacher which is somewhat reminiscent of the conflicts between the schoolmaster and the priest in French villages, they hold their classes before sunrise or at nightfall, around a fireplace built by their pupils.

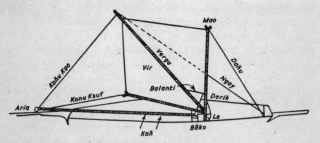

Fig. 7 The rigging of a Lebou canoe

From the yard where the group sits there rises a sad, monotonous murmur, a kind of prelude to that joyless and here unceremonious ritual with which the faithful of Islam are satisfied. In this circle of boys sitting on their folded legs and holding the flat boards containing their knowledge on their laps, I no longer recognized my young friends so eager for freedom and spontaneous expression. Now they were mere *talibe*, each struggling to memorize long chapters of the Koran but seldom managing to go beyond the first quarter of the sacred book, *talibe* for whom each conquest of the memory brought a bit of prestige and a few small presents. The more gifted among them surrounded the master when, standing in front of the mosque, he urged the villagers to greater religious fervor and less moral laxity. For a time they carried the arms of duty; they devoted themselves with sacred solemnity to a task which made them more "human" by forcing them to "learn the ways of God," while women had shown them only "the ways of the devil." But a powerful desire to escape these rigors offset this temporary gravity; their shouts were as explosive as those of any other children when they were dismissed from school.

Fig. 8 Carrying fish

I saw this scene as a caricature of the weaknesses of Islam, so great was the effect of distortion produced by the mediocrity of the masters. Only one of those I encountered added a smattering of astronomy and philosophy to his command of the Koran. I re-experienced with force that malaise I had felt during my short vists to Oran and Casablanca, and above all during my Mauritanian adventure. I had long wondered what sort of shock could shake this world out of the fixed forms in which Moslem man had become immobilized. And I must confess my joy on reading Malek Bennabi's splendid book *Vocation de l'Islam,* which reveals a subversive awareness and expresses a lucid condemnation of the moral paralysis, the "despotism" of words and forms characterizing a civilization in which exegesis kills thought and antirealism has sustained a "tradition" which

33

often masks nothing but a myth. In Lebou country it has taken all the vitality and spontaneity of Negro-African stock to keep man from becoming, here too, the victim of his conversion.

This explains how the Ge fishermen came to conceive a new sect which denies the necessity of the pilgrimage to Mecca. This innovation is justified by the discovery of a genie-fish in which the legends abound and which incites to sacrilegious courage even as it evokes ancient loyalties: "If you achieve four consecutive catches and offer up all the proceeds on the fifth catch I shall reveal to you the secret of power. If you so desire, you can become a prophet. . . ."

Let us return to the Lebou child. After he leaves the enclosure where the "master of the book" holds forth at sunrise, he hurries, after a short respite, to the official school, where he must undergo an instruction which is imported, free, amazingly secular after the Koranic mumblings, but painfully compulsory. Only at his own risk and peril does he fail to resist the lure of the banks of the branch-channels or of the mystery of the palm groves—unless the work of the fields provides him with the most convenient of excuses. What a strange aberration is this, that forced the winged helmet of Vercingetorix and the creased kepi of Faidherbe upon the memory of this young schoolboy, and erased from it the image of Dyal Diop, liberator and first unifier of the Lebou communities! I do not mean to hold a brief for "tribalism," but only to show the abuses of a system too exclusively concerned with our own viewpoints and interests.

The results are disconcerting, but our astonishment is hardly justified. You will object that eventually things change—in Mamadou and Binéta have they not colored the characters in their readers black? You will remind me, of course, that my colleagues, armed with tests and scales of evaluation, are expected to offer scientifically founded suggestions. But are we not succumbing to the illusion of our technical mastery? How can we be sure that our instruments for measuring the mind, taken out of their element, still give satisfactory results? While I was in Lebou country a psychologist, Roseline Barbé, was confronting these difficulties; she was in a position to appreciate how greatly the cultural lag distorted her methods of analysis, and she had the extraordinary courage to remain in the background, often letting the unmanageable facts have their way.

I remember the multiple precautions and hesitations of the lamented André Ombredane, who began his investigation in the Congo by rejecting a large part of the testing material with which he had come equipped. In this instance he demonstrated that a severe critique of methods may constitute a first step toward the exploration of this other who has become the object of observation, as well as a necessary condition to genuine understanding. Above all else one must beware of being carried away, as almost happened to me when I arrived at Brazzaville, impatient to put Rorschach's psychodiagnostic to use. The records of my examinations repose in a file, doubtless forever.

Precisely what meaning is conveyed by these images which we present as revelation, or by the very words we exchange with our guides once, in our dialogue with the African, they have jumped from one culture to another? To ask the question is not to doubt, with a kind of unconscious racism, the undeniable capacity for assimilation shown by the Negro, but simply to consider the possibility of a discrepancy. Observing the French diction of my Lebou friends, I noted the existence of a slight difference in our usage of the same words—but I had little leisure to explore this impression. While conducting an inquiry in Brazzaville in the schools of Poto Poto, I decided to undertake a study based on this former observation. I presented the results of the analysis in my *Sociologie des Brazzavilles noires,* so there is no point in repeating them here. But I should like to emphasize the frequency of a schematic and in a certain sense artificial use of our language, even in more advanced students. Literary teachers on the secondary level ascribed this deviation to what they termed "dictionaryitis." Words do not have the same density, nor do they always occur in the same semantic field, when they are our instruments of communication and when they become those of the French-speaking African. From the outset, therefore, we run the risk of missing the nuances.

Marked by Moslem thought and education, and by French thought and education, the Lebou child meanwhile continues to receive the imprint of the traditional heritage. In this play of unequal and in many respects rival forces, tradition is still the most powerful. It is transmitted by the women, who effectively control the first years of childhood, by the instruction imposed during the retreat of circumcision, and by that apprenticeship in public affairs which occurs within the "age clubs." But this struggle of influences, which reflects the various vicissitudes of Lebou society, does not fail to incline the personality toward ambiguity, which is the sign under which I am writing this

35

book. How are so many demands, expressed by institutions which are declining, in the case of tradition, or incomplete, in the case of Islam and westernization, to be combined? Seemingly, the only solution would be to choose one of the three paths, but this would mean a further division in a society which long took pride in its original unity.

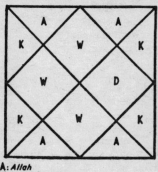

A: *Allah*
W: *The name of one of the Prophet's wives*
K: *The name of a Khalif*
D: *The desire expressed*

Fig. 9 A magic square

And yet the situation here is less serious than it is in other parts of Negro Africa. We must return to examples in which we find the effect of enlargement, examples of societies and civilizations which have been revolutionized. When I was working in Poto Poto, chance confronted me with a man not yet twenty years old whose perpetual insecurity and anxiety amazed me. He belonged to a Gabonese ethnic group now reduced to a few thousand persons; at a very early age he had fled, not the poverty and isolation of the village, but the dangers of a society in which the child has lost his points of reference and his security. No sooner had he allowed himself some modest revelation than he retracted it:

"Above all I was afraid of my uncle, but he was not the worst. The others wanted to gobble me up. . . ."

Here was the conflict in a nutshell, with a gesture which revealed a fear that had not yet been conquered. Born into a society in which the maternal uncle was dominant and in which children were hemmed in at an early age by groups which today have lost their rank, he had become a stake in the conflict

36

of interests which pitted this important personage against the father. He had wavered from one to the other. Helpless and without external support, in the end he had yielded to the pressures of the father who, recognizing the intensity of his need for education, at least permitted him to attend the regional school.

"My family [that is, the maternal relatives]did not want me to have an education. But perhaps it is true that we should not have abandoned the old ways. . . ."

The rivalry grew worse, becoming indirect and mobilizing the techniques of sorcery, which were all the more dangerous in the hands of relatives.

"I could no longer eat or sleep. I was sick, but my sickness was not of the body; my family was devouring me from within. . . ."

On the ruins of defeated societies, where individuals have lost the rules of the social game and retain only the skills suggested by personal interest, where resistance has lost access to the methods of direct violence, sorcery thrives. There is no question that by trying to destroy sorcery and with it "savagery," colonizers have restored to it that vigor which it always recovers on the ruins of civilizations. How many forces, held in check by old but delicate balances, are then unleashed! And no one can resist the temptation to push his own advantage, now in the name of tradition, now in the name of progress—the progress of "civilization," as my disturbing informants used to say, following our example.

But my Gabonese friend had no time to bother about all this. He felt that he was slowly dying. He chose escape to the city, where the law of numbers guarantees a protective anonymity.

"Here in Poto Poto I eat and sleep well. I have escaped the cruelty of a family that does not love me. . . ."

The fear is merely lulled, as was shown by his care to avoid any unnecessary contact; he left his place of work only to hurry to the protective limits of the "haven" where he lived.

"I have no friends, people are all bad. I do not like to go out because I am relaxed only when I am in my room. . . ."

Why have I chosen to play up this case, which is in no way unique, and which illustrates an unmistakable pathological disturbance? It is not just because the anguished face of the young Gabonese haunts me with a persistent clarity in spite of time and distance. He is only a symbol of African youth, which is subject to increasing pressure as the contested object of conflicting groups and is often deprived of the points of reference necessary to its equilibrium. This group is in greater danger than ever; it is beset by traps which are the more treacherous because they have become more subtle.

In an age when colonialism had not yet perverted human relations, Montaigne philosophized upon a little investigation which the modern ethnologist would do well to consider. He had the opportunity to question three Indians who were presented to Charles IX while the king was visiting Rouen; the result was the famous chapter which occurs in the first book of the *Essays:* "Three among them, ignorant of what the knowledge of our corruption will some day cost their peace and happiness, and that this commerce will be the beginning of their ruin . . . were at Rouen when the late king Charles IX was there."

In large areas we can recognize and evaluate this "ruin," which is not due simply to the exportation of "corruption," but this would not give us a valid argument for a so-called return to the past. Golden ages glitter only because they are always illusory. Everything becomes possible from the moment the new Negro generations refuse to let themselves be duped, and decide to stop being the dupes of their own weaknesses. In informal conversation with students at the old military school in Brazzaville, I had occasion to appreciate the anxiety that leads to a healthy self-examination. I was questioned and I did not avoid the responsibility of answering straightforwardly. This experience enabled me to observe their hesitation between determinedly modern preoccupations and those that tradition, that ideal position of isolation and imagined security, continues to impose. Two questions dominated the rest: What image do foreigners have of us, a new people who are awkwardly referred to as *enlightened*? And: What models must we study if we are not to waste our future? This in no way constitutes an admission of defeat. I remember the comment of my young friend Kassa, who was such a clever student and so little impressed by his success: "We are not dazzled by your great men, for we know that we have leaders worthy of our confidence."

3

Traditions

▼▼▼▼▼▼▼▼▼▼▼▼▼▼▼▼▼▼▼▼▼▼▼▼▼▼▼▼▼▼▼▼▼▼

AT THE GATES OF DAKAR

NIGHT has just fallen on the village of Grand Mbao, my base of operations in Lebou country. In the tropics, more than elsewhere, this is the moment when all life seems to be hushed. Noises cease. The bats have yet to take their squealing flight and the fireflies hover, then dart off like sparks. For a brief moment, men are glad to drink in the darkness and calm; once again they are discovering the quietness in things. Only the sea pounding on the sand imposes its monotonous power.

The complaint of a goat rises from a nearby stall.

Instantly it is answered by the terrible cry of a woman, a howl which rises and persists. In the next lane hurried steps reverberate, accompanied by whispering. An animal's cry has just disturbed one of the most delicate balances of the human organism. Konya has been overcome by her personal "genie;" her body no longer obeys her—it is convulsed.

The attack appears to be serious. The neighbor women, those who have been initiated in the everyday treatment of "possession," soon confess their incompetence; they decide to send for Tyabandao, through whom all forces can be tamed. This old woman, with her wrinkled skin, her cautious step and her untidy clothing, is possessed of considerable power. She was born to prestige, since she is the niece of Wasour Sek, a hero whose fantastic deeds are recalled by Lebou legend. She has the knowledge which gives control over the divinities influencing the women of the community: only she can treat possession which strikes for the first time, and transforms the aggressive "spirit" into a servile power useful to all. She has authority—so that she is consulted like the chief or the imam of a mosque in time of trouble—because she controls the feminine population and preserves those ancient rituals marginal, but most important, complementary, to Islam.

When she heard the complaint of the goat this evening, Konya recognized the characteristic cry of her possessor "genie;" she lost control. The initiates are worried because she was recently admitted to their association and accepted as a *lefohar,* or a woman related by possession.

It is scarcely more than a month since they danced the *ndoep* and sang the individual motto-chants of each of their companions. All the details of the ceremony are still fresh in their minds. The sequence can easily be traced.

Konya is seated in the center of her enclosure. She is surrounded by the initiates, near whom stand the *gorone** players and the spectators. Tyabandao who, as "mistress" of the cult, is at her side, first purifies her by sprinkling her with holy water. Next she welcomes her as support of the divinity and covers her with *nak,* a gruel of sweetened millet, and milk, as a sacrifice. Konya seems a part of the altar where later her genie will reside; between herself and this genie indestructible bonds, created by a real identification, are woven.

Then the *ndoep,* the sacred dance of possessed women, begins, with a choreography which is first slow and monotonous and whose triple beat is accented by the swinging of half-bent arms. Inexhaustibly the company takes up the chants, which establish communication between each adept and her personal genie and which often contain esoteric information. First we hear the fear of the newly possessed, who dreads an outburst over which she still has only an indifferent control:

I do not want to join the dance.
I want to leave it at once.
When I am older,
I will know better how to dance.

* A long, narrow drum.

40

Next, coquetry and a game of evasion which prelude the abandon to come:

> Mother of Wali, I am afraid.
> Mother of Wali, mother of Wali,
> I have known the city of the genies.
> I do not want to drink *singue*†.
> Mother of Wali,
> This year the water from the sea is coming up the river.

Then comes the invocation to the genies:

> Yoraye, Gambisal, Polbage.
> Mother of Yoraye, leave her alone!
> Grandmother of Yoraye, leave her alone!
> Leave her alone! Leave her alone!

Finally, formulas with secret meaning herald the climax of the ritual:

> The son of the bird must plow the earth.
> If he does not plow it,
> He is lost!

The dance accelerates, shoulders are shaken with an increasingly jerky motion; the right ones, which are left bare by the so-called "African bloc" style dresses, show full and lovely, glistening with sweat. The onlookers, abandoning their passive role, join in the excitement. The monotonous beating of the drums has now been going on for hours. Even the odors are becoming heavier, the smell of the spices mingling with the smell of sweat. For all the senses the excitations grow more intense; I must struggle to maintain my cool objectivity—that of the tape recorder turning with all its mechanical persistence.

Tyabandao reigns supreme. She has regulated the order of the chants. She orders an acceleration of the steps, calls for new figures. Now the arms are held over the head with the hands joined; they pull the whole body in a violent and only apparently disorderly dance. The movement must be even faster, to the threshold of unconsciousness. As soon as the personal

---

† A ritual water kept in earthenware pots.

motto-chant releases a kind of savage lust in the possessor genie, one must be ready for abandon, an abandon that overwhelms. Women collapse, and each time this happens they are immediately carried to the center of the dance, beside Konya. They continue to struggle violently, they crawl on the ground; their contracted bodies relax only to give way immediately to multiple contortions. They seem to be tiring; they ask for drink. Marem, a young woman I had already noticed for her cleverness and her modern look, comes with a gesture of bestial greed and swallows an entire basin of sea water. She pauses briefly, then returns to her interminable *corps-à-corps*. The analogy of a fight, perhaps to the death, comes to mind, and it is justified, for Lebou fighters have adopted certain of the chants of the possessed as mottos.

Marem is in danger. Will it be enough protection to repeat over and over the formula dismissing the spirit which has mastered her: "Return to whence you came!"

It is not enough, this formula which is both entreaty and command. The old women rush forward to offer their help. They apply damp earth to the nape of her neck and upper lip. They sprinkle her with fresh water. They move quickly, with precise gestures. Tyabandao also intervenes, and her body relaxes at once. Marem rises, dazed and mechanical; a friend takes her arm and leads her back to her hut.

The *ndoep* continues, as it will for two more days. The contagion affects several young women present as spectators, as if the fervor were expanding to the edge of the crowd and beyond, to the whole village which implicitly participates in this ancient ritual. Someone has just fallen, and this fall signifies her entrance into the company of the *lefohar:* it is the shock which she has undoubtedly been anticipating. Her immediate neighbors seize her and lead her to the center of the circle. Tyabandao observes her briefly, gives her the communal milk to drink, and pours some on her head, which consecrates her as a new support for a spirit. But this is only a preliminary and anticipatory ritual, simplified in the extreme, comparable to what emergency baptism is to the full Christian ritual. New ceremonies will take place in a few months; in this hope, the woman returns home accompanied by her friends.

The dance of possession belongs to the deepest strata of contemporary African civilizations. It is a phenomenon of extraordinary vigor, enduring where so many cultural traits have disappeared. Negroes who have been transplanted and dispossessed have introduced it in the New World, where it has become a conservatory of their lost civiliztions: the voodoo of Haiti, the *macumba* and *candomblé* of Brazil, and the *santeria* of Cuba, whose echoes reach our ears stripped of their sacred character, but still powerful. Certain modern Negroes whom we call enlightened continue to rediscover through it the traditional fervor. In Gabon I saw several Negro employees of administrative departments abandon European clothing to don the traditional loincloth and dance the *Bwiti*. We shall not avoid the problem presented by such fidelity by answering that the "savage" element is not easily suppressed; this would be mere intellectual laziness and childish ethnocentrism.

Time and again the ethnologist must have wondered about the element of reserve or "cheating" in these manifestations which one is tempted to link with hysteria, the *hysteria minor* of late nineteenth-century clinicians. Alfred Métraux examines such a hypothesis with regard to the voodoo cult in a fine essay entitled *Dramatic Elements in Ritual Possesion.* He shows that the authentic abandon and the submission to this real spiritual adventure cannot be questioned, but he also emphasizes how closely the seizure follows a model which is "precisely determined by tradition . . . which gives it both a sacred and a theatrical aspect." Ritual possession would seem to be an orderly disorder, a technique for communication with the divine, which differentiates it radically from nervous "disorders" of a hysterical nature. Among the Lebou, the *lefohar* woman is "seized" at the precise moment she hears the peculiar chant or cry of her ruling genie; she prepares herself for abandon, in the case of collective demonstrations, by long hours of dancing which compel her to internalize some very definite rhythms; she recovers from the seizure by means of a treatment whose effectiveness is less physical than social in nature, a sort of stop signal. Of course, there is no doubt that some personalities are more susceptible than others to the violence of possession, but this is interpreted as a gift, a way of excelling, rather than a mental illness. Only Moslem purism sees it as "the ways of devils," though for that matter the Moslems are more tolerant than our missionaries.

This problem of the sincerity of the "possessed" is also found in our own history, in the arguments provoked by examinations of "demoniacs" and "bewitched" persons. I have enjoyed following these arguments in the controversy between Jean Bodin, scholar and procurator of Henry III of France, and Johann Wier, doctor of the Duke of Cleves and author of a weighty treatise with the amazing title *Histoires, Disputes et Discours. Des illusions et impostures des diables, des magiciens, infâmes sorcières et empoisonneurs. Des ensorcelés et démoniaques et de la guérison d'iceux. Item de la punition que méritent les magiciens, les empoisonneurs et les sorcières.* * On this occasion only the doctor takes any risks. To alleviate the repression, he attempts to demonstrate the falsifications and disturbances, the "melancholy and extrabile" which determine "demoniac" manifestations. He argues heroically in behalf of respect for the human body, but his reasoning is sociologically less sound than that of the pusillanimous Bodin. The latter rejects the exclusively pathological interpretation, as I just did in the case of the Lebou, and with some heat: "Do your fellow countrymen, the Germans, have a melancholy temperament? You know very well they do not, and yet witches are common among them. In short, those whom we lead every day to the stake are 'hale and hearty' and have, I assure you, no obstruction of the spleen." He suspects an act of the will rather than submission to a physical disorder affecting the personality; he anticipates the pursuit of paths of understanding fundamentally opposed to Christianity. Moreover Johann Wier's interpretation falters when he alludes to collective attacks of possession as manifested by various communities of nuns. He sees these as a phenomenon of contagion, but his description of an incident suggesting "satanic" intervention shows how closely the nuns who became "possessed" all conformed to a single image of diabolic domination.

On one point, however, the procurator and the doctor are agreed: women, by virtue of their "readiness to believe and their frailty," to borrow Wier's phrase, are most vulnerable to "demoniac attacks." Both writers remark the role they play in the field of sorcery and dealings with "spirits." Until the late sixteenth century this is a commonplace observation which nevertheless deserves our attention. The case of the Lebou shows, almost at the source of the phenomenon, how a great conquering religion, however conciliatory on the level of doctrine, has transferred ancient religious practices to the feminine population. The cult of

---

* Stories, debates, and discussions. Illusions and impostures of devils, magicians, infamous witches and poisoners. Bewitched persons and demoniacs and their cure. Item, the punishment deserved by magicians, poisoners and witches.

the *lefohar* unquestionably remains the refuge of these practices. It contains the disparate elements of a cult of water genies, of fertility rites for sea and land, of therapeutic techniques; it preserves an authentically Negro religious behavior which has been expelled from official places of worship by Islam. However, in the case of Lebou society, there has been no fight to the death; the religion of the men and the religion of the women supplement one another in a kind of religious division of labor between the sexes. An uncompromising Islam would soon have brought on the hunting of witches and demoniacs. One cannot help thinking that the whole medieval period, which tended to execute all manipulators of "obscure forces," was trying to suppress all echoes of the pre-Christian past. In a ruthless struggle involving more than one religious conflict, human experiences were destroyed which no amount of searching or consulting of archives will ever be able to restore.

Let us return to Konya, sitting exhausted in the center of the dance. The *ndoep* is almost over and already relatives are making preparations for the sacrifice. They have brought a young bull and laid him down, and are binding his feet. Konya lies down beside the animal and both are covered with the same white cloth beneath which the young bride in an aristocratic wedding disappears during the ceremony before her departure for her husband's house. The direct allusion to marriage is unmistakable, especially when we remember that the circumcised boy is identified with the bull overcoming the heifer, and that the initiate will leave the place of her consecration to go and build her personal altar, the home of her spiritual "husband."

After a rather short interval which symbolizes the embrace of the woman and her master genie, Konya and the young bull are uncovered and restored to the sight of an audience which is overcome by a kind of communal expectation. This is because the union they have just witnessed in a sense constitutes a sacrilege, the intimate juxtaposition of the sacred and the profane. Balance must be restored and, in the phrase Joseph Chelhod used in connection with the Arab sacrifice, "a bridge thrown" between these two worlds. My allusion to this author is deliberate, for at this precise moment the ritual is modeled upon Moslem teachings. Order can be restored only by the performance of a bloody sacrifice: Abdulai, the local priest, walks solemnly over to the young bull, cuts his throat with a steel knife and catches the streams of seething blood in a gourd. The animal struggles to burst his bonds. The more the blood flows, the more effective the ritual gesture will be. Its sweetish odor dominates all others; its slow trickling becomes the cynosure of all eyes, and fascinates me more than anyone. I try to detach myself by concentrating on the role of the sacrifice in pre-Islamic Arab cults; but I cannot altogether escape an ancient fear, the memory of a schoolboy fight in which I hit someone too hard, the image of bloodshed when during the last war my comrades and I were obliged to sacrifice our first prisoners of war.

The imperturable Tyabandao seems to be indulging in a silent enjoyment, the better part of her power. She seizes the gourd containing the blood and pours part of it over Konya's head and clothing, down which it trickles already thick and brown. All night and the entire day to follow, she must preserve these stains which temporarily place her outside of ordinary life by manifesting the new status of a woman intimate with the genies. With this blood-feast the public part of the ritual is over. Guided by Tyabandao and followed by a few relatives, Konya retires to her dwelling, adopting a processional step. She will keep to her room, accompanied only by the "patroness" of the cult, during a short retreat. Tyabandao sprinkles what remains of the sacrificial blood on the floor of the room, then sets up and consecrates the altar where Konya, drawing on new forces, will submit regularly to the obligations required by her new master. The spot has just lost its profane and commonplace quality. This transformation is manifested immediately by the feast of communion, intended for the women and prepared with the flesh of the killed animal. But—and here again we see that this spiritual adventure concerns the entire collectivity—if the maximum communal intensity is now focused on Konya's home, participation is nevertheless widespread. Morsels of the slaughtered bull are given to family groups in order of precedence, to strangers and guests of the village, and also to the children who, even while they were playing, were awaiting this distribution near the door of the mosque.

This simple detail demonstrates the coexistence of the religion of the book, that imported Islam which does not always receive an unqualified credence, and the traditional religion, which has remained alive in spite of its decadence. The two cooperate to attain the same ends: to provide access to supernatural knowledge, to obtain that harmony necessary to the health and strength of the community, to pull man out of his sense of helpless weakness. Although the two "ways" have not yet diverged, Lebou society shows how much they differ in their approaches. For Islamized people, communication with the divine occurs through a literary go-between, through "techniques" defined by the Koran and its commentators, through obedience to a formalism which imposes conformity at the expense of the spiritual experience. Islam is associated here with the Koranic school and the prestige of the scholar, even the indifferent one; it remains the product of a civilization in which "literary" activity is valued far above all others. The cult of the *lefohar,* on the other hand, recipient of a very ancient heritage, in many respects resembles the religious manifestations of so-called "illiterate" peoples. Here the relationship with the divine seems much more spontaneous and also much more varied because memory, which preserves the rules of worship, is less constraining than sacred books which codify them. Supernatural knowledge, which is to be found neither in these books nor in their commentaries, must be sought directly through enthusiastic experiences capable of creating a partial coincidence between the mind and the sphere of the divine or the rationally unknown. Marx has shown how the level of techniques of production conditions the structure of societies. It would be interesting to analyze in minute detail, now that we have more adequate instruments at our disposal, how the level of techniques of communication between men has determined the character of civilizations. Sacred possession, that tool of so-called archaic societies, undoubtedly characterizes a certain era of intellectual communication.

Are the *lefohar* women of Lebou country destined to lose their prestige and become the guardians of an ever-receding past as a result of the accelerated cultural changes imposed by modernism and Islam? It is not for us to play the prophet, but merely to remember that in their evolution societies retain more elements derived from distant heritages than would appear at first glance. Even the history of the West provides no evidence to the contrary. In Africa, despite the fragility of material civilizations, the traces remain fresh.

The ancient Lebou village still appears, stippled like a neo-Impressionist painting, under the buildings of modern Dakar. Neither the mosques scattered through the various districts nor the horrible cathedral flanked by its Negro angels has dispossessed the protecting genies of the place. For Lebou of the old school, Ndak Daour and his descendants still see to the safekeeping of the people. Indifferent to the hubbub of the city, he resides in that sector bounded by Avenue Courbet, Avenue Pasteur and the barracks (a conjunction which seems deliberately ironic), while his sons are scattered among the villas hidden behind the bougainvillea.

Back in Mbao in 1945, the whole village had hoped that the end of the war would see the return of prosperity and the disappearance of restrictions. Everyone had been asking Tyabandao to perform the ritual opening of the fishing season. On the altar of Koumba Sene, the protective divinity of the village, she performed the sacrifice of a she-goat and made an offering of *nak*. Then she walked alone to the sea. She continued until the water reached her thighs, supporting with both hands on her head a gourd filled with *nak*. With a sudden gesture, she poured out the offering. Then she returned to the beach, singing and imitating the cries of mourners.

So no one doubts that for the time being Mbao is still safe from all catastrophes.

CONAKRY—NIGER

The scene changes. Shortly after the beginning of 1947 I took up residence in Conakry, but I soon felt the need to escape that city, which was then bogged down in its own lethargy and old age. I had just left the Guinea of mangroves and rice fields for a tour of the north, as far as the beginnings of the Sudanese world which stretches across Africa along the southern edge of the Sahara from Senegal to the state of Sudan itself. Termitaries here dominate a sparse and stunted vegetation and the vastness of the land remains "open," and all the more unsettling, in contrast to the same vastness which somehow closes in on itself in the forest regions of Africa.

During the first weeks of my visit to the African Institute in Dakar, Jacques Richard-Molard, who was filling in for the absent director, had asked me whether I was a man of the forest or a man of the savanna. This distinction determines a man's vocation, just as it has determined the original features of the movements of history, religions and aesthetics. The German ethnologist Leo Frobenius made this dichotomy into a regular golden rule. It represents only the most convenient of the attempts to organize the discouraging diversity of Africa.

In fact, I longed for these northern vistas, first because they

48

seemed to offer the possibility of avoiding a simplistic classification which qualified me as a narrow specialist; it was with the same sense of reshuffling the cards that I seized the opportunity for a short visit to Hawaii which I thought would enable me to spite my unimpressive label of "sociologist and Africanist." I am not partial to this parceling out of territory, with its petty border warfare, in a discipline which owes to itself to expand its comprehension by a diversity of experiences and confrontations. But this mischievous pleasure was not the only aspect of my northern journey that excited me.

I saw myself touching on the Sudan, that crucible in which a history which is not entirely hidden from us was wrought. In the distant past there existed empires from which African nationalism tries to borrow the references which will assure it some extension in time. More recently, we remember the violent resistance to colonial expeditions symbolized by the name of Samory. On the way from Kankan to the frontiers of Liberia and Ivory Coast I was to observe the ruins of an ancient *tata* (fortified town) where the Sudanese conqueror made a long visit. I found nothing but disappointment: a place devoid of grandeur, and a few traces which had managed to resist the rapid decomposition of time. What memorial do we have to this amazing military leader whom our schoolbooks conjure away and whom our official reports during the 1890s presented, according to a still-honored method, as a "puppet of no consequence?" Some information is furnished by André Arcin's *Histoire de la Guinée francaise* and evidence of our difficulties reposes in archives which are only beginning to be consulted. However, what we do know of Samory's maneuvers and the extent of his control forces us to acknowledge his military genius. In late 1893, despite the blows he had just been dealt by Colonel Bonnier's spahis, he left in search of horses from Mossi country and arms from the Gold Coast, recruited Toma pillagers at the Guinean border, set a trap at Waïma where the French and English killed each other's men in the belief that they were firing on his troops, and, maintained communications with Sierra Leone and lower Guinea. Of course local legends have longer memories, although they cheat by idealizing this figure. For us, the adventure closes with the dry little statement of an official report: "In 1898 Samory was captured by the French and deported to Gabon, where he died in Ngolo in 1900." By a coincidence it was two years after my Sudanese mission that I was to make my first tour of Gabon, which included a visit to the tomb of the fallen conqueror.

In traveling north toward the Sudan I was not only interested in discovering places attesting to a tormented history. I knew that I would find a country which had been opened early to the trade characteristic of old Africa—gold, cola nuts, salt and cattle—and a center of communications through which the slave routes also passed. Through administrative reports written during the first decades of this century I had carefully reconstructed the movement of these transactions, which fanned out to the borders of Gambia and the southern regions of Ivory Coast. The mechanism of trade revives memories remaining from our childhood reading. The image it evokes is one of severe competition and products which seem out of place in the official documents, in the style of those lists with which Jacques Prévert disconcerts us: fabrics from English manufacturers, salt, cola nuts, rubber, gold, ivory, cheap hardware, cattle, sheep, tobacco, gourds, finally *guinzé,* those pieces of iron used in traditional barter. When one studies these occasional balance sheets, one senses all the precision and vastness of the network of commercial activity in this region where the Sudan opens on the forest and finds its issue in the sea.

Manufactured products which have come from the ports in search of the crude rubber, gold and ivory offered by the markets of Kouroussa, Kankan and Siguiri. Cola nuts wrapped in a foliage known as *popo* which prevents browning and fermentation of the fruit, transported by "express" to connect with herds and salt arriving from Timbuctu. There was even competition between dealers in chip salt quarried in the mines of the Mauritanian border and peddlers of bulk salt originating in coastal regions. In short, a country wide open to people, products and competition, in which ethnology would be ill-advised to regard the peoples it meets as units protected from and unacquainted with the vicissitudes of history.

Although I had been in Conakry only a short while, I left the town with relief. I had not yet adjusted to that native poverty under corrugated iron and crumbling walls of *banco* which neither the coconut palms which crown the city in a panoramic view nor the monumental mango trees succeeded in diminishing. The bridge of Tumbo, a fragile link between Conakry, which had not yet overflowed and invaded the beach of Camayenne, and the root of the peninsula, seemed to me a symbolic shortening, the only thread by which two alien worlds tried to communicate. The tarred road was scarcely nine miles long, and you could have the illusion of pioneering as soon as you hit the first bumps. Now, the automobile quickly covers the distance to Kindia, a city under development which collided with the feudality of Peul groups which established their furthest outpost there. I say "now" in connection with memories only ten years old, with more astonishment than a former colonial rediscovering in 1939 the places he had left twenty-five years before. Highways, mines, whole new urban centers, first preparations for hydroelectric stations: all these material upheavals are transforming the familiar landscape with an amazing rapidity. The Africans are renouncing their former patience; they desire ever more fiercely and more quickly those appurtenances which render them stronger in relation to us but leave them initially defenseless in relation to themselves.

As I look through my travel folders for some notes which might recall the stages of my journey toward the Sudanese region, some of them at least seem to have an outmoded and irrelevant quality. In Coyah, where over the years political conflicts have resulted in violence and death, I observed primarily the orderly excitement of the market, the colors and odors, the unusual appearance of the displays.

Balls of dye are juxtaposed with flowered fabrics, the hardware "department" with its kerosene lamps made from old cans, and a few pairs of shoes whose soles are cut from worn-out tires: even in 1947 our "leftovers" still provided raw materials which were eagerly appropriated by the industrious activity of the Negro craftsman. The little displays which the women tend languidly are lavish with color: masses of speckled bananas, golden pineapples offered as deluxe fruits, enormous cherry-red tomatoes, dried pimentos giving off a pungent and insidious odor, and white balls of fermented manioc, which still constitutes the bread of the traditional villager and of the poor: all this suggests the scale of business. A woman selling roasted peanuts has only a tomato-paste can for a measure. The scene is commonplace throughout the Negro world; it helps one to appreciate the poverty of economies which have remained archaic in a mercantilist system.

After my stroll through Coyah, I resume my journey: a monotonous series of clay huts all of which bore empty bottles—another unusual example of salvaging—attached to their thatched roofs for the purpose of protection. It is not until one reaches the outskirts of Kindia with the complexity of its population that the houses exhibit any character that attracts one's attention. The round hut made of *banco* and opened to the outside by means of a narrow door and a series of square of diamond-shaped grooves occurs more frequently when one touches on Peul territory. Its thatched roof is arranged in graduated bands which make it resemble a motionless ballerina who is throwing back the upper part of her body. It is surrounded by a veranda of branches and dried mud. Much more often than in the coastal region, it affirms the social status or religious choice of the owner; a tall pole bearing the characteristic protective flame guards the threshold.

Fig. 10 A Peul hut in Fouta Djallon

Kindia is a crossroads where conquering and conquered groups have been thrown together, now temporarily stabilized in their respective positions, now juxtaposed in one of those hybrid villages with which the administration has experimented. These are characterized by a combination of three groups—Soussou, Peul and Malinke—which occurs even in Portuguese Guinea. Along with it, the European population has expanded as opportunities for economic development have emerged. As a matter of fact, this is a region particularly favorable to human enterprise. This "great valley of Kindia which," to quote E. F. Gautier, "articulates and renders intelligible the whole surface of Fouta Djallon," has attracted men from the most remote times. With the help of my notebooks, I recall the wealth of prehistoric investigations which were offered to my curiosity. At the time I enjoyed the collaboration of a planter who had come "for the banana" after several unsuccessful attempts to cheat the treasury of Monrovia, and who collected stone cut from each of his plantations. I noted eleven places worthy of thorough investigation, names whose resonances I still enjoy: Tasakouré Kolakouré, Sagali Fommé, Dounbéyakori, etc. Actually, I was able to visit only that rock-covered shelter known to Europeans as the "Grotto of the Monkeys," which dominates the River Santa and is located in a cliff of sandstone slabs with horizontal layers. There were some fine big specimens of globular, bifacial pieces.

Africa offers more material evidence of her distant past than of her civilized history. We succeed in grasping the two extremes when our current activities—construction of railroads, highways or harbor works like those at Brazzaville which unearth layers of the banks of the Congo—produce evidence of prehistory. Almost all of the intermediary stages, however, elude us. The ethnologist *qua* Africanist finds himself confronted by civilizations which seem to have obliterated themselves in a perpetual present and never at any time, except for a few rare and imposing ruins like those of Rhodesia and the elliptical temple at Zimbabwe, to have had the taste for monuments. Nothing is found here of what in our eyes constitutes the grandeur of the ancient Americas or of ancient Asia, that immortal architecture by which civilizations prove themselves less vulnerable than the peoples who created them.

I arrived in the region of Kindia shortly after the circumcision ceremonies. Along the paths processions of circumcised boys resembling young Tibetan monks—at least, that was my reaction to the metamorphosis of the human landscape created by their unusual silhouettes—kept up a commotion by endlessly shaking their rattles, which were ordinary sistra made of pieces of gourd cut into disks with crenelated edges. The vivid colors of the initiates' costumes lay on a drab countryside. The Soussou wear a red-and-white-striped knitted hat with a tassel and a long navy-blue *boubou* with white embroidery which is decorated at the breast with the design of the pentagram, thus combining a Moslem symbol with a variation of the tricolor. The Malinke, on the other hand, show a happy moderation; they wear the same garment, but in their case it is decorated with a single cotton cord at the left shoulder, and their white caps end in a simple tasseled braid. The style of the Soussou is, moreover, associated with a greater freedom with regard to the tradition ritual of circumcision; like the Baga of the coastal region, they permit the presence of women, whereas the Malinke have maintained the strictest segregation.

I was on one of those great axes along which Islam secured

its expansion. Even in the vast, little-populated region preceding the Sudan and the Niger River, in the vicinity of Kankan and Kouroussa, I discovered its influence in the form of a sacred geometry: those squares or rectangles of unpolished stones laid flush with the ground which form praying enclosures intended for travelers. Before leaving the region of Fouta Djallon controlled by the Peul, I had very much hoped to meet their supreme chief, Almamy de Mamou, ancient representative of a strict Islam. His neighborhood is on the outskirts of town and hidden by a screen of Lebanese shops, official buildings and identical villas. I was prepared for a strict etiquette, a decorum still honoring a political and religious power which was once considerable. Instead, a few servants dozing in a courtyard came slowly to life and showed me in without formalities, as if their master were the most ordinary local dignitary. Almamy was sitting on the edge of an iron bed with brass balls and ornaments such as were to be found in modest French homes around 1925. Five young men were crouched at his feet. In this unfortunate imported decor, he lost some of the nobility of his bearing. I soon realized that the man himself had been reduced to the scale of such a setting by the secessions of suzerains which the administration had encouraged and the insidious and irritating control which it had imposed. I remember the situation more than fifty years before: Peul country was naturally affected by the rivalries existing between the two families who reigned alternately and the feudal powers, but the dynamism remained intact, almost independent. An amazing adventurer known as the Count of Sanderval rallied these elements to some important projects of economic modernization, notably the construction of a railroad. With their consent, he envisioned vast plantations, intending first a commercial monopoly and then sovereignty of the "kingdom" of Kahel. Administrative occupation of Fouta Djallon soon put an end to his dreams. Sanderval disappeared forever in 1899, when he left Guinea. Althought the railroad was built during the first decade of this century, the Almamys were slow to receive administrative office, so that only recently was their last successor given a seat on the administrative council of a mining society.

Mamou, at an altitude of about 2,400 feet, is a starting point for the tourist spots of Fouta Djallon and especially the health resort of Dalaba, where the mountain masses exhibit melting forms and colors reminiscent of the Auvergne. This game of comparison becomes irresistible as the African landscape becomes hillier. I enjoyed the mountains of central Cameroon as much as I did the plateaus that dominate Brazzaville. It is as if altitude effects a shift in longitude which enables one to escape the violence of the tropical climate and at the same time restores a more familiar wild life. This need for self-deception is increased by the lure of spring water, which is reinforced in these regions by the hidden danger, the vegetable decay harbored by the calm and insidiously attractive rivers. On leaving Mamou for Portuguese Guinea, the traveler soon discovers that the landscape has lost all interest: a monotonous rusty plain relieved only by desolate hills of shale, where one occasionally observes an antelope in flight or a distant band of cynocephalus.*

At Kankan I encountered the great highway linking the Sudan with the forest country of the south. A curious symbol of this very ancient commercial activity and of confidence in its future is a large bridge which straddles the Milo River, but remains useless since it does not connect with any road. In its shelter, washerwomen make a colorful and charming picture. Kankan is a point of transit, a stopping place for river boats headed upstream and the railroad connecting Conakry with the Niger. In Kankan, hybrid town and marketplace, the once-hostile representatives of African diversity are juxtaposed.

Fig. 11 A group of Sudanese-type huts in Kankan

In the squares magic recipes brought by Islam are offered along with recipes of Negro magic from the forest. The successful dealers know that the more foreign they are, the better they

* The dog-faced baboon.

will do. Chances of success seem to multiply in the presence of an unfamiliar technique. Here I observed the confidence placed in magical products imported from forest regions; in faraway Montserrat, on the outskirts of the monastery which dominates a powerful landscape of ruinlike rocks thirty-five miles from Barcelona, I was to observe the prosperity of a woman selling a tisane "of forty herbs" who held an audience of visitors whose foreignness heightened their credulity. Well, here in the main street of Kankan was one of these hawkers of panaceas. He was dressed in a style which recalled the costumes of the circumcised: a long navy-blue tunic covered with amulets for sale—sachets, savage teeth encased in leather, horns filled with animal and vegetable substances. His headdress, of the same workmanship as the tunic, was a navy-blue cap decorated with two tasseled cords which framed the face. With half-shut eyes he awaited the customers who could not fail to appear.

On the highway as you leave the city to go toward Bamako, the heavy traffic carried men and produce in a multicolored medley, in which modern methods of transportation were juxtaposed with archaic donkey caravans advancing Indian file. A group of Moors, always dignified despite the filthiness of their clothing, were reaching the end of their journey: they were pushing before them flocks of sheep enveloped in a yellowish dust. They passed huge trucks loaded so high with cola nuts that they looked about to fall over: all the available space was devoted to this highly salable commodity, forcing hitchhikers off the vehicle. From time to time lines of porters formed beside the road, sometimes led by a notable still wearing his old dress sword.

As I approached Bamako, the details of these scenes of picturesque mercantilism became more typically Sudanese and accordingly less varied. The round hut of rough-cast *banco* grew smaller, accorded less prominence to the thatched roof, and became less open, presenting only a single low door. The group of habitations belonging to a single "family" also followed this trend; they formed a circle with wicker walks running between them. As one approached the infrequent water supply points, the tiny gardens with their tangles of creeping plants were likewise carefully enclosed. Hence the eye was struck by this motif of containment, which contrasted with the movement of the road: protection from a formidable sun which during certain hours of the day necessitated an "interior" life; protection from strangers who were still suspected of dangerous influences; and undoubtedly a last survival of the withdrawal once imposed by a procession of conquerors. And yet everything had changed so much! Two images return to mind. In the dense shade of the mango trees in the town squares, donkey caravans carrying cola nuts took their rest during the heat of the day. Beyond, in the flatlands bordering the river, a pair of oxen joined with a wooden yoke could be seen pulling a plow to open the ground for rice. These images remind me of those edifying allegorical figures of commerce and agriculture which, as if to preach a moral, adorn French bank notes.

Fig. 12 A Peul calabash, Cameroon

If I wanted to assign two botanical symbols to this intermediate country between the forest and the desert, I believe I would select the cola nut and the calabash gourd. The latter, hollowed out, molded and often decorated, still floods the markets despite the competition of hardware and enamelware, which find unusual uses in the hands of the African housewife. One frequently sees porters heading toward the marketplace loaded with piles of calabashes crammed into net bags like so many captive balloons. They are of a hue that delights the eye, a warm yellow in their natural state or a rich rust when their rinds have been rubbed with a decoction of millet leaves. They

57

bear witness to an ingenuity in turning a natural product which is practical by virtue of its shape, strength and malleability into a multifunctional tool. They provide numerous household implements, including colanders, strainers and mortars. The women use them as scoops to catch small fish and tiny crustaceans, and because of the ease with which they may be rotated they are the most convenient receptacle for the decantation of gold ore. They are used for carrying, "sitting" amazingly well on the women's heads. They make surprisingly good musical instruments: whistles, trumpets, horns and drums. In a bewildering series of prestidigitations which whisks them from the realm of play to sacred uses, they may be transformed into children's toys, amulets or sacrificial objects. Craftsmen use them to record popular allegories and teachings. They form the backdrop of everyday life.

Fig. 13 A Bariba calabash, Cameroon

Here is a commonplace scene: two men meet, greet one another, express happy surprise, exchange gossip; one of them takes a red cola nut from his pocket and divides it as a token of friendship. In an everyday gesture he produces this fruit, source of strength and appetite, which kindles relations with men and gods and which for several centuries has been the basis of far-reaching trade and lucrative speculation. "Cola" routes early covered all of western Africa and extended far to the north, since they seem to have reached Morocco by the fourteenth century; they branched out in a multitude of byways all terminating in those markets and stalls where the piles of white or red nuts now appear alongside the retail candy and cigarettes. Although it is always full of stimulating alkaloids, caffein and theobromine, it is not a matter of indifference whether the fruit belongs to the red or white variety. Its price varies, as does its taste—the latter variation consisting of a slight difference in the degree of bitterness encountered when one chews the nut, which always leaves the tongue rough. The social significance attached to it also varies, for the white cola may be regarded as an improper gift, a sign of stinginess, or on the other hand a specific in certain ritual therapies. From November to February the Sudanese *marka* travel in caravans from the forest regions to the principal outlets of the Sudan. They are trying to acquire modern means of transportation, but they are competing with "Europeans" who do not hesitate to work their trucks to the limit in the event of a trade agreement requiring clever manipulation of prices. Thus Bamako has become a veritable stock exchange for cola nuts.

If I had to specify the condition which the Sudanese prefers above all others, I would choose without risk of error this mental and emotional stimulation which cola achieves. It helps on long marches; with that slow rumination which marks withdrawal of the individual into himself, it accompanies difficult or important meditations; it lends warmth to human intercourse. I have tried to use this technique for achieving euphoria. I discovered a harsh bitterness, I attained a genuine acceleration of the heart, but I do not believe I was overcome. The fact is that it is impossible to treat the consumption of cola as a solitary pleasure; it bestows its full effects only in a certain sphere of social relations. All the ordeals of exaltation to which the African subjects himself, from rhythmics to ceremonies resorting to the use of drugs, are collective. The same is true of the intoxication so efficiently promoted by our exportation of allegedly delicious hard liquor. But in the case of the consumption of cola nuts there is much more than this requirement of social harmony; there is the necessity of an intermediary which seems in a certain sense to be sacred. When chewed and saturated with saliva, the nut establishes a bond between man and the divinities; the initiate uses it for this purpose before addressing himself to the mask of which he is the protector and bearer. When it is manipulated, when its cotyledons have been

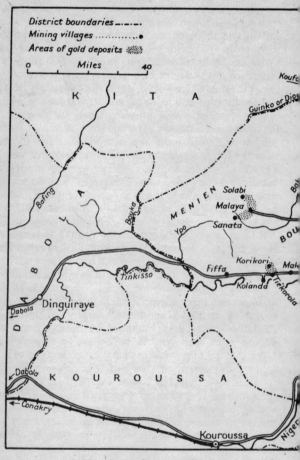

Fig. 14 Map of gold workings around Siguiri,

in the Sudanese area of Guinea

separated, the nut delivers a message. The consultant throws down the two fragments which, depending on whether they fall on the flat surface or the curved or split in two, express an elementary system of meanings. In short, this fruit of a simple forest tree resembling certain of our peach trees is more than an excuse for vast commercial exchanges; it acts as a means of communication among beings on the level of auspicious or efficacious relations. It combines a diversity of meanings and functions, as do all products of nature or human industry in societies where technology has not yet devaluated objects by mass-producing them.

THE GOLD OF THE NIGER

My progress through Sudanese country was checked at Siguiri, a post located on the Niger where the river becomes swollen with the gold-laden waters of the Tinkisso. The town, parched under its bright red poincianas, had lost some of its former importance. A fortified center built along the route of the Sudanese conquerors, in peacetime it was merely a stopping place for caravans. Heart of one of the largest groups of gold deposits, it had not known development because all attempts at industrial exploitation of the "fabulous metal" had successively suffered defeat. Siguiri remained afflicted with a drowsiness which was reinforced by the oppressive heat of these early days of the year. And my first two European meetings epitomized this solar limitation. At the caravanserai the only guest was a lieutenant of the colonial infantry who, exhausted by a long tour of duty, left his hammock under the veranda only to visit the terra cotta jar in which water was freshening or the bottle of "medicinal" cognac. In the large reception room into which I was shown by the administrator, a man who assured me from the start that although progressive, he was not above delivering a kick in the pants by way of stimulation, two young Negroes gleaming with sweat were working a heavy *punkah* suspended from the ceiling; their labor was as useless as it was interminable.

A short stretch of road led to the banks of the river (*dyeliba*). The calm greyness of the Niger impressed me more, I think, than those dark tumultuous waters full of uprooted plants which the Congo rolls as it emerges from Stanley Pool. Indeed, the Niger is richer in memories. In the schoolbooks it is the river of "mystery" which long concealed its origins from the curiosity of colonial expeditions. For me, it is still that aerial view of its gigantic mouth just before you reach Port Harcourt: a vast swarm of arms and slivers of islands in which the relation of land to water is inverted to the point where all solidity seems to belong to the latter. The Niger is also the burning issue in discussions concerning the agricultural office built on that part of the loop where the river squanders its waters beyond all limits; the idea was to transform this place which Pierre Herbart's report denounced as "the cancer of the Niger" into a "little island of prosperity." And finally, I used to wonder whether there were any but a verbal connection between the poet Paul Niger, the Guadeloupan rebel, the river I was engaged in discovering, and my own pursuit of Africa, accompanied by these haunting verses: *"L'Afrique de 'l'homme du Niger', l'Afrique des plaines désolées labourées d' un soleil homicide. . . ."**

Across from Siguiri is Somono, a village of fishermen who know the river well and are skilled in controlling it. On the whole the men appear strong and handsome, brawnier and shrewder for their continual struggle with the water. They use the cast net, the drag net and the oblong wicker trap; but it is in throwing the harpoon—one featuring a mobile point armed with either two or four barbs—that they best reveal their powerful precision. They are also shippers on the most economical of communication routes. Flat canoes and barges rock slowly against the bank, stirred by the swarming of entire families which live in them under roofs of matting. The double-rammed canoe, made of separate planks spliced together, is impelled by a triangular sail; its back half is lived in, while in front, also protected by a structure of mats, it bears a cargo of from one to two tons in which cola, rice, peanuts and manioc mingle their odors as in one of our fancy grocery shops. The barges, which have decks at both ends and are more heavily loaded—ten to fifteen tons—give an impression of security, perhaps because of their everyday appearance. They serve partly for the transport of passengers, since they cover more territory, going as far as Bamako. On board there are a few of those *dioula* traders, masters of all forms of contraband, their ample clothing—which I found in keeping with their magpie faces—fluttering in the light breeze.

* "Africa of the 'man of the Niger', Africa of the desolate plains harrowed by a murderous sun. . . ."

In the region of Siguiri, gold is still at the center of all activities. The *dioula* are clever at acquiring it on a so-called parallel market in exchange for fabrics, novelties, and foodstuffs which, like rice, sell for scandalous prices. They are skilled in attracting customers by means of loans of merchandise which lead to indebtedness with interest and finally to confiscation of the "crop" of the rich metal. They compete with the administration which is nevertheless trying to attract the gold washer with a subsidy of sugar and cloth. They maintain their control over a flourishing illicit trade in and around Conakry, Bamako and Dakar, Portuguese Guinea, Sierra Leone, and the countries to the south. In March 1947, for example, at a time when the government had succeeded in negotiating only 187 kilos of gold dust, it was estimated that approximately 800 kilos of metal had reached Portuguese Guinea alone.

I was visiting a gold deposit near the village of Doko. The sale was proceeding right outside the quarry, in a place which had something of the market and something of the booth of an old-fashioned moneylender—a sacred place where Islam, African ritual, and the prudent and mathematical religion of the Golden Calf were combined. A methodical, almost silent activity was proceeding under a fragile roof of foliage. The altar was a wagon protecting the precision scales. The officiating priests, the nearby *dioula,* dressed in their rich *boubous* and wearing colonial helmets and dark glasses, were lying casually on bamboo lounge chairs; with solemn gestures, they were busy separating iron filings from gold dust with the aid of small magnets. They dominated the scene. Around them but at a distance, the few spectators moved with an unaccustomed restraint. Women were selling little piles of fragrant mangos, or rice and millet *couscous* cooked on the spot. Butchers waited, indifferent, behind stalls where pieces of meat darkened, covered with hungry flies.

Lower down, near the muddy river, men, women and children were working among piles of loose soil, irresistibly suggesting the hackneyed image of the anthill. The technique was simple, and owed as much to the ritual as it did to the tool, although it required a long and painful labor which granted little respite from eight o'clock in the morning until six o'clock at night. For over six months this swarming of men intent on the pursuit of gold—ten to fifteen thousand might toil over a single deposit—would continue; except on Monday, an unlucky day when the place must be abandoned to the divinities, the *ginné* in charge of the metal. Only beliefs, whether local ones or those peddled by a debased Islam, could succeed in curbing this passion and contributing some restraint to the race for gold. In the presence of this metal, all social distinctions disappeared: strangers and villagers, nobles and common people, members of castes, all were capable of turning into these human moles who faced one another armed only with the speed with which they could move dirt.

In this activity which is so fundamental to the region, creative freedom recovers all its rights: the mine belongs to the man who discovers the lode, and not to the owner of the land. He becomes the chief, or *damantiki,* assisted by suitable functionaries, or *kountiki,* armed with old European guns or dress sabers, and a council of the elders, in a system combining village democracy with the power of chiefs "with customers." The discoverer collects a contribution—in these early days of 1947, fifty francs per pit dug. He enjoys a right of search. Above all, owing to his success he enjoys a prestige which assures him a more plentiful manpower eager to participate in his luck.

But does he have the "gift?" The search for gold leads to an all-out mobilization of powers: anything that works is good. One might say that the role of experimental knowledge is limited. Examination of soil, rocks and vegetation does not seem to go very far. Still, I am told that the lode of Manitoro was discovered through the presence of a downy-leafed shrub, the *soh wanie,* which serves as an indicator. But it is better to enter into communication with the sovereign divinities of the metal. Dreams are consulted, and if they show fire or red monkeys running toward a certain spot, the miners begin a series of soundings there. The old men consult cola nuts, which answer yes or no and tell where to search. However, it is the magical and religious apparatus disseminated by Islam which seems most popular. The marabouts consult the Koran as well as Oriental traditions; they conduct the prospecting by preparing collections of suras which will be washed on the spot, or magic squares which ensure success; finally, they provide the protection of animal sacrifices.

Gold has always gone hand in hand with secrecy and cunning. This was primarily to protect possessors of deposits from the greed of specialists in trans-Saharan trade. From the eleventh century Arab chroniclers have mentioned the fabulous wealth of the Sudan. Although they maintain that gold is "the principal product of the Negro countries," they are taken in by false information deliberately circulated, and curiously, they regard the coveted metal as vegetable matter. Hence, according to Ibn el Fagih, the Sudanese grow gold in the sand just as peasants raise vegetables. An Arab treatise states without the slightest reservation: "There are two aurigenic plants; you dig holes and pull up the gold roots". The dishonesty of exploiters does not imply a more rational understanding. For the Sudanese, gold is the least natural of the products offered by nature. God created it and entrusted it to the care of genies whose complicity and consent must be obtained. It remains a dangerous product, subject to a law of ambivalence which divides it into "living gold" and "dead gold." Living gold cannot be attained by men; it is concealed and possesses the power of lightning and fire; it is manifested in the violence of landslides, the splitting of rock and vitrified land. Dead gold has been partly neutralized by the effects of sacrifices; it is regarded as the part temporarily conceded to man. Nevertheless it remains dangerous and its sudden disappearance or its appearance in too great quantity arouses anxiety, requiring the setting up of protective devices.

The founding of a mine consists first of all of a ritual operation performed after consultation to determine the most favorable moment and the nature of the sacrifice. The head of the mine, acting on this occasion in his role of priest, conducts the sacrificial procedure with the assistance of members of his familial group. He asks the *ginné* who guard the gold for the right to take the metal, then recites three Koranic suras which are taken up by the chorus of those present. He has still to perform the sacrifice of foundation, which requires a red cock, a rust-colored he-goat or a russet bull, recalling the connection between gold, fire and the red appearance of phenomena. When the animal's throat has been cut, it is roasted and communally consumed by all. The liver, heart and lungs—those seats of a greater power—can be allotted only to the master of the sacrifice. Next, red cola nuts are distributed to all the men present, each of whom chews one of the halves of the nut, spits it out on the place where the animal's throat was cut, and then eats the other half. After the ceremony the sacrificer retires until the next day, thus revealing his peculiar situation, his cardinal position in the system of forces which have temporarily been balanced in favor of man.

I was saying just now that an unexpected stroke of luck may cause the danger to reappear. At the Doko deposit Ngolo, a relative of the head of the mine, has just extracted a nugget weighing over 1,000 grams, which sparkles in spite of its matrix. The news circulates, work ceases in all pits, the miners become restless and grumble, and again I am reminded of an anthill which a child is worrying with a stick. General consternation. There are only two solutions: put the nugget back in the ground, or neutralize it. The head of the mine hurriedly consults the council of elders, but he has already decided not to relinquish such a beautiful piece. He orders emergency measures: all men will abandon work until order has been restored. The nugget, fascinating and dangerous, is displayed in the center of the mine, creating around it a large no man's land. Ngolo wanders among his companions, stupefied by such a severe shock. Hastily the head musters his policemen, armed with guns, and arranges them in an alarming and picturesque firing squad; at his order all fire toward the nugget to dispel the *ginné* responsible for such dangerous generosity. I feel as if I am witnessing the solemn execution of the Golden Calf, which I imagine to resemble the statute the stockbreeders of Morvan erected on the big square of Saulieu. Ngolo worries and complains: "What a terrible misfortune to have incurred the wrath of the masters of gold! Pity the miners! What a terrible calamity!" And I expect to hear him add, for cold interest does not lose its claims, "Do not let us succumb to this temptation." A final step, the sacrifice of a young red bull, and confidence regains the upper hand and the *dioula* negotiates for the magnificent find.

The mining police have as much trouble with the dangers of the supernatural as they do with the threat represented by clever thieves. They see to it that the *tana,* prohibitions whose violation might restore to the gold its elusive and terrible mobility, are respected. It is strictly forbidden to bring into the camp grains of *soumbara* (or *nere,* as it is called), onions, dogs or potash. Infraction of these prohibitions, by upsetting that balance and harmony so difficult to achieve, would bring an era of catastrophe. An apocalypse would be unleashed combining the fire of heaven, the subversion of the earth and the fury of the waters.

There is no doubt that terror, latent but never dispelled, lurks in the minds of men who remain improverished in the face of so much deceptive wealth. What benefit do they derive from an arduous labor? A group of a dozen men, women and children may extract an average of 250 grams of gold dust in one season. This represents less than 29,000 African francs at the time of the sale which is dishonestly profitable to the *dioula,* who know only too well how to create indebtedness; and this sum is considerably reduced after the expenses presented by these men have been subtracted. There remain a few crumbs which provide only a meager improvement and are used to make those fragile jewels —earrings and pendant necklaces—of braided thread which the women wear for special occasions and which partly make up the matrimonial exchanges. Crumbs, for a dangerous work which the men regard in a certain sense as warfare. A miner killed in a landslide is a warrior fallen in battle. I was at the Doko lode a few days after such an accident, which had resulted in the death of a foreign gold washer. All the miners hastened to shore up the excavation, not in order to save a life but to prevent the gold from "escaping". When the body had been washed, it was immediately carried into the bush far from the mine. It was laid out on a bed of hastily assembled stones, surrounded with branches, and covered with a slender structure of gathered wood. Then began a slow procession in which each miner laid a stone on the body, forming a tumulus which crushed their unfortunate comrade for the second time. This very ancient ritual forbids the recitation of Moslem prayers. The man was only a foreigner, a Toma from the forest who had come for the few thousand francs he was unable to earn in his native region. It was decided that the sacrifice of a red he-goat would suffice to restore order, after which all the miners hurriedly returned to their subterranean activity.

Does not this constant fear of the mobility of gold express a disillusionment with regard to a production which in certain respects is fabulous? It is said that the Sudanese king Mansa Moussa, sovereign of Mali in the fourteenth century, was so extravagant with rare metal on a visit to Cairo that he lowered the rate of exchange. For the poor, there is another reality. After passing through so many hands and so many screens, gold leaves only an infinitesimal profit.

One must guard against looking upon these conceptions as the result of a collective aberration, a mentality hampered by the irrational. Ritual practices, which alone are capable of domesticating the metal, seem to assure protection as much as output. They safeguarded the gold washer against the greed of feudal powers and made transaction necessary. Never did Mansa Moussa, even at the height of his power, dream of tak-

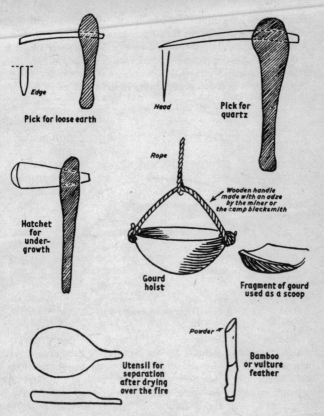

Pick for loose earth — Edge

Pick for quartz — Head

Hatchet for under-growth

Gourd hoist — Rope — Wooden handle made with an adze by the miner or the camp blacksmith

Fragment of gourd used as a scoop

Utensil for separation after drying over the fire

Bamboo or vulture feather — Powder

Fig. 15 Mining tools

ing possession of the gold mines; he saw them only as an excuse for "unparalleled" taxes and lucrative trade. Ritual practices also introduced a strict regulation, a kind of planned economy which was indispensable in the case of an activity capable of upsetting primitive and vulnerable economies. The agreements established by tradition, which reveal that African sociological sophistication which always operates in terms of equilibrium, have not as such been able to resist the upheavals created by the European presence. Commerical companies have stimulated the gold market and negotiated through the *dioula;* they have contributed indirectly to the desanctification of production and trade; they have introduced the speculative system. Thus external vicissitudes are becoming more tangible; gold washing is depreciating rapidly while the quantity of minerals in the world mined on an industrial scale is increasing; this wealth is becoming ever more elusive and more illusory.

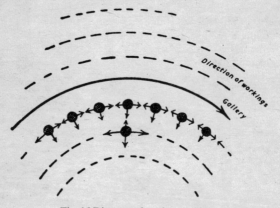

Fig. 16 Diagram of a mine-working

And yet men continue to perform this antlike drudgery, which is over two thousand years old! Beside the narrow river with its banks of alluvion, children, the less ambitious of the gold washers, or foreigners who have not obtained the right to operate on their own behalf on open ground toil away. Above, overhanging slightly, is the bed of auriferous conglomerate. Under the direction of the head of the mine, the men have made rows of pits two feet eight inches wide and two to three yards apart, along concentric lines (*safa*) intended to follow the direction of the veins. The pits are up to ten yards and more in depth, and have notches on their sides to permit the descent of the miners. The men, huddled in galleries barely two feet high, armed with pointed picks for quartz and short-edged picks for loose soil, lighted by mediocre oil lamps, are actually carrying on a work of slow destruction. Working as a team, they extract the subsoil, using only a few fragile supports called *se,* or feet, to prevent landslides. A gourd suspended from a rope is used to carry up earth and rubble. In a rapid rhythm which is accented by the panting of the man pulling the gourd, this material is crammed into enclosures made of branches. Around the edges of these are holes filled with the water used for washing; these holes are kept unclogged by means of ditches through which the fine sediment is drained. In a perpetual motion which leaves little time for play, the children distribute water and the heavy gourds of earth to be sorted. The women "wash," standing in the mud in their soiled loincloths, some of them carrying on their backs a dozing infant who is jolted every time its mother moves. With infinite patience they manipulate a receptacle containing a mixture of soil and debris; they sort, their wrist movements becoming more precise as the quantity of remaining elements decreases. They watch for the tell-tale glitter. One turn, then another, the tiny pebbles are expelled a few at a time, leaving only the dust clinging to the gold powder. They separate this after drying it over a flame in a tin cupel.

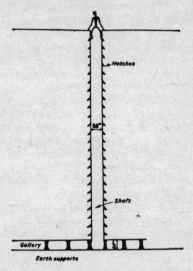

Fig. 17 Cross-section of a mine-shaft

These few grains are combined with others in a fine bamboo tube or in the hollow shaft of a vulture's feather. They are now ready for the test of the magnet inflicted by the buyer. In one day's work a woman succeeds in "washing" about a third of a cubic yard; hence her yield is one gram of gold dust—exceptionally, two grams in the case of high-grade deposits. If she belongs to her husband's team, she will receive no payment at all, but a compensation in gifts (jewelry, clothing or livestock) which will be added to her personal possessions. If she is merely the salaried employee of the head of a group, she will receive, depending on circumstances—that is, her luck and her enthusiasm for the work—between one-seventh and one-fifth of the value of the gourds she has sorted. The mine combines all phases of economics and all phases of exploitation; the fine bookkeeping of the gold weigher and the crude bookkeeping of distribution by gourds; the usurious economy of the *dioula,* who lures men into debt by keeping the miners' daily intake down to 35% of the wealth extracted, and the collective economy of the family, which allows no division; the native wage earner, and equalitarian distribution among comrades who have chosen to work in the same pit.

It is an activity largely creative of illusion. Mobilization of manpower in the mines operates at the expense of agricultural activity and the work of maintaining the villages. The number of men available permits the continuation of this pursuit of gold dust and the acceptance of low income. A constellation of activities has grown up around gold washing; a unique society and way of life have likewise been founded upon this "industry" which gave the Sudan its former prestige. All this refuses to die out, and the miners are more inclined to turn toward the past than they are to prepare themselves for modern tasks. They pay for this loyalty with an exploitation which is becoming increasingly oppressive. However, they can be proud of having "held out" where European enterprises have failed. In 1946, the Falémé-Gambia Society, by dredging the Tinkisso and employing techniques requiring the presence of seven Europeans, collected four and one-half pounds of gold, while the gold washers extracted over eleven hundred.

In this Sudanese crossroads which for centuries has been open to all conquering waves, tradition survives. It is a very ancient tradition, since we find its echo in Hanno's periplus and in Arab chronicles which describe the amazing pantomime of barter dominated by the glitter of gold in terms recalling the adventures of Sinbad the Sailor.

SUDAN—LIBERIA—KONO COUNTRY

My plans were to return to Kankan and then proceed to the

forest region of eastern Liberia and Ivory Coast. I was to meet Théodore Monod's chief assistant at that "base" which the African Institute had built facing a bleak but not unimpressive view of Mount Nimba.

During the first part of this journey, which followed an exact north-and-south course, the natural and human setting continued to be marked by Sudanese influence for about a hundred miles. The towns presented that composite aspect which I have already pointed out, but in a more pronounced manner. Not until Beyla, center of an administrative circle, could one clearly distinguish the line of contact between the Malinke and Peul invaders and the indigenous Guerzé and Toma foresters.

Well marked and often straight and firm with its facing of fine gravel, the road ran between hedges of high grass. In Africa even more than in Europe, I have always been susceptible to that sense of freedom afforded by the view of a road, that excitement which speed lends things by animating them and making them cease to resemble objects. Ngolo, the chauffeur assigned to my jeep, stiff and somewhat awkward in his brand-new dignity, took pride in this unfamiliar machine which he already associated with the symbols of power. In spite of his silent disapproval and my lack of skill owing to my recent apprenticeship, I was seized with the desire to drive. The road was too beautiful. A culvert appeared at a slight angle, I lost control, the car left the road encumbered by its trailer which could not follow, and we landed in the thick vegetation bordering a little stream. For a moment we remained stupefied, immobilized in a cloud of dust. Then Ngolo leaped up as if suddenly inspired, crying:

"Ah! Monsieur. Ah! Monsieur. It is the God."

He repeated this statement several times: "It is the God. . . . It is the God. . . ."

I was unable to discover at the time whether he believed in this supernatural explanation or whether, anxious to spare my reputation, he wanted to clear me of responsibility for this grotesque accident. In those days I had so many accidents with the car that the local authorities were beginning to take offense. As I was leaving my office in Conakry I swerved to avoid a child who stepped in front of the jeep. The narrow road projected out over an almost open beach; my vehicle hung in space by one wheel, hesitated, and turned over. I managed to jump out of the side; the jeep fell onto the shore, its four wheels continuing to turn in a strange and idiotic motion. A dozen young Negroes hurried to my aid and I recognized in their remarks the method of explanation I have just recalled.

"Sir, the genies of the water desired this!"

One of them had cut himself on the leg with a piece of the windshield. He seemed indifferent to the blood which flowed in thin trickles. When I expressed my concern I received this reply, which I still encounter with amazing regularity: "Blood is good for the genies of the water!"

Some time afterward—this time I was not at the wheel—a third accident hurled me, half-stunned, among the blocks of laterite which lined the road a few miles beyond Conakry. Such a persistence of catastrophe did more than cast suspicion on my then unfamiliar jeep; it reinforced the supernatural explanation. It compromised me, by singling me out as "chosen" by the divinities of the water and the bush—with the mitigating circumstance, however, of this luck which always left me virtually unharmed.

Such a system of interpretation not only shows how, for the traditional Negro mentality, human behavior depends entirely upon powers external to man and individual responsibility is therefore entirely relative; it also shows how an instrument transplanted into a society which did not invent it, and does not possess the intellectual understanding which would render it intelligible and ordinary, becomes incorporated into a set of indigenous meanings. There is an expatriation of the objects which we export. Their incorporation into a native context often creates effects of the bizarre or the baroque to which I shall have occasion to return. I am reminded of the remarks in which Emmanuel Mounier, in *L' Eveil de l' Afrique noire*, manifested his amazement at the reactions of certain African chauffeurs. He revealed the amazing prominence of procedures more ritual than scientific.

Later on, in the course of my travels over the bad roads of Gabon, which had been damaged by the abundant downpours of the rainy season, I was to experience impressions of the same kind. This time my Negro chauffeur was named Alexander, but his behavior was reminiscent of Ngolo's. A small, lively man, he had an assurance and indifference to danger which showed how sure he was of the necessary alliances and complicities which guarantee good roadability while they are in force. My colleague, the geographer Gilles Sautter, and myself were about to receive an illustration of this unshakable certitude.

Far from the nearest town our car, a Dodge coupé, suddenly stalled. Alexander tried to start the motor again without success. We looked for the most obvious causes of breakdown, but our experience soon proved to be inadequate. Sautter and I gave up and decided to wait for help, a hazardous business at best, while Alexander, conscious of his professional responsibilities as well as of his chances of success, continued his investigation. He declared with perfect confidence, "Leave it to me!" We left him to his diagnosis and took advantage of the mishap to prospect the surrounding countryside, which appeared to be barren savanna. On our return we did not perceive that humming sound which we were hoping against hope to hear. Instead there was scattered beside the road an extraordinary confusion of loose parts which suggested some crude autopsy. In his pursuit of the "evil" responsible for our immobilization, Alexander had not for a moment considered that the complicities which guaranteed his skill as a chauffeur were different from those necessary to the mechanic. Patiently he awaited that inspiration or external aid which would re-establish mechanical order as suddenly as it had been disturbed. Fortunately, toward the end of the afternoon a young engineer from a Gabonese firm found us and agreed to help; he appeared as an incarnation of the deity, carrying the necessary part in his tool chest.

Over a long stretch of road which was made more difficult by the dark, Alexander was trying to reach the nearest post, where we were to get in touch with the administrator, as fast as possible. The road seemed to have shrunk and the pencil of light from the headlights was dwarfed by a screen of tall elephant plants. Surprised by the light, birds took off in a low, awkward flight. The villages, few and far between, were revealed by the feeble glimmer of a few storm lanterns scattered through the modest groups of dwellings. Rounding a sharp turn, we came abruptly upon a small hamlet of a dozen huts. Before Alexander had had time to reduce his speed, he had run into a young goat which was standing paralyzed with fright in the middle of the road. We pulled up and were immediately surrounded by silent witnesses. The animal had been hit in the side and the neck and was losing blood in great spurts like a sacrificial victim; he struggled and in his death throes uttered howls that were almost human. We all stood motionless, fascinated by this quality of sacrifice. Suddenly cries came from a distant hut. The goat's owner, who had just been informed of the accident, came toward us lamenting. She announced her distress in a quivering voice. A somewhat elderly woman, she walked around the vehicle, contorting her body in the classic gesture of despair. She crouched beside the animal, looking as if she had been run over herself. Her protest was interminable:

"Ah, Nzambi. Ah, God. I am the most miserable of women. I have lost my only treasure. I have lost my support. . . . Ah, God, why must I sacrifice my support to the evil genie of the machines?"

Alexander, rigid with respect, stood watching this scene of which he was the unintentional cause. I offered the woman compensation, but she seemed not to hear. Violently she inhaled the stale odor of spilled blood, and continued her lamentation:

"Ah, Nzambi, my life has been sacrificed to the white man's machine. . . . My life. . . . My support. . . ."

We had to go, leaving to the head of the group the duty of passing on the monetary compensation, before we could pull the woman out of her state of despair. But in a case like this what significance could mere monetary compensation have? The ritual comedy of the old Gabonese woman was not directed only at compensation; it was intended to ward off an intervention of supernatural forces acting in their most dangerous form, an intervention which was all the more terrifying in that it expressed itself accidentally and through the alien power of modern technology. Thus the incident has unusual repercussions, transcending the aspect of tricky bargaining which would have distinguished it in rural France. It proved to me once again how stubbornly the processes of traditional thinking can persist in spite of the invasion of our machines. These must be assigned a meaning, and for the moment, this process of intellectual domestication cannot be accomplished by empirical knowledge which is stripped, as ours is, of its religious implications.

The evocation of some of my memories has led me to present the Negro villager's reactions to the mechanical problem, and thus to anticipate in time and space, to pass from the edge of Guinean forest country into the heart of the Gabonese forest. This juxtaposition immediately recalls how much the forests of Western and Central Africa differ, despite certain similarities in the general appearance of the trees, which bear their foliage thirty yards or more above the ground. The difference stems primarily from the form taken in each by the presence of men. The western forests have been invaded by numerous villages from which joy has not been banished. The central forests seem to have overwhelmed their human groups and pulverized them into tiny villages where depression reigns. In comparing my experiences I was very quickly struck by this contrast, which suggests how much less the natural milieu matters to people than the choices originally made by civilizations and the trials imposed on them by history. In Central Africa a number of societies seem to be characterized by defensive isolation and a chain reaction of distrust. They appear to have been diluted in too vast a nature, but actually it is under the blows of too violent a history that they have been fragmented.

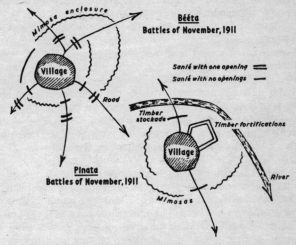

Fig. 18 Plans of fortified villages in the Guinea jungle in 1911

However, that part of Guinean forest land where I conducted my new inquiry had had its share of trials too. It has served as a storehouse and breeding ground of slaves for warlike bands coming chiefly from the Sudan. It has been open to the most extensive racial blending, with the result that a single ethnic group like the Kissi whom Denise Paulme studied so thoroughly may reveal two very opposite physical types. The area presents a composite linguistic map—with the advance of the Malinke brought by the Sudanese conquerors—which testifies to multiple vicissitudes.

These peoples have nevertheless "held out" under the impact of their ordeals by devising a military art which amazed officers responsible for conquest or pacification at the end of the last century, as is indicated by the reports of many engagements which these officers wrote. In these I have found, particularly with reference to the Guerzé, observations regarding a skilful technique of fortification: villages protected by *tata*, enclosures four or five yards high, reinforced by wide ditches armed with sharp stakes and long spearheads, and lines of defense consisting of barricades of logs or stones and bundles of thistles, protecting villages then numbering up to a thousand huts. Methods of camouflage and sabotage—stakes planted in river beds, "mined" bridges, concealed trenches—and ambush strategy appear to have been equally complex.

These conflicts, which were caused by indigenous commercial competition, reactions to the colonial enterprise, boundary disputes between the French and the Liberians—the latter were dubbed "white Negroes" (*kawite*) by the Guerzé—continued until the First World War. They were frequent, but two in particular have left a deeper impression on our memories. The battle of Boussedou in April 1907 caused the death of Dr. Walter Volz, a Swiss naturalist then "on mission" in Liberia. In the archives at Conakry, I skimmed an account of the event by Major Mourin, military commandant of Guinea:

The first riflemen of the attacking column . . . found themselves unexpectedly in the presence of a European crouched in the doorway of a hut, looking out and holding a revolver in his hand. The European spoke to them but they did not understand what he was saying; they summoned their comrades. . . . When he saw the riflemen coming, the white man went back inside the hut and climbed a ladder to the attic, from which he shot at the riflemen, firing across the edge of the roof, whose straw had been removed. The riflemen fired back at the white man and he went down inside the hut unharmed; but when he reached the floor he fell, struck in the side and the right leg by bullets which had passed through the wall of the hut. Upon entering the hut, the riflemen found a Negro who had been killed a little earlier. The white man was also dead. He was wearing red-and-white-checked pajamas, his beard was unshaven, and he was bareheaded. The riflemen state that they only wanted to take the white man prisoner, that they would not have fired if he had not fired first. . . . Besides the revolver, the white man had two loaded shotguns. . . . The scene had taken place so quickly that no European officer or sergeant had been alerted or had time to come and intervene. . . .

Dr. Volz had been regarded in the village as a kind of talisman whose presence would prevent the French from entering, so that during the battle he remained in the chief's hut with all the witch doctors. My conviction is that Dr. Volz did use his arms against us, but that he did so only because he was compelled and coerced by the threats of his guards.

I have succeeded in finding a few extracts from the travel notebooks kept by the ill-fated naturalist (*Reise durch das Hinterland von Liberien im Winter 1906-1907*). From the beginning of his expedition, whose point of departure was Sierra Leone, numerous military movements attest to the insecurity troubling the backlands on the outskirts of the Liberian border. Volz crosses the frontier; it seems too fluid and he has a presentiment that "someday there will be trouble." He makes the observation, now a commonplace, that the partition of Africa has cut into the living flesh of large cultural and linguistic units. This, then, is the context of his prolonged stay in the area lying between Liberia and the ill-defined French territory. Unfortunately for the ethnologist who is interested in Africa, the official editor of the notebooks has deleted long passages containing observations on morals and customs. He is content with indications as laconic as they are exasperating: "Description of the village . . . customs of the weavers . . . description of the tattooing of the women. . . ." I note in passing that astonishing safe-conduct which indicates Volz's status of freemason. The Liberian officers are forever calling him "my brother," but he does not let himself be deceived by this false cordiality. The local authorities are skeptical as to the scientific purpose of his trip and mistrust his activities, and in the end they offer him the job of becoming their interpreter in subsequent negotiations with the French military.

The region is so troubled that Volz has the greatest difficulty maintaining his caravan of porters. He has to agree to play the miracle doctor, secretly filling a bottle with water which he prescribes for external or internal use in exchange for carriers. He lets his men be mustered "by beating them on the shoulders with a slave whip." He places a man he can rely on at the end of the column with orders to fire on all deserters. One can feel his anxiety mount as he makes his way over less and less familiar paths, encountering peoples who have never before seen a white man but believe that the whites rule Liberia. He takes part in the alert with which the villagers prepare for war: "Two warriors gave the alarm by sounding a horn. Men rushed up from all directions armed with sabers and lances. They stood in front of the chief's house all talking at once. . . ." One can easily imagine the implications of a statement as simple and seemingly naïve as this one: "There is danger in traveling through such an unsettled country and we must treat the people kindly," especially when Volz adds some information on cannibalism in the form of the consumption of enemies and an accurate and matter-of-fact account of the method of cooking and of the considerations against eating the flesh of women because of its excessively bitter taste. This unintentional humor is obviously not free to turn to a less culinary analysis of such a forbidding custom.

Nevertheless, Volz carries on his work of naturalist. He makes map surveys and catalogues the animal and plant species he finds. He collects specimens of plants and minerals. And since the tribes, those *Naturvölker* of the German writers, seem an integral part of the natural milieu, he collects their vocabularies and records their customs, activities and hobbies. He was one of those collectors of exotic worlds and peoples who were the first to widen our intellectual frontiers and who often unintentionally become involved in ambiguous conflicts. Even today they have their heirs in those few encyclopedic minds which allay their ravenous hunger for knowledge by plucking a little of everything in regions where, for lack of information, anything gleaned has its value.

In his last notebooks there is a poignant dramatic intensity. People appear more and more in the foreground of Volz's preoccupations. They emerge with their traditional rivalries, their uncertainties regarding the conflicts waged by the powers. One senses their helplessness at this moment of colonial consolidation and enforced transition from a history which is too vast and is rapidly transforming them into instruments. The tribes of Liberia claim to have more sympathy for the French or the English, according to the region, than for the "Americans"—meaning Negroes from the United States—as if domination were less humiliating when apparently justified by racial differences. Danger is omnipresent: rivalries between the French and the English find expression in conflicts in Kissi country; rivalries between the French and the Liberians are stirred up by the anxiety of each to consolidate a still-fluid frontier to its own advantage. Volz feels himself being carried away in a sphere of confused and insidious conflicts; he tries to make contact with the French troops; he makes himself a white flag, then a Swiss flag "which he plans to hoist in case of attack." He finds himself trapped in Boussedou "as in a cloister, in a prison," without provisions, the victim of "promises which one knows will never be kept and excuses which are simply lies." He begins to foresee the tragic outcome of his adventure: "If the town is attacked and taken, I am surely lost." He wrangles with passing Liberian officers who are caught in a web of secret fraternity—"United Brothers in Friendship"—and in their illegal trafficking which is favored by the insecurity, without managing to obtain any assistance whatever. This gives him occasion to offer a severe critique of the Liberian army, which was then composed of a great many mercenaries, and to denounce the mediocrity of its officers. The last pages of his journal were written on Easter Day. They end with this sentence, which has a tragic irony for anyone who knows the outcome of the events: "It will be amusing later, for myself and others, to observe the company I was obliged to keep."

In reporting a case like this I am not simply evoking the memory of one of those scholarly explorers who gave their lives for a curiosity whose consequences they did not clearly foresee. The incident also furnishes an occasion for recalling those attractions and reactions which Liberia has provoked shortly after its birth. For more than half a century it has been arousing renewed curiosity. During my mission of 1947 I myself hoped to undertake a complete tour of the first Negro republic. I was all the more encouraged to do so because P. Maurice Lelong's two-volume *L' Afrique noire sans les blancs* had just appeared, reinforcing those caricatural traits which still compose the Liberian image for the unsympathetic foreigner.

From a reading of these travel accounts one guesses the importance of the stake: to decide what direction would have been taken by a Negro country which, apparently eluding any effect of direct colonization, would have established itself autonomously. If Lelong possesses the infinite resources of an easy irony, at least he does not hesitate to stress throughout his discussion the caricatural aspect of the "civilized world." He

81

denies that he has yielded to prejudice, but his whole approach, which makes him see Monrovia, for example, as a "sham capital," leads him to describe the society constructed by the Liberians as a "sham" democratic montage. He separates the chaff from the grain and distinguishes between the "poor devils" and those who, lording it over them, "have retained nothing of the Negro except vices disguised in the manner of the white man." In many passages the book reads like a piece of bravura.

Fig. 19 A water-carrier. Design on a Diwobli hut, Liberia

It is quite easy to detect in the background those tendencies, occasionally unconscious, which have motivated all criticisms levied against Liberian society, which serves as a pretext for the expression of the resentment and disillusionment caused by that ambiguous character, the "enlightened man." The latter is held responsible for all the weaknesses of Liberia; as if this experiment, in its shortcomings, gave one the right to express an absolute and definitive condemnation and to assert the excellence of immutable civilizations. It is really easy to omit what was wrong with the endeavor from the beginning. It was not enough to send back to the coasts of Africa a few descendants of deported slaves, who were tempted to seek some compensation for a long-endured inferiority, so that the device underlining the arms of Liberia should assume an unequivocal meaning: "Love of liberty led us here." This love led to the domination of indigenous Negroes, scandalous evidence of an outmoded "savagery." Above all, it is just as convenient as it is misleading to find in the Liberian experiment excuses or justifications for the abuses of the white colonization of Africa. All the criticisms levied on the occasion of this real test seem for the most part to be inspired by the defense mechanisms of the guilty conscience.

Almost thirty years ago the English novelist Graham Greene undertook a *Journey Without Maps* through Liberia. Unquestionably he was setting himself a test, but what kind of test? Judging from his reactions, his discouragement and anxiety when confronted by invasions of tropical fauna, one has the conviction that the writer believed in the discovery of places where man must feel "strangely free and light" thanks to a civilization less encumbered by material productions. However, he finds himself quickly besieged by an ungoverned nature. It is right after recalling the most hazardous moments of his undertaking that Greene decides he has done more than cross the frontiers of expatriation; he has "gone further in depth," he has achieved that leap "into the unknown and the unusual" about which he had previously manifested his apprehension. He abandons himself to this voyage as to a psychoanalytic cure, in the dim hope of recovering a "lost innocence;" but he discovers only the fragility of human institutions planted in "this land of Africa which always has the last word." He trembles before the ever-victorious power of nature, and the shock provides him with a cure for the disease which had alienated him from "civilization." This gives the key to his method. Once he has passed the tests, he leaves Liberia to find himself "cured" and more at home in the world to which he "belongs."

Having approached Africa with the intention of transforming his voyage into a personal adventure, inspired by the example of Rimbaud and Conrad, Greene never played on that picturesque quality that seems deliberately staged by a Negro democracy which is often compared to a musical comedy. He knows that there is no discontinuity between the obvious fantasies of the coastal civilization and the sorcery of the traditional civilization, between the tests which both impose and those with which man struggles to find a "beginning." Precisely because it seemed paradoxical to look to Liberia, which the lazy mind sees as the land of Negro artificiality, for confirmation of a relative unity and continuity in human affairs, Greene has chosen to do so.

For him, Liberia illustrates the human phenomenon in its profundity, as is evidenced by his frequent allusions to Freud. Indeed, this part of Africa, more than any other, has exerted a fascination reminiscent of that which was long the prerogative of the "Islands." The English novelist has not taken the easy path of regarding Liberia as a parody of Negro societies in the throes of modernization or, on the other hand, as a last refuge for exploration and adventure. This country has rarely been approached for its own sake, with that objective naturalist's gaze which the unfortunate Dr. Volz would have desired; it has served primarily as a pretext. This is proved by the latest "impressions" we have of Monrovia, those of the novelist Christine Garnier who, after manifesting the passions in conflict with the African evolution under the deceptively Negro name of Doellé, has recently collected the picturesque and caricatural aspects of this evolution. Her testimony, like almost all accounts of journeys to Liberia, makes me feel as if I were looking at a drawing in which I am supposed to "look for the hidden savage." We also have a few images from *Les Héros sont fatigués,* a film whose plot seems artificially tacked onto this slice of the Dark Continent. Why Liberia?

Fig. 20 Legendary figures on a hut at Yorke, Liberia

Although I have always been drawn to it, I myself have scarcely scratched the surface of this state which arouses such intense curiosity. The first "foreign" villages, approached through the Guinean frontier in the highlands, gave me no illusion of transition. I had to remain unsatisfied. Then in 1948, the steamer on which I was bound for Pointe-Noire stopped at

Monrovia to drop off a French diplomat returning to his post. The brand-new port symbolized a new era in Liberian society; it seemed to expect, on its structure of new stones, the rising of the cranes which must have covered it. Hangars, and a few other buildings, broke through the distant vegetation. From where I stood I had the impression of a décor which had been set up the day before, and the fat policemen in their American uniforms who were supervising the disembarkation also seemed too new. Even Graham Greene remarked, after noting that Freetown gives on "image of decline": "Monrovia, on the other hand, is a beginning; true, this beginning has not led to much."

Another time, crossing the Atlantic to the United States, I was on the same airplane with two Liberian diplomats on their way to New York, accompanied by their wives. Dignified, slightly old-fashioned looking and excessively modest, they were resorting to a defense reflex in order to face a society capable of overwhelming them in every possible way. Still another time, at an international meeting of specialists in African social problems, the law of alphabetical order placed me beside a young woman who was the Liberian delegate. Shy and ill at ease in one of those fitted cotton dresses unsuited to the bodies of Negro women, and burdened with information acquired elsewhere, she seemed a stranger to those arguments with which social science seeks to justify its utility. She said nothing. . . .

Once again I have allowed myself to digress. But my 1947 trip brought me to the gates of this "inner" Liberia which was said to be so savage and dangerous. It fascinated me, although the French frontier region presented the same tribes—Guerzé, Manon and Toma. These groups emerge as both tormentors and victims in the game of conquest, plunder and slave traffic which had its center in this highly accessible area. Moreover, by an unexpected military action now known as the "Guerzé Rebellion," they imposed a military intervention from August 1911 to March 1912. On consulting my historical notes, I find extracts from reports which contain the exact phraseology of certain communiqués regarding the recent Indochinese and North African campaigns: "continual fighting in the bush, against an adversary who is extremely mobile and can be taken by surprise only by night marches or reconnaissances along veritable goat paths. . . ." If the rebellion of the weak had varied little in its tactics, we have become corrupted to the point where we no longer choose to recognize them as an "adversary," a status which in those days we did not deny them.

Of this remote violence there seems to have remained only a certain cultural dynamism, and of the ancient struggle for wealth only a commercial activity manifested today in the importance of the markets. As soon as I reached the forest region I was struck by the excitement channeled along the paths and trails, by those landmarks formed by roadside fires and temporary shelters made of leaves. Long caravans of women carrying heavy burdens caught in wide-meshed nets on their heads in flat wicker baskets. Hundreds of women. A few of them, dressed in flowered print cotton dresses, formed patterns vaguely reminiscent of modern art. But most of them were covered—back, chest and face—with kaolin clay, a coquetry of magical effect which made them resemble so many otherworldly Pierrots: a paste similar to a fine fabric over prematurely aged bodies, whitish masks with holes for the eyes, delicate streaks bringing out the shape of the features and fixing the face in a kind of mineral immobility. They greeted each other by lifting their burdens with upraised arms and calling each other's names. These now peaceful roads, though they led to large and busy markets, were also the pathways to their newfound freedom.

Never have I been so happy as when mingling with the crowds in an African market, drinking in the colors, the odors and the confused din of interminable negotiations. Boola market, every Thursday on the big square where, in full view of a public thus reassured as to their good workmanship, blacksmiths make *daba,* machetes, knives, hatchets for cutting palm trees, and cotton gins; where yams and manioc, fruits and cola nuts are piled, where rows of oil cans stand beside enormous gourds with narrow mouths containing red palm oil, and glamorous fabrics are displayed among old-style mats. Lola market, more "forest" in its displays, which attracts from neighboring Liberia peasant women indifferent to boundaries, offers that pottery on which the hand voluptuously finds its place, cotton in all its forms—bales, thread, long all-white or blue-striped widths—and, amid the fabrics and cheap merchandise, a multitude of articles made of raffia: wallets, bags, garrison caps. Nzo market, a post frontier, where instead of products of African industry, cheap imported goods and, more inviting, contraband goods predominate.

My route, which since Nzérékoré had been hugging the

boundary of Liberia, now traversed the country of the Kono, an important group who resemble the Guerzé in many respects. The villages were rather frequent, full of round huts embellished on top with "teeth" taken from the banana palm and decorated on their outer walls with a sacred geometry of ochre, black, grey and white. Each village had a personality of its own which I tried to decipher from the names and legends concerning their foundation. The Village of the Unclean, the Village of the "Stingy," the Village of Hunger, the Village of Pini the Warrior Queen, the Village of Those Who Do Not Eat Snails. . . . At the beginning, beyond the memories of migrations and battles, there is always a creator of confidence and order, a man who was strong in battle as well as allied with the supernatural.

Fig. 21 Decorated huts from the Kono country

For example, Swolapakire, founder of Lola, and his father had the gift of ubiquity, which assured them victory in battle. They also possessed the power to control a flaming inferno designed to foil the enemy, so that at their command sheets of fire comparable to our curtain fire would descend from the mountainside and isolate the village without touching it. Manzaga, creator of Pora, and his son were given a gift of the same kind: one could transform himself into a child or a hawk in order to mislead the enemy, while the other could kill from a distance and command the sun, which he had the power to hold in his

87

hand. Gba, who founded the village of Gbangborossou, found a terrible power in his amazing hairiness and filth; he impressed his subjects by having his orders confirmed by the "voice" of a nearby valley which everyone knew to be uninhabited. Pakire, founder of Gueguepo, had such power as a healer that he was regarded as the greatest of warriors in the battle against evil forces; he kept around him all who wished to escape illness.

My path was strewn with these villages which retained the memory of their traditions. They formed a backdrop against which very ancient gestures were still being performed. Men standing in a circle and singing were engaged in trampling the anthill soil to make the soft paste which would cover the wattling of the huts. Women, with slow gestures, lingered over the construction, plastering it with a roughcast of black river-dirt and cow dung. In front of a doorway two young men greeted each other by first clasping hands lengthily and then snapping their fingers; old men sitting on doorsteps rested with their knees pulled against their chests, chasing away insects with a flick of the cow's tail which was a sign of their pre-eminence. Under the veranda of his large hut, a chief sat in state, stretched out in a kind of lounge chair of braided raffia, while an adolescent boy kneeling at a respectful distance awaited his orders. Children scampered off, taking huge puffs from a cigarette, while their mothers, momentarily idle, sat on the ground on the left leg with the right one drawn up and watched them, laughing. A group of men prepared to dine; each washed his hands by gently tipping the water gourd and assumed a squatting position close to the plate; each put out his hand and introduced a pellet of food very deeply into his mouth, licking his hand in the gesture of a gourmet who appreciates and savors every bite. A laborer was returning home from a nearby construction project, his day's work done; he removed the dust he had collected by hitting his clothing with a leafy branch. A few young people who were clearing a new path advanced with a steady motion, and the singing that punctuated their work recalled the choreography of some exotic European ballet; one would think it was not work at all but a realistic pantomime, and half expected to see an audience.

My notebooks are full of these hurried observations. Are they really the crumbs of ethnological research? One does not exaggerate the significance of such gestures and attitudes by relating them to a broad philosophy lived almost daily. They create the style of each human landscape. It is through them, rather than through those material manifestations which are so fragile in the Negro-African world, that civilizations express themselves as through a language. If one considers their role in social groups which are without archives because without writing or monuments, one realizes that they are first of all the memory of these societies. They form the individual from early infancy. They ensure continuity. For individuals away from home, they remain conventional signs capable of evoking a common heritage. This humble fabric of everyday life has held fast in spite of the rents made in it by ancient tribal wars and colonial conquests. It rather resembles that very flag of civilization which no defeat can utterly destroy.

A hunting expedition encountered on the edge of the forest takes me far into the past. The only "modern" note consists of a few long flintlocks whose butts are ornamented like bows and which are loaded with a shot in which wire fragments replace lead. Otherwise the men, each of whom carries a leather-sheathed knife at the neck or under the arm, are armed with bows, clubs with large heads, and double-edged axes. Some are leading on rattan leashes skinny dogs which are even more remarkable for their muteness than for their scorched and dirty coats. Children follow, each carrying a fiber bag of boiled manioc for the dogs which slaps against his shoulders, suspended from a slender headband. The equipment follows a traditional specialization. The flintlock is designed to hit gazelles and buffalo; the club is for small animals like the delicious savanna rat; the bow is fatal to deer after the tips of the arrows have been coated with a poison derived from the sap of the *dogo* tree.

The expedition mobilizes all the men in the village of Bakore. It is prepared to ransack the large section of bush between the highway and the edge of the forest. I am witnessing the drawing up of a regular battle formation; all is in order, and every position is manned in a prebattle silence. Several lookouts are stationed along the highway, while a network of them closes in the length of the forest, near the supposed points of escape. The men are concealed with a skill of camouflage which makes their detection difficult. I see them only by coming upon them accidentally, and this confusion with nature caused by their costumes of branches combines with the tension of the watch to give them a disturbing appearance. It is as if elementary forces, too long contained, are about to be unleashed.

The bush is dry and rustling in the sunshine. The barely perceptible breeze presents no threat to the enterprise. A few animals can be heard fleeing through the grass. When the leader of the hunt gives the signal, fires are lit along the highway; the flames spread crackling, swerve, seem to falter. Then all at once the fire takes on extraordinary proportions. High, glowing flames rise, releasing clouds of charcoal bits and acrid smoke which obscure the sky; they meet with a roar, leaving a fine ash and charred stubble in their wake. The heat is almost unbearable. The onslaught of the flames grows more intense, and I feel as if I myself am caught in a trap of fire. But the fire proceeds according to a necessary order, and with a merciless precision. Above the savanna, birds of prey wheel endlessly, come to compete with man for some of the smaller game. A buzzard takes aim, swoops, and disappears with a lizard he has caught in the confusion.

Shots are fired. A few dogs give chase, setting their neck bells ajingle, brush past the flames, and disappear. Men and children scurry about, shooting and ransacking every last corner where the small animals lie like wreckage; they check the traps—high screens made of branches which conceal the springes behind their mouths—set between the slope and river. There is no escape for the terrified victims. The gathering proceeds with unforgettable thoroughness, overlooking nothing that is edible. Slowly the thick smoke dissipates, and the fire subsides.

The men begin to gather near the edge of the forest where the catch is piled. Animals that have been killed with poisoned arrows have already been eviscerated. The bowels hang from the lower branches in sinister garlands. A gazelle is crackling over a wood fire: a preliminary singeing, then the animal is gutted and divided according to very strict rules. The knives disembowel and dismember—the same knives which dancers from the forest used to throw back and forth in a passionate ballet, alternating them with small children, in front of the cafés of Conakry. There rises an odor of warm ashes, half-burned grass, blood, and the stale smell of the little piles of warm viscera. The men are excited; their hunger for meat, so soon to be satisfied, intoxicates them more than palm wine.

Nothing now remains but a vast burned plain over which the last fumes writhe in fantastic forms. The fire has stopped at each of the previously determined points: the control has been perfect. I am reminded of those "men of fire" who, from the forest to the plains of the Sudan, in a kind of carnival stunt, roll on the burning coals, rub their faces with the glowing embers and crunch them up like so many pieces of red candy. Evening falls, intensifying the odors of recent burning. The uproarious band of hunters heads back toward Bakore.

If the forest, with its border of savanna, and the river are central to economic activity, they are also at the heart of religious life. Like that stream, the Zíe, whose legendary waters and forbidden fish establish relations with the ancestors, they are the support, as well as the secret refuge, of the sacred. At their contact power and fecundity are found or increased. The society of maskers is still associated with the forest. The rituals of excision somehow involve the proximity of water.

In these days of early April the daughter of the chief of the village of Keoulenta has released long-dormant ritual mechanisms by asking to be excised. This signal has been awaited impatiently by her companions. They have been anticipating this ordeal which will change them into women in the social sense and provide them with a second name which will confirm their adult status. A female witch doctor, a kind of chambermaid and flatterer, has dressed the young girl and, for the first time, braided her hair in the style of the women. Nyanle parades in her clothing of new cotton with gestures which combine a naïvely self-satisfied vanity with a bearing of unmistakable grace. She finds herself in the center of the dance (*kuruba*), the public prelude to the secret ceremonies and initiation required by excision.

The dance and the gastronomic festivities involve wide community participation. Through multiple invitations, they provide an occasion for reinforcing friendships. In this cheerful atmosphere social ties and neighborly relations acquire a new vigor. A similar function was filled by those rustic celebrations which, overshadowing religious obligations, marked First Communions in the villages of my native province and during which families reconciled old quarrels. It is as if on these special occasions when the adults welcome a new generation in a specific ritual, people are led to repair, at least temporarily, a damaged unity.

In the yard of Chief La, which has been decorated for the occasion, the dance continues until the final hours of the night. It will continue until the young girls have gone to the place of their retreat. Musicians from neighboring villages have hired out their services and received a payment of chickens and rice.

They stand inexhaustible in the center of the open space. One is playing the *konbara,* a cylindrical drum with skin stretched across each of its ends and decorated with strips of leather, which hangs from the right shoulder by a cotton strap. Another is beating the *baralon,* which hangs from the neck by a little cord; it is a long, cup-shaped tomtom, with a latticework of leather and a wooden base, which is attacked with both hands. A third has slung over his shoulder an empty oil can which he is striking with two small sticks. Since it is an exception to the traditional rules, this makeshift instrument allows freedom of improvisation; he takes the role of the drummer who imposes his variations upon the prescribed rhythms.

In the movement of the dance everyone shakes a leafy branch, as if the sacred grove where the women hold their secret meetings had been transplanted to the public square. These branches will be left on the roofs of the nearest huts when the festivities are over and it is time to rest. Nyanle, accompanied by her "witch doctoress," who has just put the finishing touches on her dress, enters the circle. The excitement redoubles, combining song and dance, amplifying the rustling of the leaves flourished overhead. The very setting of initiation is imaginatively recreated, and during this make-believe the young girl experiences a sense of communion and receives a preparatory instruction which will provide precious memories at the time of her isolation.

By means of this preliminary communion, the pain to be endured is somehow domesticated, shared, transformed. A chant in archaic language consisting of three short fragments sung in three parts monotonously evokes the theme of suffering:

Zo mu zo / awe zo e / e wein wein zo

The repetition seems interminable. It insists with an insidious power which increases the physical effect of a choreography which is itself interminable and unvarying. I do not doubt that such a procedure is effective in the long run; a real preparation for surgery which divests the clitoridectomy of its frightening character. We have just discovered some equivalent procedures in the psychological treatment and exercise preparatory to painless childbirth. If progress is possible in the realm of mastery and utilization of the body, it is from those civilizations poorest in the instruments born of technical imagination and experience that we must learn its secret. This should en-

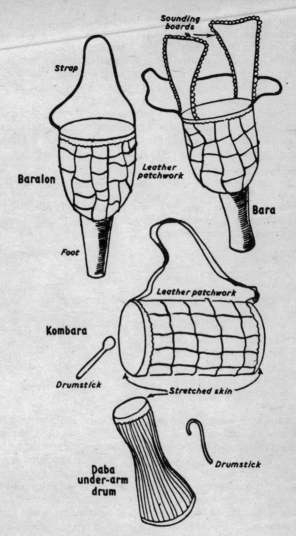

Fig. 22 Musical instruments from the Kono country

courage us to be less presumptuous, by showing that we have explored—and with what disquieting success!—only a limited sector of human activity. Methods and treatments of unimaginable intricacy and effectiveness are offered us by men who are too conveniently dismissed as savages because their hands are empty of complex tools and their sky unclouded by the smoke of factories.

During the manifestations preceding the ceremony of excision, preparatory chants play a cardinal role. There are three of them, and they have an obligatory quality because of the feminine symbolism peculiar to this number. The first, which I just recalled, endlessly evokes the theme of suffering. The second, which seems esoteric, enters the scene under a misleading name: that of the bird-*mwoni,* the only man who, in his capacity as priest-doctor (*zogumu*), will participate in all of the operations and all of the ritual. The chant begins with a cry of invocation and the response of the "bird":

> *Mwoni weu!*
> *E de!*

It continues with the conventional dismissal of this disturbing personage:

> Go away.
> Stay where you belong.
> Can you tell me
> how my heart and belly
> will know peace?

The last allusion concerns the regulation that, beyond its general educational value, initiation imposes in the realm of sexual relations. The phenomenon is better understood when we remember that these preliminary gatherings enable family groups to arrange for the settlement of dowries or to conclude new matrimonial agreements. The ceremony polarizes collective forces, reanimates the flow of exchange, reactivates reciprocal obligations; in fact, the guests never come without a load of gifts—sheep, chickens, rice, red oil, silver or cola nuts— carefully wrapped in small packages of leaves.

The third chant is even more cryptic than the preceding ones:

Me and you,
both of us,
we are equal,
yes, we are equal.
What is it one must not do?
All men are equal.
What must one not do?

It is difficult to come by a satisfactory explanation of this
passage. Its real meaning is nonliteral. What kind of equality is
meant, and equality among whom? Equality before a tradition
which, after being prohibited because of its physical risks,
reappears with new vigor and purpose; equality in the face of
pain and a surgical procedure which is known to involve danger; equality of the current generation with preceding ones, for
it approaches the ordeal with like courage; equality in the face
of death: my commentators suggest all these interpretations,
but without guaranteeing any of them.

The dance continues tirelessly, frequently independent of
the singing. It provides an opportunity for escape from the required movements—as if one of the participants suddenly
wished to release the emotions rising within him, to express
himself in the most eloquent language the African knows. In
the Negro world there is no important act which does not possess its peculiar choreography. Dance remains the preferred
medium for the expression of lyricism and the most solemn
medium for communication with the powerful or the "powers"
that control human action. It is part of that language of gesture
whose importance I have already discussed. And I am pleased
to find a similar observation in Richard Wright's *Black Power:*

There is in the African a latent lyricism which tends to express itself in movement, so that every gesture, every attitude of the body takes on a special significance which
belongs to a language of which I caught only a few words.

I too am confronted by a choreography which reveals only a
few words among the multiplicity of its meanings.

The night advances, but it is as if negated by this excitement,
this interminable beating of drums. All temporal points of reference are gone. At times, everything seems to be subsiding.
Some of the dancers have laid aside the leafy branches which
enhanced their gestures; they seem exhausted by their efforts.

The musical accompaniment is subdued. Then suddenly, the dance revives with a burst of fresh vitality. . . .

As soon as this public preliminary to the ritual is over, the candidates for excision are led to the place of retreat: a hut built in one of Chief La's fields beside a stream and surrounded by a high fence of raffia-palm leaves with a single exit facing the bush. Here in this sacred space, now the feminine nucleus of the society, the young girls will remain secluded for nearly six months.

Some of the relatives have cleared a path to the spot with machetes. At intervals along its axis are areas which form so many barriers to a communication which is ritually dangerous: first of all, the fireplaces where the women will prepare the initiates' meals; further on, the space where the food will be distributed, which constitutes a kind of parlor; finally, a good way off, the temporary building where the young girls will live with nothing but a floor mat and a blanket apiece, and where they will receive the prescribed instruction. Here reign Gonoune, a dignified matron surrounded by her already initiated disciples, and Sougoula, a man whose family for generations have been masters of the treatment indispensable to excision.

Fig. 23 A *bounga* excision knife

Gonoune has secretly had the village blacksmith make the crude razor which is used to perform the clitoridectomy. By making offerings and sacrifices on her mother's grave, she has obtained a guarantee that the operation will proceed normally, with the consent of all the powers involved. Thanks to the connivance of these powers, she controls the whole biological life of woman, from excision, which reinforces and socializes femininity, to practices relating to fecundity and childbirth. She prescribes and supervises the physical test which will prove that physically and morally the young girl has become a complete woman. Nyanle is in a privileged position to face these tests: a trusted servant accompanies her into seclusion to keep constant watch over her health and to give the necessary care.

The ethnographic film puts our sensibilities to a rude test when, sometimes with the help of color, it catches these scenes

96

which arouse in us not so much uneasiness as real horror; we are inclined to see them as a kind of human "butchery." But why should we believe our sensibility to be ill-prepared for such treatment of the human body? We ought rather to ask ourselves what reasons preserve this tradition, reasons sufficiently imperious to drive the "victims" to demand such a formidable shock. The retreat of excision throughout its duration clearly accentuates the value assigned to the feminine element of the society. During this period the maskers of the men's society, absolute incarnations of "masculinity," are categorically forbidden to appear. A case of infraction occurring in Nion, a village in the district of Bossou, resulted in the death of the guilty party. Thus the rituals of excision periodically impose a relative disappearance of the men which is quite the reverse of the usual situation. They increase the unity of the female group and create a better equilibrium in relations between the sexes. An "answer" to masculine initiation, this feminine initiation is, moreover, characteristic of a number of traditional civilizations of the Negro world.

There are, nevertheless, more personal reasons why a young girl undergoes this pain and discipline. If she is sincerely anxious to meet ancient obligations, the young Kono girl regards excision primarily as a way of acquiring universal recognition as a full-fledged member of the community. She emancipates herself from childhood without those expedients by which young people in our societies try to wrest this recognition of their adult status, which is conceded to them only under duress.

Initiation primarily concerns relations between the sexes. It is preceded by a period of freedom during which the young girl delights in amorous adventures and seeks conquests through sheer coquetry. Initiation defines the necessary relations between husband and wife. After the sexual impulses have been disciplined, marriage generally follows, which satisfies all aspirations to fecundity. Here, neither guilty experimentation, haphazard instruction nor chance encounters attend awakening to the sexual life: on the contrary, the development of the instincts follows a plan whose effectiveness is unquestionable. The initiatory enclosure is also a school where the meaning of rights and duties is learned and obligatory behavior is explained. In this respect, these establishments recall our boarding schools for young girls: friendships are formed and memories are accumulated, to fade afterwards according to the accidents of existence. These observations, however disorganized, should nevertheless correct that impression of "gratuitous" savagery which these practices often give.

Six months later Nyanle, already idealizing this retreat which she will come to regard as a pleasant holiday, will find herself once again the center of collective festivities celebrating the return of the excised.

The results of my investigations in Kono country—especially the discovery of the masculine initiation into the ritual of Poro and the knowledge required for the wearing of the sacred masks—confirmed my impression of the renewal, albeit temporary, of fundamental traditions. Beyond the cry, *Nyon ki ekoulo ke pereka*—"The mask is brought out to entertain"—and pantomimes performed at my request, I discovered an activity that was less vulgarized, less like a Bastille Day parade. The torch of tradition has been seized by young hands, for ends in which political preoccupations play a vital role, ends of which the ancient creators of the sacred choreography could have had no inkling. Is not this, with the maskers' glorification of red, its final avatar?

4

Lost Arts

I DETEST objects, above all those regarded as works of art, when they are divorced from the human context which gives them their full significance; objects under glass, as helpless in the presence of sightseers as the dead in the presence of the crowds on All Saints' Day. Both are "defenseless," so that we have unlimited freedom to consider and treat them as we please. They become pretexts.

We are accustomed to a civilization in which material creations are endlessly multiplying and diversifying, imposing their ever more compelling presence and the most powerful forms of alienation man has ever known. We can hardly pick up a newspaper without being reminded of our enslavement to machines and to the riches they manufacture in order to arouse our greed. We claim to be a civilization of labor, but we suspect that our servitude is increased the more extensively our societies are invaded by the products of this labor. We have, without exactly being aware of it, an account to settle with the objects of human industry, an account which reflects our inability to achieve social relations well suited to their massive invasion.

We are tempted to take revenge upon objects at the expense of those that are offered to ensure our education and enrich our contemplation. Objects alienated in time or space, separated from their human environment, retain an absolute passivity. And the further away from us they are, the freer we feel to take liberties with them. We invest them with meanings which satisfy us at small cost to ourselves; they become symbols of savagery, images of perfect craftsmanship or excuses for inner liberation.

Such has been the case with the collecting of those "curiosities" which have launched Negro art. Is it not significant that their discovery around the time of the First World War coincided with a crisis that revealed the weaknesses of a civilization purporting to be both industrial and liberal, that is, with the Russian Revolution? What was the purpose of this revolution in taste which, as Apollinaire put it, insisted on "regarding Negro idols as genuine works of art?" What motives drove the young Surrealists to steal masks and fetishes from the confusion of the old ethnographic museum of the Trocadero? The idea was above all to gain possession of symbols of total subversion, to defy a civilization which had been indicted, to transform the objects into instruments of liberation after satisfying all their demands, direct or implicit. The masks, statuettes and ornaments, removed from the dusty storerooms of museums, exposed to the light of exhibitions, brandished as the badges of disgrace, became, once they had lost their *raison d'être* and original meaning, liberating forces. Anything was permissible where they were concerned, since no one knew anything about them or the men who had made and used them. The mere fact of their appearance had a subversive value, and European littérateurs who were pushing Negro art relied on this value as some new weapon of intellectual warfare. One thinks of Picasso's alleged outburst: "Negro art? Never heard of it!" Indeed, everyone found a different use for the objects which the colonials brought back in quantity, none of which had anything to do with the aesthetic conceptions of the African Negro.

Let us not forget the controversy this art has provoked up to our own time. We shall see how the "pieces" of which it is composed have been used to justify contradictory arguments not to be explained away by that phenomenon of misapprehension underlined by essayist Alioune Diop: "There is no interpenetration between the mind of the artist and that of the European public. Only the object binds them together—accidentally."

During these early years of the century, out of a protest against our society, Negro art was flung like a shout of refusal.

For several years the fragile symbol of traditions which are declining, it is starting to become an instrument of conservative thought. The work of certain African intellectuals brings out this latest misinterpretation. Even Cheikh Anta Diop, that impassioned advocate of the Negro origins of civilization, fears nothing so much as an idealization of the past inspired by ancient masterpieces which would divert attention from present tasks. Nowadays the excuse of art conceals under its glorification of traditional values a taste for "fixed" societies. By a very understandable progression, the Negro "fetish" has won a first victory—the right of African cultures to be recognized as civilizations—but in a second phase it has become a symbol of all the obstacles to progress. If the Negro's attitude toward the productions of the past is never innocent, the European's is even less so, for he has set the example of deception.

Fig. 24
A wrought-iron axe of office,
Nigeria

Fig. 25
A baton of office,
Angola

By a kind of exaggerated animism, I find it hard not to begrudge the objects their passivity, their compliance. The liberties the foreigner takes with them are also liberties taken with the men who made and used them. For this reason, I dislike

101

them, seeing them as trapped in this context which transforms them into helpless accomplices.

During a brief visit to the Musée d'Homme just before my departure for Africa, I had occasion to test my reservations, which amounted almost to aversion, to these collections so painstakingly assembled in order to construct an image of exotic civilizations. By an effect of prolepsis, they seemed to be already dead. I could not bear to see them utterly contained, as in a digest, within a few showcases arranged with laudable pedagogical care. Their slightest material value, made more obvious here, inevitably asserted itself at the expense of their immaterial value; and I asked myself whether we would agree that a complete picture of French civilization could be presented to the eyes of strangers in artfully arranged showcases. The balance will be restored only when the exotic peoples have created our ethnography and expressed in museums their representation of our societies and our cultures. And yet, there will always be something disturbing about these exhibits of foreign peoples—this immobility, this formalization which seems definitive and misses what is intangible but in my eyes essential: the various changes by which a civilization reveals its vitality and its history. Anyone who has seen the attempts of the Museum of Natural History in New York or the brand-new Musée de Neuchâtel to make their exhibits speak is even more familiar with this irritation which is impossible to avoid, and so overwhelming in my own case, before the passivity of objects "on display."

Before going to the site of my first investigation, I had imposed on myself a humility before these products which constitute the materials of ethnographic research. I forced myself to compose, according to the rules, those species of cards of identity which always accompany them. I classified. And I still remember vividly my attempt to work my way through a collection of axes—utilitarian, ritual and ceremonial—which seemed endless. All individuality and profound meaning of the objects seemed to disappear in this effort of meticulous tabulation, just as the most personal characteristics are destroyed in police files. In the course of this undertaking I never reached the men who created these tools or objects of artistic value; the more I concentrated on the objects, the more the subjects disappeared as if behind a screen.

I approached Africa with the determination not to let myself fall into the trap of objects. I remained on my guard. I wished neither to pounce upon what is immediately available—the material manifestations of Negro civilizations—nor to take part in a campaign of dispossession for which the Africans are beginning to demand compensation.

It was in Kono country, in that part of Guinean forest land discussed in the preceding chapter, that I managed to surprise works of Negro art in their present context. I had been at the Mount Nimba encampment for several days when one evening a young man from a neighboring village came to see me. He demanded a private interview, speaking with that excitement which love of secrecy often gives the Negro. We retired into one of the rooms of the large hut and my interlocutor was careful to ascertain, in an unmistakable pantomime, that we were indeed alone. Then in a solemn tone he said, "Do not speak, it is dangerous, and look!" adding, "I bring you Nyon Néa."

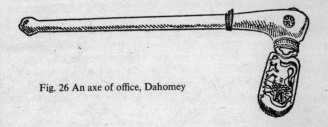

Fig. 26 An axe of office, Dahomey

Out of an old torn jacket, bundled up under his arm, he produced a mask wrapped in a piece of raffia cloth. The conventional features, which I later learned to recognize, had been respected: an oblong face whose contours were accentuated by parallel streaks, harlequin eyes which were mere slits, and a prominent mouth, graced with aluminum teeth. But it was a slapdash affair, carved out of coarse and mediocre wood, all smeared with a shade of purple ink inseparable in my mind from memories of rural grocery or stationery stores. In spite of the conventions that had been respected, nothing remained of what gave the traditional forms their value; and in the absence of the black dye which traditional patience knew how to make, the artisan had settled for this ink purchased from a village dealer. The object resembled a schoolboy's exercise. I refused to believe that it could still be the repository of those forces which resided in the models of the past. This seemed too much of a caricature to be associated with the old formula for the transfer of power: *Seme yabe nyon ploki zuki eto yike zu;* May the force (*seme*) which was in the old mask enter the new one!

I tried to question my interlocutor. According to him everything was in order: yes, the sacrifices had been performed (although the mask bore on its brow neither bloodstains from the sacrificial chicken nor fragments of ground cola chewed by the officiating priest); yes, the mask had received its name, "She-who-gives-peace;" yes, its first public appearance had taken place. Suspicious claims all, but I decided to persist.

"Who is Nyon Néa?"

"The wife."

"What wife? Whose wife?"

"Ah, you see, boss, nobodies like me don't know about the masks the way we used to in the old days . . . maybe it's the wife of the initiates."

We had to leave it at that. My interlocutor had only one thing in mind: he wanted to sell his mask, and this concern was confused with some tale of witch-doctor fees to be settled. I gave in, wondering whether by some subterfuge these objects, which had become ugly and available to anyone who wanted them, might not avenge themselves on me. It took time and my friend Bohumil Holas' splendid book on Kono masks to teach me a little more about Nyon Néa. Mother of the initiates, she swallows them and gives them second birth. She destroys children and brings forth adult, socially equipped men. But in public, skilled in the dance, she again becomes the graceful, submissive and gentle wife whom every man wants to have under his protection.

Actually this was not my first encounter with the masks of the forest region. I was at Conakry when President Auriol, during his African tour, received delegations from all over Guinea. There was no lack of folklore, and those in charge did not fail to present the *Nyomo Kwouya,* a festive mask found among the Guerzé and Kono, and popular in a large area that even includes Liberia. The mask is called *kwouya* ("the long") and its presence creates a distortion of our perception of space, for the axis of vision becomes vertical and the landscape seems to become flat. Raised on stilts several yards high, the masker rises in tiers starting with an interminable pair of trousers—the second tier extends from the waist to the dancer's feet and resembles *sans-culottes*—then a skirt of raffia fibers, a striped shirt with elongated sleeves, a braided face guard and finally the headdress, heightened by woolen tassels and a shock of tin-foil hair. He indulges endlessly in the most amazing acrobatics, towers over a dwarfed humanity whom he does not hesitate to overpower with his exuberance, hops like some one-legged monster, crosses his stilts, and writhes atop his contraption in a jingle of bells. Once in a village in the district of Vépo I saw him sit down on the roofs of the huts in an attitude expressing a hilarious contempt for the human stature. He likes discord: his shrill voice seems mocking, and his accompanists merely beat time on little drums hanging from their necks. Nyomo Kwouya has been secularized to the point where he is merely the great public entertainer. His exploits inspire young Kono boys like the feats of our champion cyclists. He commercializes his performances, offers his services to administrators in search of local color for official entertainments, travels hundreds of miles to reach fairs in large towns. His photograph sells well. It

Fig. 27
The masked
Nyon Néa

Fig. 28
The masked
Nyomo Kwouya

is almost as if his enormous stride has given him a head start on that path of sacred decline which all wearers of masks have taken.

As soon as they learned that I had bought the horrible purple-faced mask—although I in no way violated the so-called se-

Fig. 29 The masked *Nyon Sinoe*

crecy demanded by my interlocutor—the villagers decided they had discovered one of my weaknesses. Out of their baskets, where they keep the unusable ancestors of contemporary masks, they took a few pieces to try to sell. They delegated emissaries who were prepared to organize a performance of the sacred dance. And I can still see some of the men who, half driven by the hope of gain, half uneasy despite their alleged skepticism, came to me to offer discreetly the purchase of those amazing miniatures, the *lougo,* reduced replicas of the basic masks. This is not without significance. If, as Bohumil Holas insists, it is still true that one villager out of two carries this personal protection on himself, there is still no doubting the adulteration of the practice. It is inconceivable that an individual would sell his *lougo* if he continued to regard it as the repository of his personal genie. For many young men, this genie has vanished unless, according to the teachings of the missionaries, he has been transformed by donning the protective wings of the guardian angel. Certain facts do not lie; they show how close these gestures are to that everyday personal magic which we occasionally observe and use ourselves. A peasant touches his *lougo* to win an argument, as we do a piece of "rough and unvarnished" wood. A soldier takes it to the front with him in order to have a familiar image to restore his confidence and help him counteract the danger of being away from home. A young chief turns to his *lougo* as a French peasant woman addresses the image of her familiar saint, to solve his everyday problems. But these are mere vestiges of a belief which once engaged the whole man.

I easily obtained an interview with Nyon Sinoe. The masker arrived from Keoulenta with his interpreter and some friends who helped him put on his costume out of the sight of the women and noninitiates. A confused murmur announced his approach, then cries resembling cooing. A·disorderly excitement: the masker appeared in the open space in front of the large hut; he advanced with an abrupt, jerky motion, pretending to seize bystanders. It was a game of attack and pretense, feigned anger and feigned fear. At one point the masker seemed to be subsiding and then, for my instruction—or so my interpreter, Lagwa, insisted—he came forward in the opening dance. One man ventured the first words of a chant, then the spectators came in on the alternating responses with an impressive solemnity:

"Excuse me, Master of the cult, excuse me!"
"*E yo,* Master of the cult."
"Good evening."
"How is it with the things of this world?"

"Excuse me again!"

"*E yo,* Master of the cult."

"Good evening."

"How is it with the things of this world?"

The chant ceased, and the masked man made his way toward me. I felt that the rustling of his raffia robe precluded a conversation of veiled meanings which I could not avoid. Never have I felt so stupid as I did during this initial confrontation. I did not know how to behave; I found myself both skeptical and impressed by the appearance and bearing of this personage. I did not know how to carry on a dialogue with an informant who was no longer a simple villager. Unlike the spectators surrounding us, so at ease in their attitudes, I did not know how to enter into the sacred game. Everything about the scene was disconcerting: the impossibility of remaining indifferent to the sensation the mask aroused in me, in spite of myself; the respectful familiarity with which the participants established their relationship with this personage.

Nyon Sinoe stopped a few steps away and faced me. He spoke in a hoarse, almost inarticulate voice, addressing my interpreter. Lagwa removed his cap and listened with surprising attention and immobility. The sense of my stupidity weighed on me so heavily that I lost patience.

"What is he saying?"

"He greets you. He asks you how things are in the world you come from. He hopes that you will love the people of Kono country, that you wish them no harm."

Then he seemed to take no further notice of my presence. His attendants arranged him on a new mat, spreading his dancer's robe around him. Solemnly he waved his cow's-tail fly swatter, observed the audience, and took advantage of this unexpected appearance to lecture some of the young men present, who listened with perfect deference.

I waited, attempting a clumsy sketch. The image of Nyon Sinoe is that of the authoritarian old man with all the outward signs of power. His face, which is concealed by a luxuriant black beard, is constructed on the line of the superciliary arches, which is prolonged by a large prominent nose. The cheeks are hollowed out and the eyes, framed by a rectangle bordered with aluminum, are mere slits. Two pennants of white cotton hang the length of the face and accentuate the vividness of the red material that covers it. In a sense, I saw him as a pontiff asserting his majesty with the most splendid of tiaras. I wondered at the amazing skill that could assemble such modest materials to create this complicated and magnificent headdress: a cylinder of wicker covered with green cloth, decorated with composite motifs in which the square and the symbol of the lizard dominated and flanked by a plume of white ram's wool, rested on a crown whose leather base was garnished with rosettes and fringes of cowry shells. A little red cloth suspended from the mask fell over the shoulders. The upper part of the body was covered by a full smock which hid the wearer's arms under two stitched panels resembling wings. The identity of the wearer had been spirited away; the metamorphosis was complete.

It seemed impossible to start the interrogation: Nyon Sinoe did not appear in full regalia for such an unspectacular purpose. For the moment we had no means of communicating; we seemed to be spying on each other. Suddenly inspired, he decided to show me his power, to demonstrate the cries with which he impressed new initiates imprisoned in the sacred enclosure. He began with a series of cooing noises and little cries; then, becoming more savage, he emitted harsh sounds that started deep in the throat and ended in a kind of trumpeting. This vocal demonstration had an unmistakable physical effect on me. I observed my companions, especially Lagwa; they remained phlegmatic but respectful.

Nyon Sinoe wished to retire; he claimed to be exhausted. He started to leave the big hut, then retraced his steps and addressed me. The guttural voice seemed angry.

"I thank you for the offering you have made me. But you took a picture."

"Well?"

"You have kept me with you; you must compensate me."

I had not thought the incident would end so soon in haggling, in such a rapid return to the commonplace.

Later, as my investigation proceeded, I analyzed these impressions of my introduction to the system of the masks. I could not help asking myself whether this really had been Nyon Sinoe, the Red, the Terrible Father, or a fraud to deceive the foreigner? The answer was simple, and could be divined from the half-incredulous, half-apprehensive reflections of my youngest informant:

"We no longer believe in the *nyomo* in the way our ancestors did. We want them with us because they are good for our people. They are our force against the foreigner. . . . And then, we are afraid of the masters of the cult, who are still the keepers of the poisons."

This took me far from those metaphysical justifications according to which Nyon Sinoe ensures the glorification of masculinity, as Nyon Néa does for femininity. He—Nyon Sinoe—presents some of the faces of the Father and in this way performs a work of illumination which psychoanalysis has been able to rediscover. He shows him not only in his dominating, grasping form, but also in his aspect as protector, benevolent towards his descendants—the initiates and maskers who are dependent on him. He symbolizes force in a society where warlike ability was long the necessary condition of all survival; ruthless trickery, also, based on skill in using the techniques of poisoning. He is the guardian of traditional religious life, he supervises initiation, he kidnaps disobedient boys; at one time he executed initiates who divulged the secrets of the associa-

Fig. 30 The masked *Pwoin Sinoe*

tion. He is the very cornerstone of the old social and cultural order. Moreover, he is the most powerful and at the same time the most contagious source of energy. The chant describes him as *Mangana, mangana tini ngon* (Stain more indelible than filth, more indelible than fire).

In the clearing around the big hut the sacred presentation

continued for several days. It excluded neither competition for prestige between villages, nor refinements on the part of the maskers, who sometimes made me feel as if I were watching a procession of comic mannequins. Nyon Pwoin Sinoe, the Warrior, presented a flat, oblong face whose eyes looked out beneath a strip of red cloth, and whose howling mouth revealed teeth made of chicken feathers. On his forehead he had ram's horns in imitation of those once worn by fighters and the symbol of their office. He offered from several neighboring villages a diversity of names: Invisible Genie, Gust of Wind, He-who-brings-shame-to-the-enemy, Roaring Mouth.

Next came Nyon Pwoin Néa, Wife of the Warrior. Her face did not differ very much from her husband's, although it was more apt to be bordered by three streaks within which the eyes stood out against a background of red cloth edged with aluminum. The visage gleamed with a beautiful metallic luster and was framed by two large fiber braids. Nyon Pwoin Néa, whose voice is low and almost whispering, behaves in a peaceable manner. She submits to the rhythm of the music which accompanies the dances, whereas her impetuous husband will tolerate no constraint and spends himself in immoderate and violent gestures. It is she who preserves fertility and protects human lives in the confusion of battle. She is mother of the villages and guardian of the dead. Her names are more evocative of beauty and feminine grace than of sacred discipline: Little Eyes, Black Beauty, Murmuring Forest, Togba-the-Dancer. . . .

Behind this parade of stars there existed a choreography of minor maskers whom my companions hesitated to present, so second-rate did they consider them: for example, Kwi Néa, jack of all trades and jester of the stars of the sacred dance, and Mamoungonyo, surly and grumbling in charge of material order and the war with dirt.

I can still see these masks lined up in my office at Conakry on my return from this trip, their brows stained with cola-nut dust received in offering, stripped of their finery, inert, ready for the descriptive labels and the obscurity of museum files. Near by sits the pile of notes I have accumulated. My window looks onto the sea and that backdrop provided by the little native port and the cemetery. With ironic intent, my memory discovers the first stanzas of the *Cimetière marin,* and with malicious attention, as if these objects seemed suddenly more hateful. I repeat a couplet:

> *"O récompense après une pensée*
> *Qu'un long regard sur le calme des dieux!"**

But what wretched gods are these, descending with slow or hurried step the path of their decline! They are dying one by one: Nyomo Nkwouya, the Stilt Man, so far from his former power that he no longer merits even the ritual offerings—a *déclassé* aristocrat turned wandering acrobat; Nyon Pwoin Sinoe, the now genial Warrior, whose ridiculous battles of the old days the young people no longer hesitate to deride; and all the female maskers, drooping and molting into an image of charming, gentle, confident femininity; and bringing up the rear, Mamoungonyo, without voice or musical escort, whose function is simply to remind villagers that the meanest of men must still be less dirty than their dogs. Only Nyon Sinoe, the Red, retains some of the old prestige. Even so, they whisper behind his back although they continue to fear and respect him in a different way as the last segment of the old structure. But he had better not have too many illusions. Already his peaceable brother, Nyon Sinoe of the simple black-stained face, is becoming the maid of all work of Kono villages; a character too popular to remain long in the realm of the sacred, one who is willing to be the everyday refuge of people in trouble.

This decline of the gods follows the direction of those forces which are transforming Kono society. Tribal wars have disappeared to make room for more insidious conflicts; the initiatory enclosures have been momentarily deserted; foreign beliefs have been imported together with new methods of therapy; traditional authorities have grown weaker and the people, tempted by the opportunities opening up all over the country, have crossed once forbidden frontiers. If the fabric of relationships created by the choreography of the masks is becoming as threadbare as an old garment, it is because the old social pattern itself is dying out in favor of other forms.

The society of the maskers is tending more and more to become a kind of museum, a source of evidence. It serves to idealize a past which helps Kono peasants to resist foreign influences (ours) which are less and less tolerated. It constitutes the archives of a people who, since they have no knowledge of writing, have not been able to record their history in libraries. It reveals traces of influences undergone: the secondary masks,

---

* "O compensation after thought / A long look on the stillness of the gods!"

in fact, form a constellation revealing Sudanese, Liberian and Eburnean contributions to this composite civilization. In it one can still trace the old moral and political codes which the sacred figures were supposed to enforce. The Father, the lineages and familial groups, and the Warrior are central to the system: they see to it that fundamental obligations are respected; they organize social life around themselves. The sacred couples impose a certain image of man and woman; they illustrate the prescribed relations between these two alien elements which nevertheless have been united since the world began. In the secrecy of the initiatory classes, the maskers are the principal educators of new generations: it is they who *make* respectable people. They protect; they check deviations from custom; they guide individuals through the multiple vicissitudes affecting their lives. They maintain a certain order of the society and at the same time are the product of a meditation upon that society.

Obviously they are more than this, but only in a subordinate sense. They arouse aesthetic emotions for the artist as well as for the spectator who is judging their workmanship and evolution. They have given rise to a popular imagery which causes their silhouettes to appear on the outer walls of huts. They furnish a reflection not only of the society but of the image which man draws of himself, for himself. In this sense they are the products and the instigators of powerful emotions. The society of the maskers constitutes the sole book of wisdom for peoples without written works or monumental creations. In the heart of a human universe which is so tightly enclosed within such narrow limits, and whose frontiers are subject to the pressures of a savage nature and hostile strangers, the masks also permit an illusory escape. Somehow they reconcile these two forces. In an essay entitled "Les Masques," Georges Bureau asks the question, "Why did the Negroes once wear masks?" and decides that the answer lies in the individual's desire for escape, his desire to "increase his range and his powers." But this study also suggests the danger of focusing one's attention on this aspect of African civilization. The masks become a pretext, a base on which we construct our own fantasies; we lose sight of what is essential.

In this case, what is essential lies in relations between individuals, between people and things, relations of which the society of the maskers is a kind of reproduction. These relations are fundamental to that society, and changes in them affect it, in

113

spite of its appearances of immutability. In civilizations whose material structures are fragile the decline of the gods is a more serious matter than in our monumental civilizations. Neither imposing temples nor imperishable books remain to bear witness to their past royalty—only these costumed characters whom the young people are beginning to ridicule. They are still performers of miracles: a man laid down his mask, turning it toward the east, threw down the cola cotyledons—*tougélé touka*—to ensure aid in his race for money, and the sacred figure obligingly accepted the offering of ground nuts; but more often they are merely players of tricks.

This Kono civilization is not one of the worst affected—far from it! I can still see the indignant expression on the face of my friend Bohumil Holas, the ethnologist of Ivory Coast, who had to collect hundreds of masks and fetishes which the villagers had thrown onto the garbage heaps outside the towns—dregs of a past that was now dead. In the workrooms of the Museum of Abidjan, with patience and love he is constructing the archives of an Africa which has turned its back on dreams and mirages—and has still to learn to take pride in such a heritage. And I am sure my colleague's Negro assistants look ironically upon this scavenging activity as a harmless eccentricity.

In all fairness let us acknowledge that forces alien to the Negro world have added to this tide which is sweeping away the traditional arts. Islam, in bringing the Book, banished images which had been venerated until then. Missionary Christianity was necessarily violently iconoclastic. Let us change the scene: I am at the Catholic mission at Libreville, looking for manuscripts and archives relating to the Gabonese Fang. I meet with nothing but understanding and erudition until I make the mistake of lamenting the lost arts. As if I have raised the devil himself, a priest thunders:

"I have burned or destroyed thousands of fetishes. I regret nothing!"

"And has Christianity gained as a result?"

The question remains unanswered. It is a curious illusion to believe you have dealt paganism a blow by destroying its most obvious props. The beliefs continue by going underground or resorting to a less obvious symbolism. Fires lighted to the greater glory of God are contagious, and fascinate the Negro founders of those "separatist" churches which I was later to encounter in the Congo; it is as though their spirit were projected outward upon anything that resists their campaign of spiritual

Fig. 31 Doorway surround, Bamileke country

conquest. History tells us of their incendiary rage in Angola as early as 1872 in a movement justly named *Kiyoka*, from yoka, the act of burning. They continue to appear sporadically in the Congolese zone. One day in March 1950 when I was about sixty miles from Brazzaville, I suddenly found myself in front of a still-smoking fire on which were lying several half-burned statuettes and some amulets which had been reduced to ashes. The new prophet had fled upon hearing of my arrival. He had just laid down the precept, "We must renounce the fetishes of our fathers," and the last vestiges of the ancient art were being slowly consumed. In their struggle against idols, the instigators of religious dissidence, some of whom find justification in a passage from Leviticus, rival the first missionaries in zeal.

But the destructive activity may be more indirect, more gradual. When the Kingdom of Dahomey fell under the pressure of French colonial expeditions, it inevitably took with it some of the artistic activities associated with the political and religious systems that supported it. We know the sum of the vanished riches: copper statuettes cast from lost wax molds; wood sculpture, royal thrones and statues plated with copper or silver; bas-reliefs of clay decorating the walls of royal buildings; appliquéd hangings. A plentiful creativity, for the most part intended for an aristocracy which the colonial peace deprived of its privileges and originating, in the case of those best satisfying aesthetic criteria, with "families" that guarded the traditions of art.

A few ethnologists have tried to evaluate the present situation objectively. Wood sculpture reveals a decline in vitality which is related to the pressures which the traditional religions have undergone. Paul Mercier tells that while he was visiting a region that had once been rich in skilled craftsmen, he had no difficulty acquiring the statues that stood in the chief temple of a certain village. The notables gave their consent, specifying that they would obtain new ones, which were hastily redone. This illustrates a casual attitude toward traditional aesthetic requirements and toward the gods received from the past. But it is not only the divine consumers of the products of craftsmanship who are on the decline; Europeans and a Negro bourgeoisie have supplanted the old aristocrats. These two groups are imposing their tastes and becoming the inspiration for objects which, since they must be exclusively works of art, have lost that authentic beauty which the old utilitarian objects always possessed. Commercial necessity is also responsible for the inferior quality characterizing the work of coppersmiths and jewelers today. In the absence of the material assistance of patrons, they work for the local market and exportation; they retain the items that sell best, filling the stands near the hotels with silly figurines and "souvenirs;" they work without creative pleasure, indifferent to the solicitations of their new clientele. Perhaps they find some consolation in observing that this pitiful state of Dahomean art is not due to their compliance alone. The sculptors and workers in appliqué have likewise been forced to give in to the exigencies of supply and demand.

Fig. 32
A carved Bamileke drum
sketched by R. Lecoq

Fig. 33
A Bamileke mask
sketched by R. Lecoq

All has changed, but all may not be lost. The clay palaces started to disappear while history was being made outside their walls. For several years, however, official services have been capturing sections that could be preserved in cement and the Dahomeans are beginning to travel the road to the museum at Abomey in a sort of pilgrimage into the past. All artisans have not entirely lost the aesthetic inspiration. Mercier mentions one now working in the village of Athiémé who sculpts masks which are completely independent of ancient canons in that they are designed for no ritual purpose. This man's work consists of "strange faces, whose features are tormented, distorted, twisted, often haunting." Thus an isolated artist succeeds in creating an original style and producing images in which Afri-

117

ca presents her anguished countenance in the face of the uncertainties of her new destiny.

I am quite aware that the world too early predicted the death of Negro art, which acquired its universal value in the studios of men of "audacious tastes." There remain a few civilizations which are creative by traditional norms, for example, the Bamileke, a mountain people of central Cameroon whose artistic vigor was demonstrated by Raymond Lecoq in a volume of the *Présence Africaine* series. This society has grown under the sign of exuberance and tenacious industry, and a fertility which has created one of the greatest population densities recorded in tropical Africa: seventy inhabitants per square kilometer. A spirit of conquest led the Bamileke to subdue peacefully, by economic influence, large sectors of southern Cameroon and of the town of Douala. There is no denying the dynamism of this ethnic group which, proud of its traditions and preserving its originality, has nevertheless proved skilful in assimilating modern contributions. Its equilibrium and vitality are revealed by the strength of its art, which thus proves to be one of the best indices to the health of a civilization.

Fig. 34
A Bamileke sculpture
sketched by R. Lecoq

Fig. 35
A carved Bamileke vessel
sketched by R. Lecoq

These creations, which without being monotonous reveal a definite unity of conception, and are as diverse in their materials (wood, ivory, copper, terra cotta, pearls, fiber, paint) as in their uses (architecture, furniture, religious sculpture, utensils), serve a double purpose: they glorify and strengthen the power of the chiefs and they testify to an agricultural economy which is determined to subdue a difficult nature. Lecoq's inventory of human and animal representations is significant in this connection. The figures depict the chief with his most characteristic attributes, symbolize his victories, and evoke attitudes of respect imposed by his presence or his role of justiciary. The animal motifs—panthers, buffalo, elephants and snakes—are primarily concerned with the so-called "totemic" alliances contracted by founders of the chieftainries. The art is intended to be an expression, as well as a material aid, to a specific social organization, and it marks those instruments and rituals responsible for preserving this organization. It justifies this organization by teaching a language which is comprehensible to all and permits explanation of the prescribed behavior. It constitutes a book in which one can read the history of Bamileke country, as well as techniques for maintaining the status quo and ensuring fertility to man and his labor. If one were to rely solely on this "text," one would not doubt that it was the product of a hierarchical society with an essentially agricultural economy.

As of today, Bamileke art has retained all its power. Both the dynamism of the chieftainry and the force of popular sentiment have operated in its favor. But there are other factors. Precisely because power seemed more diffuse in this society, it has not been dominated as has the Kingdom of Dahomey, for example, and at the same time it has been protected in a purely geographic sense. Above all, by its conquering activities, it has offset an inferiority experienced within the limits of the colonial situation. Confident of its enduring vitality, it has had the will power not to regard itself as definitively defeated. And this example shows how closely those areas of the Negro world where artistic activities remain strongest coincide with the distribution of those tribes least subjected to, or best defended from, the constraining effects of colonization.

At the time of my visit to Central Africa I only scratched the surface of Bamileke country. I penetrated the heart of regions in Gabon and the Congo where a once flourishing art has completely disappeared, thereby accentuating that sense of cultural desolation which the traveler feels there. From time to time chance unearths some fine piece which has survived devastation and neglect: for example, an ancestral figure made by the

Fang of the Bitam region north of Gabon, found by an administrator in one of the supply rooms adjoining the official buildings.

It is one of those sculptured images—the last, perhaps?—which exerted their charm on Parisian painters of the Fauve school. The statue represents a woman of hieratic bearing, powerful neck and unforgettable face. The attitude is one of immobility, withdrawal: arms held along the sides and hands joined in a line with symbolic tattoos which form a kind of pediment over the prominent navel—that root of the race, that center of the ancient Fang world. It is tempting to emphasize the severe and rhythmic volumes, their expressive distortion, that architecture by which the object arouses an aesthetic emo-

Fig. 36 An ancestral Fang figure

tion. This, however, is not its true meaning. But how do we find it? The face, from which the image draws the essence of its quality, remains impenetrable. It is traced in a concave oval crowned by a head of hair arranged like the peaks of a diadem. The eyes are hidden under the curve of the eyelids, the gaze is turned inward; over the sockets looms a forehead of powerful amplitude. Something stirs us, makes us eager to question this Negro version of the Sibyl. In vain! We feel free to construct theories upon this enigma: hence the scramble of history leads some to the Egyptian origin of Negro civilizations, and others—

like Cheikh Anta Diop—to the Negro origins of Egypt, mother of civilizations.

I have neither the ability nor the taste for this sort of thing. For me, the statue presented the simple problem of what reaction it would impose, when it appeared, upon my Fang informants. First they manifested astonishment; then a slight withdrawal. One of the young men ventured to observe:

"It is a *bieri*. The heads of families used to have them in their huts."

From the hodgepodge of discarded archives the administrator produced the crate containing the ancestral image. I noticed that the latter was resting on a bed of red-stained crowns of skulls stacked like crockery and sprinkled with a fine black powder. My companions moved back another step, encouraging me to try a revealing experiment:

"Take this stuff to the car."

My mock casualness provoked first general indignation, then a confused protest which I had great difficulty silencing. I elicited only one stubborn response:

"We cannot touch these things!"

"Why not?"

"Ah! Because we cannot. . . ."

And so forth. One of my informants, conciliatory and anxious not to offend the European mania for explanation, ventured a remark which he believed was calculated to close the discussion.

"You see this powder, it is black *nsou*, the deadliest of the poisons made by our fetish makers. . . . Don't touch it, or you too will die."

"But you see very well that the *nsou* is in the bottom of the crate!"

It was no use, and I had the conviction that there was little point to the argument. In spite of the general annoyance, I persisted. The discussion seemed destined to terminate on an "explanation" repeated endlessly, an explanation which remains for the ethnologist the mark of a failure which is often temporary.

"Young men have no right to tamper with things having to do with ancestors. They do not know how to go about it; it is dangerous for them."

"Things having to do with ancestors"—this *bieri* which had turned up in a crate which had contained canned goods? This detail gave a ridiculous quality to the anxieties of my companions. And yet, for a long time the *bieri* was the image most charged with political and religious meaning, the instrument most propitious for assuring basic communication between the living and the dead. Atop a basket containing the crania of the successive chiefs, it formed the altar of the group and the symbol guaranteeing the legitimacy of the power held. In it the race found its root and its spiritual sustenance. In a certain sense it represented the "fatherland" for groups which, before the establishment of the French peace, were characterized by the mobility of the conquerors and the precariousness of their ties with the occupied land. It disappeared, first as a result of missionary activity, and then under the impact of the multiple upheavals Fang society had undergone; continuing to exist in secret, it had become an instrument of magical power. Therefore it overwhelmed indifference with fear.

All this was present in the minds of my informants, who were frightened by my audacity. It was impossible to get them to move. The administrator decided to call upon a guard of foreign descent. I can still see the man, frozen in an attitude that was all the more deferential since he was expecting an order he wished to avoid.

"Take this to the car."

"But, sir. . . ."

"Don't argue with me, pick up the box!"

The guard ran off at a fast trot without touching anything.

"Where are you going?"

"To get the chauffeur, sir."

"Come back here and take care of it yourself."

The man ran off again, this time toward the police station. He tried to explain as he ran: "Bad business, sir . . . we'll need a gun. . . ."

The tension mounted. Finally the guard, holding the crate, which was more dangerous than a box of grenades, in one hand and his gun in the other, scurried off with a grotesque and disjointed gait in his eagerness to put down his burden. I immediately took the precaution of sealing the crate securely and burying it under the rest of my baggage. The anecdote has a sequel: the objects disappeared during the last leg of my journey in Fang country. All my efforts and threats were unable to retrieve them. This outcome, which still has the power to exasperate me, leaves the field open to anyone who wishes to extract a moral from it.

My fund of information on the Gabonese arts was very limited. With a greater sense of distance I could confirm Fernand Grébert's remark of twenty years ago: "In order to appreciate their vanished arts, descendants of the man-eating Fang will have to come to Europe to our museums to contemplate their ancestral skill." In almost all of the villages, blacksmiths and sculptors have laid down their tools. And in my files I find notations devoid of real interest.

Fig. 37
Bakota funerary
figure, Gabon

Fig. 38
Mpongwe mask
from Gabon

My relative familiarity with the syncretic cult of *Bwiti* led me to visit several temples on the road that follows the Ogooué toward Libreville. The central pillar which supports the temple and represents one center of the sacred place is sometimes decorated with a crude polychromatic feminine figuration; generally speaking, it carries signs which are an open book to the eyes of initiates—bird of death, saw of destruction, python, rainbow. Even these minimal artistic requirements are difficult to meet and some of the founders of temples must have gone far afield in search of the last artisans.

Aesthetic preoccupations tend to center around houses and clothing. At the time of my investigation, a clannic initiative in certain regions of Fang country was promoting an architectural

123

revival which was felicitous when it rediscovered the traditional geometry of hammered bark or colorful braided bamboo but somewhat less so when, as I observed near the Cameroonian frontier, it unreeled on walls of dried earth edifying frescos lifted from some mediocre Bible story. These architectural efforts are even more depressing when they inspire a species of "interior decoration." Color plates and illustrations torn from magazines, reproductions from scholarly books or catalogues replace the old wall decorations, while embroidery learned in workrooms is invading bourgeois homes. Then there is the ornamental use of certain of our waste products, boxes with pictorial advertisements or gaudy wrapping paper. The deterioration of taste is still more noticeable in the urban centers. All this has a meaning difficult to define in terms of our own criteria, which are often based on ulterior motives. One might speak of an African baroque in which the objects disseminated by our industrial civilization are incorporated into a context of values and meanings which is often alien to the utility habitual with us. There is an alienation and "Africanization" of our familiar objects which contributes to the emergence, as yet awkward and hesitating, of an aesthetic peculiar to modern Africa.

During my last days in Gabon I had the brief illusion of a more elating discovery. I came upon a small short-handled mask hanging from the wall of a hut. I later found it to be a piece of junk, but it resembled those images which without great conviction are assigned to the Mpongwe or some other tribe of the lower Ogooué. My excitement was all the greater because, contrary to my habitual reserve, I have always had a passion for these little-known works. I love their infinite interrogation and their mysterious irony. Try to imagine these human—possibly feminine—faces, white as Pierrots, with their elongated eyes set between the delicate arch of the brows and the crimson disdain of the lips, each bearing a cluster of frontal tattooing and framed by a complicated crestlike headdress. These masks baffle one with their Oriental features, the uncertainty of their origin and meaning—are they the faces of albinos or the visages of ghosts?—and their use. Anything that might have aided in their interpretations is gone. Their disdainful expression seems to mock our helplessness.

The modern Congo is scarcely less disappointing, except for Bateke country where, because of its isolation and difficulty of access, the traditional temples are not yet deserted. However, among the Bakongo living near Brazzaville I was to remark an astonishing invasion of cement into creations which were unquestionably appreciated as art. I am speaking of works associated with a revival of the ancestor cult which have drawn their inspiration from European cemeteries. I remember my astonishment on remarking the contrast between the fragility of the homes of the living, many of which are still of mud, and the monumental solidity of the "houses" erected for eminent dead. Funerary edifices of vast dimensions, requiring quantities of a rare and expensive cement, loom even in distant villages. They have absorbed considerable savings, all the more precious as they belonged to the poor, as if the most profitable investment were still the one the group makes in honor of its dead.

In Vindza, ninety-five miles north of the capital, the impressive home of a still-powerful chief with the magnificent name of Kongo presents three centers of prestige: the overdecorated house proper, where Kongo only receives guests; the informal courtyard enclosed by narrow wooden benches and shaded by a thick mango tree; and the tombs of the chief's ancestors and parents. These monuments are protected from dirt by a fence and covered by a thatched roof. One of them rises in steps supported by a low wall; it is surmounted by a cross with a niche containing a flowered earthenware plate (symbol of the household objects once left on the tomb) which is still the place for offerings. This is the tomb of Kongo's mother. The other structures have a more ordinary form which, however, is less commonplace in my eyes. On a thin slab bearing in relief the motif of the Christian cross rests a massive affair resembling our coffins in shape but raised at one end to suggest the position of the feet. In other villages more elaborate stylization gives rise to a form which is a curious blend of the rough outline of a recumbent body and the shape of a canoe. One is tempted to look for a necessary connection between the ancestors who were the first occupants of this territory and the ordeal of crossing the Congo, the most serious obstacle to their advance.

The cross, which is Latin or Greek according to the locality, predominates. It does not signify a large following for missionary predication. Kongo, who is so anxious to have the support of his dead, is the most feared of the "fetishist" chiefs. The cross has been adopted as the most effective symbol for evoking ancestors; it ensures the success of those whose duty it is to address them. It seemed to underlie the strength of a civilization—ours—which presented itself as both Christian and materially triumphant. In the beginning all our advantages seemed due to our religious techniques—that is to say, from the Congolese standpoint, our methods of communication with the dead. The cross became a "fetish" without destroying the teaching propagated in its name. The association dates from the sixteenth and seventeenth centuries in certain parts of the Congolese region. Modern Christian missions were forced, especially in Angola, to conduct veritable campaigns for the destruction of these *nkangi* (crosses), so closely associated did they seem with paganism and various magical practices. *Nkangi* figured notably among the badges of chieftainry and judiciary power, within a system involving offerings and sacrifices.

Fig. 39 A concrete funerary statue

In Boko, another district in the vicinity of Brazzaville, I had occasion to observe more literate examples of this funerary art in which the age of cement joins hands with the old ancestor worship. The tombs are often flanked by guardianlike figures which are cast on their pedestals in comical attitudes. Here, two little fellows covered with red, white and blue stand, one with

126

his arms crossed, the other caught in a gesture which combines the military salute with the stop signal of a traffic policeman. There, perched on a concrete base, is a figure whose face and sprightly attitude recall the antics of Felix the Cat. But it is above all the tombs of the chiefs which reveal this luxuriance of form and color. Take, for example, the monument erected to Biza, *mfoumou* of revered genealogy and an early instigator of anticolonial resistance. Although it is very wide and high, the tomb does not differ appreciably from the models already described. On the other hand, it is rich in accessories daubed with crude colors: a whole set of furniture is represented with particular attention to the living room, which indicates the social importance of the deceased; round about, petrified animals remind one that this was a man of property. A structure with a roof of corrugated iron protects the whole. Near by, the precarious dwellings of the living cower under roofings of dried grass damaged by the elements.

Fig. 40 New Year card by Poto Poto painters

All this requires our attention rather than our criticism. A modernist art interested in being *imperishable* is being born. This renaissance is expressing itself in terms of certain relations which society cannot allow to disappear without risking its own

127

death: those established between the lineage, the clan territory and the ancestors present in their tombs. In the villages of the chiefs these monuments dominate the whole landscape and unquestionably constitute the spiritual center of the group. It is in the hands of the ancestors that the future of the Bakongo continues to be wrought; it is on them that prosperity depends and that the social structure rests. History consists of the legends peculiar to them. The future cannot ignore them without fear of seeing the social fabric torn in all directions. These remarks do not apply to this Congolese region alone; they show more generally that in its least vulnerable expressions Negro art remains above all a meditation on death.

Around a quarter of a century ago, after trying to trace the vicissitudes of this art, Georges Hardy concluded: "Today, after a hundred years of Afro-European conflict, we have a vacuum, or close to it." The balance sheet no longer looks so discouraging and the curve plotted by this author may be extended at either end. First of all, toward the present: in this connection I have just mentioned aspects which must be filled in. A free art is emerging which no longer capitalizes so outrageously on the falsely naïve and the falsely exotic as in past decades. To return to Brazzaville, of course there still exist those "artists," specialists in door-to-door selling, who offer bad frescos on burnt wood, masks and statuettes made to order, and realistic "calendar" paintings, but they are no longer alone. The Poto Poto school of painters is developing in a contagious manner, by expressing its beliefs, its dreams and its humor. The imaginative projection which the painting requires, the concern for significant or descriptive detail, even the blunders, which attract our attention, the forms of abstraction which prove the last to be the reflection of an old reality—all these suggest the riches to come. One senses the possibilities for immediate effectiveness of such painting, its influence, born of its spontaneity, upon the ways of seeing and believing still imposed by the ancient cultural heritage.

Hardy's curve can be extended at the other end, by pushing back the origin of Negro art. When I was living in Jos, a mining town on the central plateau of Nigeria, Bernard Fagg, founder of that town's Museum of Prehistory, put me in touch with evidence of a very remote past. Thanks to the collaboration of some tin miners who could look beyond the rich carapace they had torn from the earth, this great archeologist discovered the most ancient specimens of African art. In fact, they must be placed within the five centuries preceding the birth of Christ. The terra cotta objects unearthed by the excavations, evidence of a civilization which was naméd the Nok culture after a neighboring village, reveal an amazing skill in portraiture and an ability to treat the human body in supple forms which recall Indian sculpture.

Fig. 41 Terra cotta head from Jemaa, Nok culture

Our knowledge broadens with time, increasing the discontinuities. We cannot re-establish the connections. At least we can be certain of one thing: the arts of Africa are infinitely more diverse than our painters and amateurs of Negro art imagined in the early nineteen-twenties, with a diversity which places them beyond controversies over realism and idealism, beyond attempts at formal classification. By changing, they endure; we are beginning to understand this today in spite of the gaps in our scholarship. The periods of eclipse seem to have been merely periods of transition during which Africa was recovering her balance in order to begin again. When we lament the lost arts, we are dwelling on a certain image of Negro civilizations which have already been swept away by the tide of history. The art which is evolving can only be an expression of the present state of Negro societies and cultures. It reflects their vicissitudes, bears the mark of their weaknesses, their promises and their aspirations. It is still clumsy in its indecision, confusing in its ambiguity. Its slow transformation heralds other, profounder changes. It cannot, in its ancient guise, resist the impact of the "metamorphosis of the gods."

▼▼▼▼▼▼▼▼▼▼▼▼▼▼▼▼▼▼▼▼▼▼▼▼▼▼▼▼▼▼▼▼▼▼▼▼▼

NIGERIA: TWO AGES OF AFRICA

I WAS speaking in the last chapter of the town of Jos, the tin capital of Africa. An airplane flying over the outskirts of the city reveals to the traveler, as it rocks wide strips of landscape, a region revolutionized by human industry. Across a now barren bush, the large breaches opened by the miners are very evident. They are sometimes arranged in steps, giving the impression of a gigantic amphitheater, and are surrounded by heaps of loose soil which are flattened by the altitude. Railroad tracks and an excellent road which seems to have fairly heavy traffic run straight, avoiding these chaotic zones. Next, the eye falls on a compact group of monotonous buildings: a camp for native workers.

However, it is only on ground level that the real scale of these exploitations can be grasped. Tractors and modern cranes with long steel arms extract, push and transport tons of ore and "sterile" earth. The latter is piled in curious pyramids; it is used to reconstruct the natural surroundings in accordance with Nigerian legislation, as if the European businessmen were trying to prove to the natives, the real owners of the land, that nothing has happened, nothing has been taken. An engineer

131

commenting on this obligation told me without irony, "In this way, we further the agricultural and pastoral vocation of the natives." Through the mines over considerable distances runs a network for the canalization of water. High-pressure jets resembling blowpipes cut out wide sections of soil. Water, indispensable to the concentration of the powdery ore, is inseparable from the powerful machines which shift enormous masses. These two elements, the jet and the crane, are the double trademark of mining country.

The quarrying has an offshoot: processing factories for rare ores. I had occasion to visit one of these. Closed in, its single exit barred by a heavy iron door, it seemed to harbor some momentous secret. Its defensive isolation seemed to indicate the superimposed nature of these mining activities, which form a kind of small island of modernism; it also seemed to reveal fears regarding the possible subversion of African masses who have remained outside the system and its advantages. The equipment, which was comparatively antiquated at the time of my visit in December 1949, continued, like that of the mine, to combine the mechanical power of water with that of machines. Repeated and systematic washings and screenings were accomplished in a confused din of flowing water, moving metallic belts, and shuddering separators. After these operations, the chemical department subjected the ores to warranty tests.

I cannot help evaluating the effort which has permitted the importation of these technical procedures and this equipment, this deliberate expansion of mechanized civilization. And yet, how am I to dismiss an impression I have had since my arrival? Civilizations are juxtaposed without interpenetrating—that of the tractor men; that of the feudal Moslems, former conquerors; and that of the indigenous "peasants," doubly vanquished. This list has a significant sequence. It indicates the order of appearance of those groups which have or had control over this vast region, the domination of one group ending that of another. Moving backward from today to a remote past, we find the bearers of mechanical power and the bearers of the Book, then men who could have imagined neither the machine nor the book. The whole history of a large portion of West Africa is written on this soil.

This coexistence of different ages is reproduced accurately within the tin economy. The airplane does not reveal it. The spectacular upheavals caused by the machines of the large enterprises conceal it. Nevertheless, a manual quarrying of ore proceeds in the shadow of these machines. The natives extract the tin by a technique identical with the one I described in connection with the Sudanese gold mines. One finds here the same network of narrow canals, the same methods of washing, which after patient rotation leaves a few pinches of metal in the bottom of the gourd. The means of transportation is still the basket carried on the head. The heaps of loose soil thus removed take on the appearance—so persistent is the image of mechanized mining—of molehills which have grown to unusual dimensions. It so happens that a lone European is trying to bring a little progress by organizing a pumping team which gives the water the power necessary for more intensive production. The thirty or forty natives who work for him pay for this improvement in their very ancient techniques with a social transformation which turns them into salaried laborers.

These activities, which represent a certain profit when considered as a whole, add their production to that of the great enterprises. Thus, under the patronage of the financial groups which possess the tin of Malaysia and the ore of Nigeria, the "partnership" of the tractor and the gourd is formed. True, only the frailest of bonds—not to mention the obvious inequality of the relationship—can be established between these two methods of production so different in age. Modern mines need only a limited number of totally proletarized workers. Near by, archaic Africa is forced to shift for herself by picking up what crumbs she can. Those economists who have dealt with the study of underdeveloped countries are familiar with the phenomenon. They speak of the "juxtaposition of economies of different types," but such abstract formulation destroys the dramatic character of the situation in question. And Governor General Ryckmans' courageous admonition to the leaders of the Belgian Congo has today a tragic echo: "We have reached an impasse; next to prosperous European enterprises, the native economy vegetates."

The juxtaposition manifests itself directly on the cultural level: there is no lack of accidental contrasts similar to those I mentioned at the beginning of this book, not to mention the very plan of the town of Jos. The modern city has been built around mining activities. It adjoins the buildings erected by the feudal Moslems without establishing any but circumstantial and official contacts with these people. The first occupants, whom the English residents inaccurately call pagans, are these people who have remained on the outside. There are, in short,

133

two separate classes of citizens, distinguishable by their occupations and religions, and on the margin, the peasants who live under this twin domination. Each of these groups remains turned in on itself. To pass from one to the other over a short physical distance gives one the sensation of a daring leap through space and time.

It was unquestionable during my stay at the splendid Hill Station Hotel, surrounded by domesticated rocks and gardens, that I was most aware of the impenetrability of the white world. Here everything is organized in luxury and calm to make one forget that one is in a foreign country. Even the natural configuration of the land is used as a screen, a means of concealment; beyond the huge terrace, one almost expects to see a typical English landscape. The Negro servants seem to glide noiselessly in order to make Africa more unobtrusive, while the colossal and magnificent "majordomo" is transformed by a costume evoking an imaginary Orient. On the evening of my arrival the hotel had been given over to the "miners" for one of these periodic evenings when they recreate an artificial atmosphere which makes them forget the place of their implantation—a *nuit blanche,* literally.

Those converted to Islam also have a unique architecture which isolates them and acts as a screen to keep out foreign eyes. The "pagans" are withdrawn at a distance in actual fortified villages. Yet another leap through time was made possible by the organization of an outing for the members of a scientific conference meeting at Jos. We met the pagan peasants at every stopover on this trip, which seems in the minds of its organizers to have been a kind of pilgrimage to the sources. After we left the car beside the road, there remained only a few miles of hard walking. What with the aridity, the sparse vegetation, the rocky debris and the disappearing paths, I re-experienced my profoundest African emotions. I fell in with the game of finding the oldest living Africa. Suddenly a dried-up river appeared with a fallen tree forming a bridge; further on, a path rose toward a pile of rocks upon which huts were perched and where naked children ran away screaming.

The habitations resembled miniature fortified castles. A cluster of small towers connected by narrow passageways opened onto a little courtyard a few yards square. In these miniature houses kitchen, bedroom and attic were so many identical rooms. Inside I noted traditional furniture greatly reduced in size, handmade household utensils and those large terra

134

cotta jars in which the millet beer indispensable to human and sacred intercourse is prepared. No product of English industry was visible. In the narrow and difficult alleys where we stumbled down the crude stone footing, we happened to meet one of the inhabitants, simply clad in a loincloth; he recoiled and turned away, avoiding our eyes. He defended his human dignity before the onslaught of cameras and the enthusiastic assault of visitors in a hurry to record their observations and

Fig. 42 A Sudanese village of early type:
the Dogon of Ireli

make a few sketches. Better than many of my colleagues, I sensed this resistance and respected it; for it is less serious to lose a "scientific" notation than to miss the reaction by which a human being, however unpolished, rightly shows that he is a man. The ethnological commandos have never shared my view. These raids on villages which are regarded as veritable cultural storehouses always miss the very thing they set out to catch—a certain "quality" of societies and human relations.

On a square a few old men were dozing on the large flat rocks that served as grinding stones. This attitude of withdrawal caused their wrinkled skin to sag even more than usual until it resembled some curious garment. In this spot, which represented the center of those social and religious forces which sustained and inspired the group, they were the guardians of the temple. A circular building with large apertures and bearing on

135

its walls the skulls of slaughtered oxen contained the slab upon which sacrifices were performed. Our presence barely disturbed these sleeping or meditative old men. What dreams and thoughts held them in this indifference?

They are the guardians of a very ancient civilization which has its counterpart in northern Dahomey and Togo in the Sudanese region. Theirs is a culture not lacking in remarkable contrasts: poor in farming implements, these men have managed to take root in a barren and hilly land, to invent agricultural techniques based on cereals which are the finest known in the Negro world; bare and unadorned, these peasants have created an architecture which is less fragile than that of Negro peoples externally less archaic. They give the impression of stubbornly defending a very old cultural success. The secret of this success —and this will please Arnold Toynbee, who sees human history as an unending series of challenges and responses—is certainly related to the violence of the hardships they have suffered: those inflicted by conquering and converted Negroes who forced them back toward marginal regions, and those inflicted by a natural milieu difficult of exploitation. But their success is also explained by the scale of their undertaking. Confined within limited areas and forced to work only small strips of cultivable land, they concentrated their efforts in the struggle for survival. They built a society that makes a virtue of miniaturistic subtlety. In withdrawal and defensive adaptation they found amazing strength and a new architectural ingenuity. The movements born of colonial history have so far stopped at the foot of their rocks. Of course the time-honored formula is of no great help today; despite their remoteness, their villages are being contaminated; the germ is present in their society. Their culture has all the succulence of fruits past their prime.

Against one of the walls of the temple, an enormous jar covered with stains from the native beer seems to have been abandoned. This splendid achievement reveals a great skill in the modeling and firing of clay. Its sides bristle with large thorns like the husk of a horse chestnut, and its neck bears the head of some legendary animal whose large open mouth is used for pouring. The stylization of the design amazes and disturbs. By a kind of "internal evidence" which specialists have noted, it suggests some relationship with terra cotta fragments found in neighboring regions and used to identify the Nok culture which, however, precedes it by two thousand years. This reflection makes me realize with a kind of giddiness what an extraordinary flight into the past the study of such a civilization entails: a voyage without points of reference, or very nearly, which has all the earmarks of an authentic "journey to the end of the night."

Around us and the still mute and imperturbable old men a few young men were moving, trying to attract attention. They had spent the night here, coming from Jos and the mines. They were showing off their clothes, their brightly colored scarves and their dark glasses, amid this humanity which, even naked, was culturally richer than they were. If these so-called "enlightened" youths—and what a leap they had taken!—wished to fortify themselves in the village for a few days, it was because they were aware of their weaknesses. They were returning to the support of their families. They were renewing protective contact with the divinities and local genies by coming to observe the old practices. They no longer believed in the same way their fathers did, but for the moment they had no other source of confidence, no other reservoir of energy. They seemed more foreign here than we did, becoming our false accomplices by soliciting cigarettes and favoring us with a few scraps of elementary English. They illustrate yet another flight through time, the reverse of the previous one, but just as hazardous.

Our journey continued into the Bauchi Plateau, whose "pagan" tribes were more contemporary with us. They resembled the Sudanese tribes which I have already discussed; they did not have the unadorned grandeur of the more primitive groups. The organizers of the excursion had arranged for a demonstration of the masks belonging to the male society which was so massive that I have never seen anything like it. The sacred figures appeared from all sides uttering their characteristic cries, shaking headdresses of amazing magnificence featuring colorful sculptured forms that revealed an extraordinary skill in abstraction. In a confusion such that the eye did not know where to look, they recreated the myths they embodied. Guardians of the club, men camouflaged by foliage and armed with branches, chased away the women and children, to whom knowledge of the masks was still forbidden. My traveling companions, however, perched on rocks and trees, sought the best angles to take pictures from.

All these accumulated impressions, which resemble a cinematographic montage with its trick of snatching us from our familiar surroundings and catapulting us through time and space, offer a simple reflection of reality. All these scenes could be experienced simultaneously by someone possessing the gift of ubiquity; and yet they represent ages very remote in terms of human relations and cultures. Sociologists and historians of colonization have created the concept of the "plural society." Although such a notion is accurate, it cannot give any idea of the importance of the phenomenon. The division exists not only because of the races and religions brought together or the economies transplanted, but also because the human groups juxtaposed only seem to be contemporary. These remarks apply to the limited area contained within a radius of ninety miles around Jos. And it remains to be seen what bond or unifying principle can be imposed which will not cause the weakest to be overwhelmed. Even on this scale, the problem is without immediate solution. One can imagine, then, the magnitude of the task facing the African founders and leaders of the Federation of Nigeria.

THE CONGO: ENTER THE NEGRILLOS

Overlooking Brazzaville the Bateke plateaus, so named for the best known of the tribes that inhabit them, attract visitors because of their moderate altitude and the vast blue perspectives of their valleys. For European citizens too long confined to the white world of the city, they are a place to get away from it all. They are relatively easy of access, at least up to a point, in spite of their out-of-the-way situation with regard to economic routes. There are several stopping places marking the ascent: Gîte at thirty miles, Case Barnier, and the post of Mayama on the banks of the Djoue. The river separates real lovers of the bush from casual tourists; it also marks the point after which urban influence on the villages begins to decline.

After that the road deteriorates, skirts the abandoned administrative center of Pangala, and comes to an impasse at the Léfini, a northern tributary of the Congo. Now the landscape shows less evidence of human intervention; the forests on the slopes and beside the rivers become deeper and more luxuriant, and the palm groves become more extensive. One must travel for a long time to reach the village groups, which are broken into many hamlets or encampments; they own wide

138

tracts of land which have enabled them to elude the control of the administrative and scientific departments. In this marginal region where human groups seem to dissolve, three ethnic clusters are in communication. Their propinquity and their occasional co-operation often conceal antagonisms which are still alive. The Negrillos (who are known here as Babinga) are Pygmies, generally half-breeds, who have broken down into little groups living near the villages founded by their masters; they are mobile because unencumbered by material wealth, fugitive, and dominated by a fear which their owners take great care to keep alive. The Bateke, originators of an aristocratic society and former owners of the land to beyond Brazzaville, "possess" the Negrillos as well as the land. Their withdrawal to this mountainous region is a result of colonization: it expresses a desire to cut off contact and to protect themselves by means of a defensive recoil. The Basoundi, the third term in this human equation, have advanced by profiting from this surrender; farmers and traders, skilled in exploiting the advantages of the colonial system, they have followed a patient policy of peaceful invasion. During the last few decades they have taken part in the resistance movement, a *volte-face* which has not reconciled them with the Bateke, who continue to despise them.

In 1949 and 1950 I did extensive research in Basoundi country. It was through certain of my informants, who were participating in a strategem of seduction aimed at the Negrillos, whom they were hoping to lure into dependence upon them, that I came in contact with this tribe. I made several visits to Mindzo, where Kome Mpoutou, one of my best assistants, was living. Eventually, by demonstrating my understanding of his needs as an elderly alcoholic, I won the friendship of Kouka Nganga, the village chief. This man, exhausted by the abuse of palm wine and imported liquor and slovenly in his dress, derived a certain nobility from the wearing of a fanlike white beard which made him look like some saintly character out of the movie *Green Pastures*.

He had confided his policy with regard to the Negrillos in the hope of receiving my support with the local administrator. His method was not without ingenuity and he did not hesitate to explain to me later, "When I gave the *malaki* [a feast celebrating the end of mourning and in honor of the ancestors], I invited the Babinga. I treated them as equals and they were proud. Now that they have come to my village, they must obey me. We can no longer refrain from an exchange of riches. If

139

they are obliged to give in, because they are too poor, I will have assumed authority over them, at the expense of the Bateke."

"How will that help them? They will simply be changing one master for another."

"That is not true. We shall treat them better than the Bateke do, and we shall teach them modern life. The Bateke do not want to know 'civilization;' they are men of yesterday."

"And what advantage will you derive from this maneuver?"

"I will have become a more important chief. Everyone will talk of my skill and cunning. Above all, I shall no longer be obliged to go to the plateaus to buy game meat; the Babinga will bring it down to the village."

The whole matter rested on this double causality: the economic motive, to break the monopoly of the market for meat, a rare and consequently costly food, which the Bateke controlled since they possessed, in the Negrillos, the best hunters in the land; and the political motive, to weaken the Bateke, their contemptuous rivals for the past century, by impairing their right of sovereignty.

One morning Kouka Nganga came to my hut accompanied by several boisterous and talkative young relatives. I was amazed at the excitement and even more so at the transformation in my visitor: he had put on a new khaki uniform and was wearing an old-fashioned soft hat which resembled the headgear of certain European rural types. He was sporting a carved cane in place of the old badges of power. To tell the truth, I was worried by what looked like the official protocol portending an important discussion. After civilities that seemed interminable and the communal consumption of *malafou* (palm wine), the first drops of which everyone, myself included, offered to the ancestors, the matter became very simple. The point was to present me with an invitation which, as I saw it, was not consistent with the rules, but was excused by my disinterested concern for the affairs of the country. Without hesitation I agreed to a request which anticipated my own plans, and was told:

"As you know, the Babinga have lost their chief, a rich man who cannot be treated like an ordinary deceased person. They are planning the *malaki* of the end of the mourning, starting tonight. They will also announce his successor. I have just received the news and I ask you to come with me."

"Is it far?"

"Oh! Not very. If you walk fast, you will arrive before nightfall. The Babinga are no longer so afraid of being near the roads."

In accepting this tempting offer, I became a party to the old chief's political stratagem. I added the weight of my prestige to his advantage. I transformed him into a man capable of bringing a European in his retinue on this solemn occasion. His calculation was not so far off, as I noted when I observed the black look with which the Bateke chief, owner of the Negrillo encampment, favored me on our arrival at the place of the feast. I saw no point in passing up this unusual opportunity. I even had the sense that in some small way I was contributing to the Babinga's appearance on the scene of modern Africa.

It was a noisy crew dressed in their Sunday best that started along the narrow path; two drummers on their way to join the other musicians hired for the occasion brought up the rear. The sun beat hard upon the parched savanna. Everything seemed lifeless. Cultivated fields disappeared very soon, and an occasional bundle of knotted grass marking a hunting boundary was the only reminder that men exercised some control over this desolate landscape. The path was hilly. We kept going up and down, occasionally skirting strips of secondary forest which were trying to win back the flanks of valleys worn away by erosion. Our band began to string out; shouts of encouragement were addressed to the stragglers. I felt that I was being observed and I realized that my companions were watching me with amusement for the first signs of fatigue. With that obstinacy which, persisting until my vision was clouded and I heard a dull hammering in my temples, caused my friend Pauvert to accuse me of a "passion for masochism," I forced myself to maintain a rapid pace. I repeated under my breath some refrains which helped me keep to their rhythm: "The road is long, long, long. . . ." Then the outline of a rather large forest appeared, but its dark and massive shape impressed me less than the anticipation of its coolness. A calm and shallow river, flanked by small rice fields, forced us to look for a ford. Abruptly, the excitement brought me out of my mechanical torpor. We met other groups. Shouts, calls, messages ran through the forest. Kouka Nganga stopped me with a sudden gesture.

"Look! The Babinga are arriving for the feast."

They walked catlike, without rustling the undergrowth, lined up in double file like strange, silent schoolchildren. They amazed me with their ability to blend into the natural setting,

141

revealing a faculty of imitation of which we no longer possess the slightest trace. I observed them with intense curiosity. They were puny in appearance, and yet their height seemed to exceed four feet nine inches, which indicated, as did their dark skin color and other physical traits, the extent of crossbreeding with the Negroes who became their masters. They wore either raffia loincloths knotted at the waist or castoff European clothing. Their women, whose skin seemed more wrinkled, carried small burdens on their heads in *moutete*—the usual long wicker baskets acquired from their Negro masters. They glided by our halted troop without a word of salutation, without a sign, without a look. Kouka Nganga watched them go by, reliving his dreams of ownership.

We had reached our destination. In a vast clearing which had recently been enlarged, an authentic *kermesse* had united all the ages of Africa before its makeshift scenery. The Babinga encampment was located a little to one side. Except for the habitation of the chief, which was built in the Bateke style, it consisted of a few huts which resembled little tunnels covered with dry grass. Inside each of these, in a space a few feet square, the whole family lived, gathered behind a fire of embers burning in the doorway. The room contained almost no objects: I could distinguish only a few bark mats, an occasional gourd from which a child picked a crumb of food. Near by, some yam plants showed that the Negrillos were beginning to farm, but they still depended for manioc, the basic food in the forest country, upon the Negroes who exploited them.

Outside of hunting implements—the short lance, the knife, the crossbow and the fiber net—these men possessed almost nothing. They were unprovided with material goods, thrown back upon the resources of intelligence and guile. The forest was their real home, and their contribution to civilization consisted in their ability to control it. Almost with their bare hands they were more skilful than any other people in exploiting the natural surroundings which had been given them. They were unexcelled in the hunt, and they had been named Babinga from a corruption of *Ba-mbenga,* which means "those who live by hunting." In the appropriate seasons, men and women knew how to fish the water holes without tackle. Women and children in silent bands made the most profitable hauls, returning loaded with fruit, leaves, edible tubers, insects and worms. Their gastronomy was direct; it did not consist in artifice. They gathered honey, which was used for the feeding of young children, and a myth represented them as former blacksmiths who had given up ironwork for the gathering of honey, as if all the avatars of their civilization composed a lesson in the glory of renunciation. But this incontestable success—which shows that every society, even one destitute of material productions, is nevertheless *human* and how, in spite of its material handicap, it achieves impressive victories—has another side. Competent in dealing with the equatorial forest in which they have been leading a nomadic existence for centuries, the Babinga have proved helpless before the more powerful men who have crossed their paths. They have become the "property" of the Negroes who have lured them on with that same mirage effect which marks the beginning of every colonization: the glitter of cheap goods and the prestige of a superior technology.

On the edge of the encampment a temporary village with squares and paths had been built. Shelters of branches and palms provided resting places for whole families who had come with blankets, storm lanterns and gourds full of traveling provisions. All the Bateke and Basoundi peasants in the vicinity were here, settled in their respective "quarters," and surrounded by people newly arrived from town who were parading their finery, complete with new shoes and dark glasses. On the largest of the squares a tradesman had set up his stall: printed fabrics, cigarettes, chewing gum, etc. These luxuries were unpacked under the gaze of the Babinga, who kept their distance. In this bewildering *kermesse* in which everyone seemed to be doing just as he pleased, a strict order was nevertheless being observed, an order which kept different ethnic groups in their places, avoiding intrusions by means of constant supervision. It took care of precedence: in the center stood the temporary dwelling of the Bateke chief, "boss" of this Negrillo encampment; in the various quarters, the placid notables avoided the throng and sat in state on native armchairs which had been transported by their attendants. Although everyone had his share, the good things to eat and drink—palm wine, dried meat and prepared manioc—followed a system of distribution that was based on social status as well as on the value of the counter-gifts contributed to the *malaki*. For the *malaki*, which involves not only an exchange of goods but competition in the exchange, requires meticulous bookkeeping. A young clerk, unexpectedly coiffed in a kind of Tyrolean hat and with a money bag slung over one shoulder, was recording the value of the gifts and collecting the monetary contributions. I saw him in the role of one of those local officials who collect taxes from the tradesmen amid the hustle and bustle of a Parisian market. The two "chiefs of the *malaki*," the Bateke master and his Babinga subordinate, watched him closely.

My arrival had simplified or violated the protocol of reception. I constituted an apparently unexpected element of discord, although the "bush telegraph service" had quickly transmitted the news of my change of position. I brought my gift to the leaders of the feast, but it was a gift with no possible counterpart which placed me outside the system and in a sense gave me an easy victory of prestige, since it excluded the possibility of reply. The Bateke chief was annoyed by this situation, which placed him, in his own eyes, in a position of irremediable inferiority. He sent a great quantity of food and palm wine over to me, whereupon Kouka Nganga, anxious to insult his rival, whispered:

"There is too much water in the *malafou*. You can see for yourself that he is a miser and a bad master for the Babinga."

The guests continued to arrive *en famille* in large bands. They greeted the two "chiefs of the *malaki*," and had their gifts registered with suspicious insistence. Then the men presented their wives to the musicians even before they had laid down their burdens. The picturesque crowd, rich with the color of the cotton fabrics, noisy with shouting and singing, stirred with a localized activity that suggested a theatrical montage in which the various scenes were being shot simultaneously. Here, people were eating in a picnic setting; there, they were dancing.

Only the Babinga entertained themselves "without laughing, without talking, without singing." They stood in a circle composed half of women and half of men, in the center of which an instrumentalist played the four-stringed rattan harp. They danced by stamping and clapping their hands. At a certain point one of the men entered the circle and all the participants began to utter a long unnerving cry. I was unable to grasp the meaning of this choreography. To hide my inadequacy from myself, I pretended it was the original version of one of those games to which our children are the unconscious heirs.

A few young Babinga attempted in an awkward parody to imitate the dances of their Basoundi neighbors. The latter accompany their movements with a monotonous, insidious chant characterized by a short, constantly recurring motif. The dance repeatedly throws the sexes together in a violent gesture which is closely followed by withdrawal. The drummers occupy a lat-

144

eral position. Men and women are divided into facing rows. They look at one another and mark time in place by stamping in triple time. Then suddenly each man rushes to his partner and embraces her, simulating the act of copulation. They separate, and there is more stamping. Then the woman throws herself upon her partner in turn and forces the fictitious coitus upon him. Again they separate. And this double attack begins again. We should guard against seeing these games as a simple technique of sexual stimulation. They indicate the condition of societies in which all effectiveness of human action is of a biological rather than a technical nature, cultures in which, as Engels put it, "reproduction of human beings" greatly overshadows "production of the means of existence." In such a context, the prototype of every effective act is the sexual gesture. To simulate this gesture shows recognition of a fundamental law—indeed, a condition for the continuation of the living natural world—and gives assurance of fruitful and harmonious action.

The Bateke in their "quarter" remained calm. They sat on the ground in small groups listening to the songs which their "witch doctoresses" were singing in their harsh voices. A notable got up, readjusted his draped loincloth, ordered a large glass of *malafou* and slowly began to drink. A woman rose and walked toward him in an attitude of humble submissiveness. She straightened her body with a sudden movement and addressed to the man her song of praise: "You are stronger than the lion of the plateau . . . Your ancestors are among the greatest our people have known. . . ." The notable listened continuing his interminable sipping. The woman surrounded him with her gestures, recreated noble deeds illustrating the glory of this undisputed master, guiding her song by the rhythm of her accompanist. Not until the man, satisfied, had deigned to take the last swallow of palm wine, would she subside, exhausted by her laudatory pantomime.

The sudden nightfall, humid and heavy, at first put a partial stop to the celebration. The families recongregated around meals consisting of the food provided by the two chiefs. A few young people still lingered at the dancing areas. The light from the storm lanterns magnified the scene with their play of shifting and distorted shadows. A couple went off to the forest to make love, then another. In the shelter of her hut, a Babinga mother was gorging her infant child with honey. Sounds had become muted.

145

In a quiet spot, Kouka Nganga had achieved his purpose: he had cornered the Babinga chief, whom he was hounding with questions:

"Why have you not come to talk with me? What is the matter with you? Do you wish to renounce my friendship so soon? . . ."

The little man was trying to avoid the issue. He was uneasy, afraid of being overheard by his Bateke master. Once again I found myself confronted by the problem that motivated my investigation, that of the evolution of the Negrillos who were anxious, by a difficult juggling game, to terminate their long servitude.

The procedure was simple. Kouka Nganga had presented me with all its elements, and I do not believe his list exaggerated: the Bateke appropriated part of the tax levied on their Babinga encampments; the Bateke "stole" the slaughtered meat and sold it at their own profit; the Bateke exploited the Negrillos to clear and cultivate plantations; the Bateke did not treat the Babinga like men: a Babinga's hut, the place where he had sat, the food he had touched were contaminated. The Babinga were sufficiently untouchable that a distance was kept which gave them a sense of inferiority, but not untouchable enough to be economically unusable.

The situation does not differ appreciably in the northern part of the Congo Republic, especially around Likouala, where André Hauser was working from February to May 1951. The same relationship of servitude is imposed on a larger scale in the district of Dongou, where 10,500 Negroes "possess" some 5,000 Negrillos. The same impatience to end this unequal relationship is found there too, although in this region of extreme poverty the gap between the two civilizations is much less marked and intermarriage is beginning to increase. In fact, the inequality has become greater as the economy of the market has advanced, pushing ever further into the past that tacit agreement which had determined the initial symbiosis between the Negroes and the Negrillos. The copal, areca and palm oil produced by the Negrillos are not sold for their profit. However, they are susceptible to the temptations of the merchandise introduced by trade; the more desire they feel for these things, the more aware they are of an exploitation which increases and continues to leave them naked and unprovided. Hauser has estimated that the sale of products provides an "employer" owning a dozen Babinga with an average annual income of 12,000 African francs—a modest income which nevertheless seems considerable in the eyes of men who have recently emerged from their forest nomadism and whose freedom has been sacrificed to the gods of the market.

The Babinga would like to penetrate the screen which their Negro masters have erected between them and the administration, and establish direct contact with impartial authorities. They are trying to get closer to the commercial centers. They are venturing beyond the limits of the forest, to the thresholds of the dispensaries and, in a few cases, of the schools. Certain stronger individuals have succeeded in improving their condition, but often at the price of a complete rupture with their place of origin which even includes a change of name. Such is the case with a Babinga from the vicinity of Brazzaville who, under an adopted surname, had built up a large clientele as a "fetisher" in the capital and beyond the river. Several of his clients who had been saved through his intervention called him Babinga the Miracle Man.

Every human society, when examined in terms of an oversimplified dualism, presents a conflict between two principles: that of heterogeneity, manifested by social differentiation or the antagonisms associated with it, and that of homogeneity, revealed by unifying factors such as beliefs and practices or common interests. Every society is viable on its own scale if the second of these principles outweighs or balances the first, which brings us back to the problem I have been discussing. In contemporary African societies it is easy to see the privileged position held by the elements of division. The European implantation, besides introducing a new term, has created more intense relations between the various Negro cultures, accentuated their profound differences and the gaps which separate them. Although particularism no longer finds expression in the game of tribal war—and perhaps primarily because of this—it remains very strong. The influence of effective unifying factors is much more difficult to observe. The modern economic structure common to all introduces causes of exploitation which, as may be observed in exaggerated form in the case of the Babinga, tend to rest upon the old unequal relations. The Negro religions do not have a unitarian nature and Christianity, which abounds in prescriptions incompatible with the old African heritage, also appears suspect because of its association with the colonial system. The new civilization which is trying to grow under the influence of ours remains for the moment so poor that it can scarcely help to overcome the extreme cultural diversity of the Negro world. Into what units, by what means could these fragments be joined in order to build a modern society which would be relatively homogenous and sufficiently creative to add its own note to the chorus of great civilizations?

In the dancing areas movement had resumed. The same partners would repeat the same steps until the early hours of the morning. I felt tired and hoped to find a little peace by walking in the night. A nephew of Kouka Nganga's decided to accompany me and show the way to his village. As soon as we entered the forest the noises of the festival were deadened, as if they had fallen into absorbent cotton. A rustling of foliage betrayed a fleeing couple. My guide burst out laughing and jeered at the two young people, whom he was able to recognize. Afterward there was nothing more to be heard but the hum of insects. I felt the need to ask a question:

"What do you think of the Babinga?"

"Oh, those people are like savages. They all smell bad. . . . You saw yourself, for the *malaki* of a Babinga you pay only twenty-five francs. If the man had been a Negro, we would have had to pay five hundred francs, maybe more."

GABON, EQUATORIAL ZERO

Coming from Brazzaville on the highway, it was not until Lambaréné that I felt I had reached the Gabon of my imagination. It had been a long day's journey. I had driven part of the night before I distinguished the faint lights, reflected in the Ogooué, which revealed the proximity of this center, known for the intensity of forest cultivation in the region. I only caught a glimpse of it. Because of the late hour it was impossible for me to take the ferryboat or even find a canoe in which to cross the river. There was no sign of a human being on the bank. The darkness was so profound that it obliterated any separate form. Only the Ogooué, whose large calm presence I sensed, cast a faint shimmer. The heat was still oppressive. The atmosphere was heavy, with that humidity that makes you feel every moment that you are living in a world covered with pitch. A few palm trees stood beside the road, their branches drooping, their leaves motionless. In this setting, words like sleep and torpor came to mind and all at once acquired an almost cosmic resonance.

148

I discovered an empty shed; behind that, I came upon a wooden house built in the old colonial style with a stairway leading up and a balcony that shook dangerously. The premises were deserted, but the house was open in accordance with a tacit and still prevalent custom of hospitality. The home was poor, barely furnished and covered with dust. I choose a room containing an old wooden bed with a worn-out mattress and a piece of ancient and useless mosquito netting and a straw-bottomed chair that had seen better days. The room was sinister with poverty and neglect. What man could endure such deprivation, worse than that of the natives in their traditional huts? I learned the next day that this was the house of Isaac the half-breed, who lived on the meager income he earned from his artistic use of *okoume* wood. I did not have an opportunity to meet this person, but he immediately became part of my life through his legend. I learned that he had been initiated into the so-called Bwiti, a religious society about which I shall have occasion to speak, and that he had accepted all its obligations and had acquired an eminent position in it. Thus, beyond this poverty which had made such an impression on me, there emerged a man who was more concerned with his spiritual loyalty to the old Africa than with the road to prosperity in the selling of colonial woods.

The site of Lambaréné is one of the most oppressive I have ever known: a leaden sky, a river whose banks are without color, African houses scattered over too vast an area and devoid of their original style; everything conspires to unnerve as well as to depress. One quickly senses that here civilizations have been corroded and peoples debilitated in less than a century by contact with our economic, administrative and religious imperatives. Already the trade which has been so advantageous to the petty monarchs of the coastal region has exhausted them. You step off the ferry onto a shore road, a kind of marina along which the stalls of the native tradesmen are lined. There is no animation, no shouting, no lengthy bargaining. The men live at a reduced rate, far from the seething crowds which immediately impress one in the centers of West Africa. The poverty is all the more striking and distressing since it is no longer mitigated by the picturesqueness of the exotic decor. Behind the European homes and buildings is a little village populated by Galwa: undistinguished wooden houses whose common design is borrowed from us, and whose walls are covered with color photographs and pictures torn out of illustrated magazines. Through its half-open doors can be seen interiors which are all the more wretched for their bourgeois pretensions. The last survivors of this greatly depleted ethnic group live in an artificial setting of poverty-stricken modernism which has its counterparts as far afield as Haiti.

The Fang and Galwa are short and stocky and often have coarse features. They are not a very photogenic group, and one can understand the anxieties of Claude Vermorel, the director who came to this area to make a film on the woodcutters. I was told that he had to borrow from the army several riflemen from other regions; the local physiognomy failed to meet the demands of cinematographic aesthetics.

Equatorial Gabon is drab and grey, or *chiaroscuro* in the shelter of the forest. And yet it has always spelled adventure for the Europeans who came to settle there; it has played a role of catalyst, as if the environment forced men to exaggerate their originality to the point of caricature. It is a land rich in characters. A number of foresters have their legends. Even the administration manages to stand out unexpectedly. I still recall fondly the district director, a passionate naturalist whose only real contact with Gabon was through the magnificence of its butterflies and birds and who was obsessed with the capture of a rare specimen, the lyre-tailed honey guide. We went into the forest to catch, with learned ingenuity, the characteristic sound this bird is said to make with its tail: *"Nyété! Nyété! Nyété!"* repeated a dozen times with rising, then falling dynamics.

On my first day in Lambaréné the weather was particularly capricious, threatening, and oppressive. This did not improve the rooms of the only hotel where I was staying, boxlike affairs with corrugated roofs and dilapidated furniture that reminded me of those pieces that are held but never picked up in furniture stores. I had an impression which was to strike me often during my stay in Gabon; it seemed to me that an old capital had steadily deteriorated until it had acquired this ancient and exhausted face which I now saw. Everything seemed of another era, tired from too long service, corroded by a destructive climate. Thus I grasped two of the three elements of the Gabonese problem: the illusion characteristic of certain African groups and of the European colony as well, an illusion which consists in living on a past whose riches have long since been consumed; and the difficulty of combatting a nature which feeds insatiably on the corruption of all human achievement. The third element is the dispersion of human groups, their

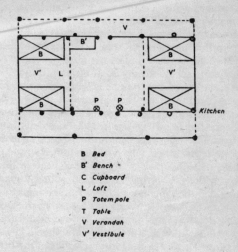

B	Bed
B'	Bench
C	Cupboard
L	Loft
P	Totem pole
T	Table
V	Verandah
V'	Vestibule

House of tongued and grooved planking

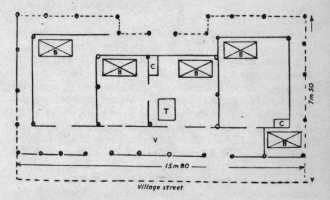

Fig. 43 Plans of old Fang houses of the Libreville region: moderately rich, and wealthy

fragmentation across a country which is much too vast and engulfs them.

As I was feeling unwell—my stomach out of order, my skin covered with a fungus which grew in little reddish clusters—and weighed down by these depressing ideas, I decided one afternoon to pay a visit to the doctor at the administrative hospital before the storm broke. I had been told that he was a newcomer, a "civilian under contract" from the north of France. I wanted to meet him as much from curiosity as from necessity. All at once the sky darkened; I had just enough time to get there before the rain and the thunder started. The doctor received me in his office, which was crammed with papers and pharmaceutical samples. A single storm lantern illuminated the room with its flickering flame, casting monstrous shadows. The man had the large round face, the blondness and the accent of a northerner. He huddled in his armchair, suddenly silent after detailed inquiries about my duties and the reasons for my visit. I could see him clearly only when a flash of lightning bathed his face for an instant with light. Abruptly, he began to speak without pausing, to deliver the most extraordinary monologue, which was accompanied by the roar of the thunder:

"I, too, monsieur, have studied philosophy. The queen of the sciences, the mother of us all. Remember Spinoza's *Ethics:* "The object of the idea which constitutes the human mind is the body, which is to say, a certain mode of extension." Ah yes, the body. And yet, monsieur, from philosophy to medicine, what a fall! In this country the mind wanders and the body deteriorates without your being able to do anything about it. . . . Look, they sent me to a hospital without equipment. What you see there is fake, unusable. The sterilizer is institutional—it would make a good cupboard. Do you take your meals at the hotel? Then you run the risk of appendicitis. I'll operate on you—you'll stand a good chance of dying from lack of asepsis. *Dies irae, dies illa* . . . No, I'll send you to see Schweitzer. See what I have come to! I am turning into a decoy, whereas they want me to be a competitor. . . . You complain of your stomach, that's no laughing matter. Ulcer of the colon can carry you off in no time. Go home and take care of yourself, have an X-ray. . . . This country is not for Christians!"

I left the place stunned, less by the threatened catastrophes, which I hardly took seriously, than by the total disorder I had just witnessed. In the space of a few weeks this man, in his bat-

152

tle against the torpor and decrepitude of Gabon, his struggle to perform a task he soon found to be Herculean, had been reduced to a state of delirious frenzy. On a second visit to Gabon, I inquired what had become of my strange doctor: the administration had sent him back to France. In the end he had spent his days in a game inspired by William Tell, shooting empty Perrier water bottles off the heads of his Negro servants with a pistol. The case is exceptional in its acuteness, but it is instructive for the effects of exaggeration it illustrates. It shows how rapidly Gabon can use up the men placed in its service. It takes a particularly strong personality, or powerful material interest, to remain sane in the face of a natural and human milieu with an amazing capacity for destruction and the added advantage of being enormous.

I could give dozens of these picturesque portraits. I shall add only one, because it provides a sequel to an episode in Marcel Sauvage's *Sous le jeu de l'équateur: Les secrets de l'Afrique noire.* I am talking about "Totor the Convict," whom I met in his camp some twenty-five miles from Lambaréné, not far from the road to Libreville. Here is the picture Marcel Sauvage drew twenty years ago: "A man of short stature, the body of a skinny urchin, bony, his skin scaled by the sun, with a black face and black, heavily shadowed eyes which burned like coals under an old felt hat." Today the man is even smaller and more dried up; his hollowed, wrinkled face gives an impression of exhaustion and the sunken eyes seem to devour the rest of the face. A full beard, orthodox clothing and a white colonial helmet create a less unusual silhouette; he might be an old missionary burned by the equatorial sun. I had the conviction that "Totor" had become the bearer of a wisdom that remained his secret and his dearest possession. This wisdom was born of hardship, of his contempt for the several fortunes he had made and squandered, and of his life as a tracker in the equatorial forest where he had made a world of his own. This wisdom had made him a man of regular habits, the man the administrator meant when he described him, all dressed up for the occasion, as the most punctual of his taxpayers. A man one is allowed to criticize, now that his violent reactions have subsided.

I heard his cracked, husky voice issuing from the house before I saw him: "Who's that character?"

He appeared, followed by several young Negro women in pretty flowered cotton dresses and a few of his native hunters. Ruler of a little forgotten kingdom, he too constituted a scene

153

out of the past. He gave me his hand, which I found bony and tough as leather.

"Greetings! You have come to see Totor?"

"I read about you in Marcel Sauvage's book, and I wanted to meet you."

He seemed to reflect for a moment, then replied simply, with a note of gentleness in his voice, "Ah, yes, Sauvage. . . . Come in and have a drink."

He lived in an enormous Fang hut of hammered bark with large doors and windows. On the door a big white cross had been drawn with chalk. Inside, new but very rudimentary furniture, guns hanging on the walls, liquor bottles lined up on a chest, merchandise for the local trade. Women and children ran in front of us. He chased them away, shouting, "Outside! Outside! Here is the *schtrasse**. . . ." Then turning to me and indicating the children, he added, "They have the seed of Totor in them."

We began to drink. He launched into a self-satisfied monologue in which were mingled scraps of daydreams, the reflections of a disillusioned cynicism, and the anxieties of a disordered life that was nearing its end.

"You mentioned Sauvage. I gave him a chop and a salad to eat. You don't realize it, but in those days that was unheard of. . . . You know my story: I killed a woman, but I did not steal. That takes another kind of courage, understand? . . . The 'doe-feet'† are worthless boys, without morality. In the days of free France some of them turned up here. I took one into my house, entertained him, gave him liquor. When he left, he took my savings. . . . You see what they're like. . . .

He filled the glasses with a trembling hand. I wondered how he still managed to hunt. I remembered what I had heard about this: "He's a big talker, but it's his Negroes who bring down the game." He resumed his story, striving for certain effects which betrayed the ham in him:

"Those in the *schtrasse* aren't bad. They have some consideration for me. . . . The others think I'm a has-been, a wreck. . . . You, you've been to college; me, I've been to the great school of life. I know more about her than you ever will. . . . You came here to study the Negroes, they'll always know more

---

* Slang term designating government agents.

† *Pieds-de-Biche:* slang term for burglars who have served a prison sentence.

than you do too. . . . I'm an old codger now, I'm waiting for the Great Reaper. . . ."

The moment I left the house to take my departure, his whole "clientele," his wives, his children and everyone else's reappeared, shouting. He made a gesture to drive them away, then he pointed to them:

"Look how fat they are. . . . When I bag an elephant, they swarm over the meat like maggots. . . ." Suddenly he disappeared into the house, gone without a word of farewell.

Here is another case which may seem excessive, but is just as instructive as the previous one. Beneath the adventurous surface of such an existence, it shows the asceticism which Africa eventually imposes on her victims. In his portrait of "Totor the Convict," Sauvage quotes a revealing remark: "In Gabon," Totor told him, "I pressed my nose to the windowpane." Other horizons suddenly appeared, and this defeated man sensed, to use Rimbaud's formula, that it was still possible to "change one's life." But it makes little difference to the Africans that their country lends itself to personal and redemptive adventures. It is not the salvation of a handful of offbeat Europeans that moves them, but their own, and in the most material sense of the word. In this connection it should be observed that Totor's relations with his "loyal natives" were in no way exceptional. In all forest and mining activities of average size an authoritarian paternalism has developed. The guarantee of protection, of enough to eat, is taken in exchange for labor and an outspoken and unswerving loyalty. The dependence is absolute, and is associated with an intimacy which does not exclude brutality. Thus within the context of activities manifesting a rudimentary economy (woodcutting, hunting, barter), old social relations resembling feudalism are reappearing in simplified form—relations which manifest, supplementing the easy adoption of polygamy, the equivalent of the *droit de cuissage* (right to sexual intimacy). Gabon is still overlaid, as with a loose network, with these societies from another age. One must not think, however, that the pioneers with "clienteles" have helped to lay the foundations for a new Brazil; they have been too few and have come too late in the course of history.

I have never traveled through this country without being haunted by the theme of isolation. Too few roads, and bad ones, span regions which are inadequately populated. Too much water and too many forests create frequent impasses.

The human groups seem disturbed, isolated, withdrawn—yet this defense mechanism has not prevented the total disappearance of tribes honored by the first chronicles of exploration. This previous colonization, which, though over a hundred years old, was quantitatively and qualitatively deficient, became marginal and obsolete as soon as Brazzaville became the capital of equatorial Africa. Surrounded by more dynamic countries—the Republic of the Congo, Cameroon and even Spanish Guinea—this territory was divided by the attractions exerted on its inhabitants. On the level of culture, as of economic activity and political influence, Gabon reveals a disconcerting multiplicity. Despite the administrative fiction, unity hardly exists save in that coastal region sometimes referred to as Old Gabon—the Gabão of Portuguese sailors.

It is in isolation that extraordinary personalities are created or preserved. This is precisely what I was thinking as I waited for the ferry to return to Lambaréné. The river surrounds the administrative center. On that bank, on a small stretch of land which the forest has relinquished, I saw in the distance the luminous buildings of the Protestant mission. A few poor houses, the homes of the ferrymen, announced the end of the journey from afar. The men sang in chorus an alternating refrain intended for my edification:

Who steals the manioc?
The militiaman! The militiaman!
Who gives us presents?
The white man! The white man!

They repeated the lesson endlessly. Albert Schweitzer's old pelican, solitary and unexpected, glided slowly over the Ogooué in search of prey. I knew that we were not far from the hospital where the doctor had cleared the forest and built a world apart.

I mused on the utter solitude of Albert Schwitzer. I should like to have met him and been able to do him justice, but at the time he was detained in Europe. What an amazing man, to whom all material support, encouragement and fame came from the outside! Here he remained the prisoner of his world of invalids and hospital equipment, of his splendid isolation and of his human failings. The man was even greater when one considered him beyond the banks of the Ogooué. There he had appeared in some sense sacred, even before he was widely recognized as an exceptional man, whereas on the outskirts of Lambaréné I found him oddly vulnerable.

Nobody questions the long effort of will power and self-sacrifice that has permitted the building of a modern hospital center "on the edge of the virgin forest," but everybody judges the man himself. One has only to mention his name to provoke violent reactions. Without crediting ancient grievances which recall African incidents of the First World War, it is curious to observe the unanimity with which he is condemned for his inability to transcend the limits of his work and his lofty passions. I imagine him imprisoned within his relentless dedication, his metaphysical system, and his musical monarchy, become remote and alien. All this is unforgivable in the context of a small colonial outpost where a feverish sociability tries to conjure away the chains of loneliness, and the warmth of those parties and celebrations through which the Europeans try to find some fundamental cohesion could only create intolerance for his austerity. But his lack of cordiality toward anyone outside his domain is also seen as indicative of a harshness shown those who live under his law. I have heard of the difficulties that one of his assistants, who was upset by the severity of his rule and frugality of living conditions, had in recovering his freedom. This man, whose devotion stopped short of total submission, was obliged to make his escape with the help of a native canoeist. Some people criticize Schweitzer for having shown little or no curiosity about Gabonese civilization, for always seeking his spiritual nourishment outside Africa, and for rarely turning his attention to the problems raised by African societies whose destinies are uncertain. The attack is justified, though it does not always come from those who have the most right to make it. The physical ills of men are so tremendous that they conceal the social ills, although the latter are equally fatal. It remains incontestable that outside of some antimodernist ideas based on the notion of salvation by a return to rural and artisanal traditions, Schweitzer has not applied his extraordinary talents to solutions for restoring social well-being to the peoples of Gabon. He remains a man turned nostalgically toward the past. This, and the fact that devotion is rarely rewarded by recognition, may explain the apparent ingratitude of these people. They react against his authoritarian behavior and refuse to forgive him for making them pay for the healing of their wounds with drudgery. They feel, according to some of my African friends, that although he sees them as bodies to be repaired or souls to be saved, this man has not treated them as they would have wished.

I have no desire to feed an ill-timed controversy which already has its propagandists. But I have felt that this indirect judgment based on the attention focused at Lambaréné upon this exceptional personality reveals problems of a more general nature. It shows, for example, how the Gabonese experience brings out the exaggerated characteristics which distinguish unusual personalities. Is it really impossible to maintain a balance? Is it impossible, in the very words of Schweitzer's close friends, to act otherwise than "for better or for worse"? The vicissitudes of religious passion are in a sense intensified by the African vastness and by the colonial game. Certain of my companions point this out; they ask me to look beyond these petty externals, to raise judgment to its true level, that of grace. The fact remains, however, that the reputation of the doctor of Lambaréné rests on Africa and the Negroes. These are the inevitable points of reference, if one is judging the man's actions and not merely the great spiritual adventure of which he is the originator. Any other line of reasoning leads to the loose thinking of those who see Africa only as a pretext.

In a human setting like this where social relations assume a very elementary aspect, individual expression encounters narrow but stubborn limitations. Conflicts of interest and antagonisms become more violent. In exact proportion as the European population is reduced and divided in its aims, clashes between individuals take on a peculiar violence. Individual influence tends to become exclusive, multiplying the phenomenon of "clienteles" which I have already discussed. The whites have imposed this type of relationship all the more easily because the natives themselves disliked multiple commitments. This explains the increase of rivalries and the lack of consistency in the distribution of European contributions. New divisions are being superimposed on the old ones; they now find expression in electoral contests, whereas in the early days of colonization they took the form of struggles for economic pre-eminence or spiritual supremacy.

Further investigation in Gabon was to confirm this impression of division and separation. The large, loosely connected regions which make up the territory seem generally to be mosaics of populations still weakened by their particularisms and broadly covering the zones of isolation created by geography. The phenomenon is all the more pure in that local history reveals no trace of tribes having, through force or influence, a unifying effect. On the contrary, this dispersion over a vast natural setting containing large vacuums of population has provided the most constant means of defense—in the era of the Negro slave trade and the recruiting of manpower, during the setting up of the administrative machine and periods of crises in relations with Europeans. Isolation and instability are the "techniques of protection" employed by tribes whose social structure is capable of breaking down without being destroyed.

The obstacles a situation of this kind presents to programs of modernization and technology can be imagined. The cost of these undertakings, in a country where human settlements are lost in space and distances are accordingly multiplied, is out of proportion to the anticipated results. In 1950 some metropolitan societies using the latest mechanical methods constructed the first miles of a road (the first that deserved to be called usable) connecting Libreville with its backlands. The attempt proved disastrous, and forced the abandonment of projects which were to have traced upon the territory a network of communications indispensable to its difficult unity.

During this same period a young man from the Agricultural Department, who later succumbed to exhaustion, made a heroic effort to open a road between one of the finest natural palm groves in southern Gabon and the modest regional markets. He used techniques recalling the age of pioneers: spades and machetes, armies of villagers turned laborers: the hard way. He was intoxicated by the idea of being an instrument of progress, by the power he discovered he had over a great number of workers whose inspiration and hunter-hero he became—for he supplied his men with dead game.

I know nothing more moving in this part of the world than a new road cut through the mighty forest. In high spirits we started over the first usable miles. They ascend a group of mountains overlooking the large plain which is the site of the administrative post of Tchibanga, in two flat tracks which the truck followed bumpily. The cut was neat and new; here and there severed roots had laid their snares. It was easy to imagine the labor that would still be necessary to combat the ravages of erosion, the exuberance of a vegetable world which was capable of destroying this fragile and rudimentary road in a few months. The mobilization against nature must be perpetual; it demands a constant collective effort which could only be sus-

159

tained by sure profit. But when this natural palm grove, called Moabi, is covered with forty miles of trails and roads, it will produce five hundred tons of palm oil and a like quantity of areca annually. An optimistic estimate which, based on 1950 prices, would mean an income of ten million African francs for the 10,500 villagers, or less than 1,000 francs apiece. The improvement would apparently be considerable, on the order of one to ten; but this benefit is inadequate to maintain the intensity of labor necessary to new conquests.

These are dramatic illustrations of the impasses in which stream either organized or haphazard attempts to modernize the territory seem to end. Such undertakings are profitable neither for the old metropolis, which must acknowledge that its financial aid is a gift pure and simple, nor for the natives, who for the moment are conscious of a great effort culminating in disproportionate results. On both sides the temptation becomes great to give up, casting responsibility upon the partner for misfortunes undergone. Perseverance is impossible if the immediate material benefits (and we have just seen how often these are deferred) are all that is at stake. The Gabonese must be stimulated by a kind of "pyschological New Deal" capable of orienting them energetically toward the future. Independence must create the salutary shock.

But I am leaving the Moabi road behind—literally, for the usable section stopped after about a dozen miles and we abandoned the truck on the banks of a peaceful river. Beyond, the forest had recently been cleared; enormous stumps were everywhere; fallen trees, showing traces of the fire which had been used to undermine them, barred the way; crews of laborers were attacking a job that was made ridiculous by the size of their tools. We soon lost sight of this Africa where men were beginning to cut down the obstacles. Only the path formed a complex network, like a diagram of social relations, across the thickest part of the palm grove. Dense clusters of trees with dark trunks, many of them covered with moss and loaded with dead branches, created an impression of gloom. Sounds no longer carried. We came upon numerous villages where our guides amused themselves by making tours of inspection and performing antics which provoked much loud laughter. The migration of groups from the savanna along the River Ngounié and from the coastal region had resulted in a partial domestication of the forest and an amazing invasion of palm trees. The human groups had spread by extending clannic boundaries,

160

projecting the network of familial and tribal relations onto the land. They had made desperate efforts to control a space too vast; always the forest had imprisoned them, isolated them, and kept them confined in a solitude which was aggravated by petty conflicts.

The further we progressed in this difficult region, the more unavoidable these reflections became. The narrow, bumpy roads rolled by in sections; sometimes they were covered with a sticky clay which caused our column to slip and slide about grotesquely; they led up to steep-banked streams spanned only by narrow tree trunks. The villages became more infrequent, precarious and solitary. In one of them a European engineer temporarily connected with the palm grove seemed trapped, defeated by a sense of the absuridty of his tools and by his own melancholy. Far from him, in the middle of a more sparsely wooded area as bleak as a desert island, a family of American missionaries was oddly ensconced in its comforts, including an enormous icebox which had been transported on human backs, and dominated a handful of natives who were as much the minister's "clients" as they were his disciples.

In a natural setting like this all human endeavor seems doomed to come to a sudden end. The symbol, in my eyes, of this danger which perpetually threatened the individual and his societies, a young madwoman accompanied our party constantly during its final stages. In spite of her distracted expression and her grimaces, she was beautiful in a short print dress that revealed her thighs. She walked ahead of us, howling incoherent songs, brandishing a stick which she caught in mid-air in a gesture that suggested some fantastic drum majorette. She vaulted obstacles, writhed violently, disappeared only to appear again splattered with mud. In a village where we stopped for the night, she knelt in the middle of the square motionless in the rain. For hours on end she shouted prayers and confessions of sexual guilt. One motif recurred constantly, which my guides laughingly translated as, "The long penis of the gods has made children in my head." Nobody paid any attention to her, nor did anybody think of chasing her away or mistreating her. Late into the night, as I lay trying to fall asleep, her interminable howling rose above the sound of the rain to invade and torment me.

I encountered this same passion for road building in an altogether different region, a spot wedged between Spanish Guinea and Cameroon in the cacao country of Woleu-Ntem. With no help from the administration other than some borrowed shovels, a group of villagers organized into "work societies" were preparing an access to the commercial routes and their markets. For them, "civilizatión" (this is the word they used with respect and envy) would begin as soon as the transport trucks could come right to the town's single street. The schemes of these Fang peasants, whose magnificent art I have already discussed, did not end with a more profitable economic activity based on a better network of communications. They had more comprehensive ambitions. They became not only the builders of villages which were better designed and less confined within their ancient boundaries, but also the organizers of a society desirous of meeting modern requirements. With a restlessness betraying their desire for change, they were attempting to revive large clannic groups and to reunite villages that were too dissimilar by providing them with better equipment.

Shortly after I arrived in the chief town of the region, I received a visit from a large group of leaders of this movement. Haltingly, but not without persistence, they called me to witness their efforts and their need for progress. A certain Pierre Afouganou, who boasted the title of "inspector" of an important tribe, particularly impressed me. I paid even more attention to him because he had been presented to me as an "enlightened" man. Indeed, he must have been possessed of a great passion, for he had had the courage to go to Spanish Guinea to inspire related clans with this restless desire for modernization. His proselytism could easily have cost him dearly in a country which does not tolerate native movements and where recourse to violence is not hampered by unnecessary precautions.

To plead his cause, Pierre Afouganou had put on a khaki suit which bore the insignia of his new rank on an embroidered tab. He was cramped and ill at ease, and undoubtedly worried that he would not succeed in convincing me. In spite of his difficulty in expressing himself in French, he revealed an eloquence which was all the more effective for its unusual turns of phrase. Even as I followed the chain of his reasoning, I recorded fragments of his discourse, which I now find in my files:

"The ways of the whites are good for living. We desire them to become our ways. . . . We must unite as brothers of the tribe, otherwise we shall remain as weak as children. . . . The old say that it is well. It is as in the past, when we were men to be feared. The young say that it is the road to civilization.
162

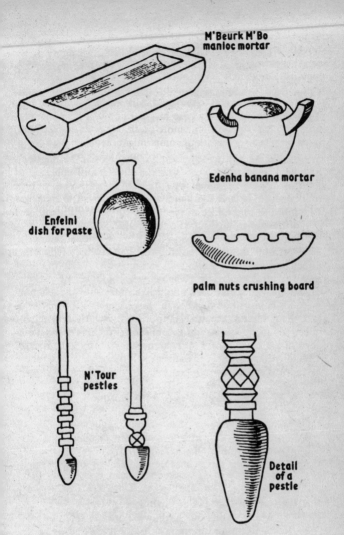

M'Beurk M'Bo
manioc mortar

Edenha banana mortar

Enfeini
dish for paste

palm nuts crushing board

N'Tour
pestles

Detail
of a
pestle

Fig. 44 Old Fang pestles and mortars

. . . We must unite under a single leader. . . . To prevent us from reuniting the tribes is to leave us in savagery. If we could do this, all would be changed; up to now, nothing has changed. . . ."

Such are the arguments of a doctrine which in 1950 the administrators regard as "another myth," and a dangerous one. And yet it recognizes the fundamental problem facing all Gabonese tribes: the necessity of forming large groups sufficiently unified to regain their vitality and capacity for adaptation. Without being aware of their underlying motives, Fang peasants have acquired a conviction that the lack of cohesion of their society explains their weaknesses, the persistence of outmoded rivalries, and their alienation. They want to find new strength; but in the face of this desire for reinforcement local authorities rebel, anxious and uncertain.

The founders of the movement lack neither passion nor skill. They resort to those methods of propaganda which seem most effective. They are creating an ideology which, adapting itself to the cultural level of the Fang villager, combines rational justifications with themes of a mythical nature. They use teaching methods modeled on those of the missionaries. As a matter of fact, the indoctrination is accomplished by a curious system of questions and answers reminiscent even in its tone of the pedagogy of the catechism. From the notebook of Ndon Mba Joseph, dignitary of the Yemisem tribe, I quote the first of these categorical imperatives, which are written in French:

What Every Yemisem Should Know

Q: What is the enemy of our tribal religion?
A: The enemy of our tribal religion is disobedience.
Q: To what tribe do we belong?
A: We belong to the Yemisem tribe because we are of one blood.
Q: Where were we born?
A: Missam Mivoro is our birthplace.
Q: After celebrating our birth, what are our first duties?
A: Recognition and harmony.
Q: What way of life must we follow?
A: We must follow the European way of life.
Q: How are we to follow the European way of life?
A: We must work to earn money.

These declarations, with their injunction to follow the example of the colonizer on the level of material achievement, are directed primarily toward the goals of social reconstruction. To this end they exploit the emotive power contained in notions of tribal fraternity, common origin, consanguinity and "religious" respect for tribal unity. Without weighing the risks involved in this manipulation of obscure and volatile forces, they appeal to an idealized past to arrive immediately, by a kind of dialectic movement denying the phase of colonial alienation, at the epoch of modern civilization. There is a lack of harmony between end and means, an ambiguity echoing the one existing in reality, which has led observers to see these attempts as essentially "reactionary" or, on the other hand, essentially "revolutionary." Both are right, in that the two tendencies coexist, reinforcing rather than resisting one another, within this endeavor on the part of the Fang to regain control of their destiny.

The rules which each tribe tries to establish—in the most diverse realms, ranging from the campaign against adultery and excessive dowries to the regulation of petty commerce—present the same ambivalence. The tribal legends, which constitute the deeds of foundation of the new unities, are occasions for downright fraud. They are doctored, marked by Biblical echoes, confused in their style. They are like an image of this disturbed society and a projection, in the psychoanalytic sense, of the anxieties of their authors. I shall give a partial transcript of one of these texts which for the Fang villager have the importance of our historical archives.

The Legend of the Ndon Tribe

This is the origin of the Ndon tribe and of the clans belonging to it.

David was not at variance with Jesus Christ. God loved David because he worked well. In those days all men were polygamous; they were too fond of women. Before Christianity, David had eight hundred wives. Most of the people did not want to obey God. They lived in a village called Sidon; it was a village of evildoers. They committed many sins. The young men consorted with one another without shame. Finally, God sent David and his militia to destroy this accursed village. His men numbered six hundred.

One day at dawn, King David walked out of his house and stood on his veranda. A charming young girl came out of her house quite naked and hid behind the banana trees. When David saw her, he uttered a cry of amazement and said, "Never since I was born have I seen a woman as beautiful as this one!" This woman was the wife of a militiaman who was away on duty and had left her in the village. David sent a soldier to tell the woman that he wished to see her. . . .

When she knew that the king was alone and unattended (his servants had gone to gather rice), she came to his house. He took her and made her lie down on his bed. The adultery was consummated, and the woman became pregnant.

Pleased with his good day, King David went to take a walk at the other end of the village. There he found certain men who knew how to explain dreams. A man named Isane asked King David whether a man who possessed eight hundred sheep would abandon them to borrow one from someone who had only one. David replied, "If you meet such a man on the road or anywhere, seize him and bring him to me." Then David uttered a cry and said to himself, "These men know what I have done!"

When the militiaman returned, David offered him a bed. He summoned the woman to tell her the news. The woman wanted to enjoy her husband. Her husband replied, "In time of war, the regulation is that a solider must never pay his respects to a woman." To soften the heart of the brave militiaman, David was obliged to sweep the room in which he was to spend the night with his wife. The militiaman always answered the same thing: "Only give me a mat, I will sleep on the ground." David left no stone unturned. He wrote a letter to the leader of the troop, commanding him to place the young man in the front line. On the first day the militiaman was struck in the forehead with a bullet and died. Suddenly, God opened the sky, took the man in his right hand, and a huge white cloth descended between David and him. God said to David, "Why have you acted thus?" David replied, "Have mercy on me!" It was then that God ordained that a man should have only one wife.

After Adam, there were only two women. One was named Ye and the other Esa. All those tribes whose names begin with Ye, like Yengwi and Yemedzit, are descended from Ye; all others, like Esakotame and Esengi, are descended from Esa. Adam begat Mvon Adam, Mvon Adam begat a son named Nsouno Evo, son of Evo Mvon and Adam Nzame, Nsouno Evo begat Nguene Nsouno. They dressed like the poeple of the North. These men built a great tower to glorify God. But God sent his Angel to destroy this tower without warning. When they returned from their labors, they found the tower demolished. These men were scattered by tribes. One cried, *Ndzo!* and fled; another said *Aye!* and fled; the white man said, *My God!* and fled; the Fang said, *Na ako!* and fled. And they were scattered, each speaking his own language.

Nguene Nsouno begat Mbo Nguene, who had two brothers and committed adultery with the wife of one of his brothers. Nguene Nsouno tried to kill him and he was forced to flee. He found a man of the Biyengo tribe who told him, "Stay with me." Then he gave him a wife. Soon afterwards, the man died and left him in command of his village. . . . He kept everything he received from his work for a dowry. He married a woman named Boulasse and took her to live with him. During the wedding, she was given the surname of Ndon. The woman was soon with child. She brought forth a first son, Ekar Mbo, then Akougme Mbo, Ekagne Mbo, Eviame Mbo, Ovougne Mbo, Etone Mbo, Medjima Mbo, Membo Mbo, Evangue Mbo, and Afome Mbo. Akougme Mbo crossed the border and came to settle here, in Gabon. . . .

Clearly this passage has salvaged few elements from ancient tribal legends. One recognizes, on the other hand, the Biblical sequences which have provided its organization: the episode of David the adulterer and murderer from the Second Book of Samuel, and that of the Tower of Babel from Genesis. The genealogies linked to Adam reveal an interpretation of the origin of man based on three genitors: a son of the first man (Mvon Adam), Eve (Evo Mvon), and the first man as son of God (Adam Nzame, *Nzame* being the Fang word for the Supreme Being). There is even a conception of the Trinity derived from Genesis and the story of Christ which meets the requirements of the genealogical imperative. All this has a meaning which we must discover in spite of our amazement. The Bible, which presents the Africans with a society comparable to their own, provides a possibility of transcending the inferiority they have suffered, of denying their state of "savagery." By identifying with the people in the Book, they can re-establish an equality which in their eyes is the condition of all future progress, and which is specifically mentioned in another fragment of the legend: "One day it shall come to pass that a white man and a black man shall be alike. Indeed, we wish to know this miracle." This attitude is a commonplace for a large portion of Christianized Africa from the Equator to the Cape. The reference to the Biblical type of society plays the same role here as the reference to ancient Egypt does in certain Negro intellectual circles: both make it possible to participate from the beginning in the grandeur of undisputed civilizations. It also appears that the themes retained allude to current problems—especially those of polygamy and the increase of adultery.

This doctored legend, whose primary purpose is to restore the self-confidence of the Fang—in contrast to the literary creations of the first colonial period, which expressed a sense of malediction—provides not only an account of ancient migrations, but more importantly, a renewed sense of the kinship existing among all the clans. It emphasizes those elements having unifying power. Its purpose is to justify efforts at reunification. To understand clearly its importance and meaning, one must regard it as an ideological manifestation aimed at specific contemporary goals, whose formula is adapted to a peasant society little affected by our rational instruction.

The manifestations of this Fang movement, which began around 1948, are disconcerting to the casual observer. Take, for example, the titles it has instituted, which are curious for the "ranks" they have borrowed from colonial administrative and military organizations and for the multiplicity of the functions provided for. In addition to the "president in chief" and "vice president" having authority over all members of the tribe residing within a single district, there has arisen a whole hierarchy of "governors," "majors," "assessors," "commissaries," "inspectors of commerce," etc. with fairly well-defined political, judicial and economic prerogatives. These innovations, which some have ridiculed as a childish parody and others have feared as signs of subversive intent, have a highly interesting psychological aspect. They show a new desire for terms vividly expressing the idea of power and a need to "possess" the name in order to arrive, by a kind of magical process of the imagination, at the reality. They reveal a desire to present the clannic movement as an enterprise which not only revitalizes ancient social structures, but ensures progress by endowing the Fang with "civilized" instructions. And the very multiplicity of new titles seems significant of the need for prestige and responsibility of an ever-increasing number of villagers.

The organizers arouse intense collective emotions at *esoulan,* gatherings at which the tribes affirm or recreate their unity. The square of the village chosen for the occasion is decorated with arches of braided leaves, slogans and symbols, and colored flags and pennants. In the middle stands a shelter made of palm branches where the dignitaries sit, dressed in new clothes and armed with their distinctive insignia. The atmosphere is as reminiscent of Bastille Day as of traditional African festivities. Groups of peasants in their Sunday best arrive, noisy and laden with provisions, and are soon reviewed by "commissaries" who take their official duties very seriously and harassed by "treasurers" who levy contributions to the tribal fund. All able-bodied adults are present—for their absence could mean a fine or, in the event of a second offense, dismissal from the tribe—surrounded by rowdy and curious children.

The festivities open with a highly symbolic performance. All the participants embrace one another in an extraordinary confusion to indicate not only their "fraternity" but the absence of any "evil thoughts." Then the dance, the *enyengue,* begins. A common innovation which I have already discussed is the presentation of a specific choreography which stimulates social relations and maintains a certain fervor. Although it has become mixed, the dance has been divested of its sexual symbolism under the puritan influence of the missionaries. According to the definition given by its creators, it is a series of figures in which "the women no longer strip." I find it monotonous, unrhythmical, and relieved only by the undulating movements of the women, who wave colored handkerchiefs. It provides more than one occasion for joyous communion; it has value as homage and as public recognition of the authority of dignitaries and influential guests; it creates a solemn atmosphere for the deliberations by which tribal matters will be settled. In several regions where the influence of Christianity is more profound, religious songs follow the initial dances. These songs, in which Catholic and Protestant choirs alternate, rise, nasal and constrained, following a declaration of loyalty to an unusual trinity

169

consisting of God, the Administration and the Tribe. The Ye-misem have ostentatiously woven this threefold obedience into a motto:

> The highest, higher than the head: God three times Holy.
> In the middle, as high as the heart: the Administration and the French government.
> Below, on a level with the knees: the Tribe.

But such recognition remains ambiguous, in spite of its imperative form. God does not have the exclusive Christian face which would rule out believers in the traditional cults or the modern syncretic cults. The administration, for its part, mistrusts an affirmation which opposes the introduction of new authorities hostile to the official leaders. The tribe, revived after a long period of decline, imposes an abnormal unity by

Fig. 45 A Fang ritual object, copied from Bakota objects

traditional criteria. The clannic movement would like to reassure by appearing submissive; but it cannot avoid that dialectic which decrees that colonized peoples can reorganize only by opposing one another, by trying to achieve a greater margin of political and cultural autonomy.

While the festival continues and the women prepare the communal meal which is to ensure a symbolic mingling of bloods, the dignitaries work out the "modern" laws of the tribe. They are surrounded by young literati who form an embryonic bureaucracy. They decide on matters of agricultural and commercial activity, hygiene and education, division of duties and procedures for established powers, and above all, matrimonial regulation. If the clannic movement, by conferring certain responsibilities upon the Fang woman, grants her a position she did not enjoy in the traditional society, there nevertheless persists a widespread antifeminism. The most serious disorders are attributed to women and to adultery, which is considered the first of the plagues that have fallen on the land, and seems to be explained only by the compliance of wives eager for unpunished adventures. Nor does the new law, which takes a progressive approach to the problem of the dowry and the "inheritances of wives," hesitate to restore the punishments designed to curb infidelity.

The dignitaries have decided to make an example. The dancing stops. The victim is a young woman from a nearby village who is too susceptible to the magic of a uniform and cannot resist the advances of soldiers on leave. She is led to the center of the square, jostled, and surrounded by old peasant women who insult her. The men start digging a kind of ditch in a muddy place. In spite of her struggles the woman is stripped of her clothing. Naked and trembling, she hides her face in her hands. She is left this way for some time under the stares and gibes. Then, at the order, she is dragged to the ditch and pushed in. She sinks up to her waist in the sticky clay. She flounders helplessly while balls of mud strike her from all directions. Filthy, miserable, her mouth full of mud, she begs for mercy and promises to reform. Not until much later, after night has fallen, will she emerge, dazed and defeated by an elementary law which is quick to appear in any society in the throes of reconstruction.

A year later on a second visit, I again encountered this passion to construct a viable society with greater freedom to control its future and better adapted to its present obligations. Frustrated by official reservations and opposition and prematurely exhausted, the clannic movement had been reduced to a campaign for the reunification of related villages. But the dynamism had not disappeared; in confusion and ambiguity, the Fang were still stubbornly seeking a solution to the impasse.

Under arches of braided palms, before lines of schoolchildren and gymnastic exercises, before assemblies of notables, everyone wanted me to judge and witness this resolute desire for adjustment and progress. I did so, in the hope that the equatorial torpor would eventually be overcome, and that this example would encourage other Gabonese peoples to seek, even in error and excess, a renaissance of civilizations once rich in original products.

6
The Cities

▼▼▼▼▼▼▼▼▼▼▼▼▼▼▼▼▼▼▼▼▼▼▼▼▼▼▼▼▼▼▼▼▼▼

IMAGES IN BLACK AND WHITE

MY encounters with African cities—Dakar, Conakry, Brazzaville and Leopoldville, Lagos and Ibadan, Douala, Libreville, Abidjan, and of course Saint-Louis, transfixed in its centuries-old splendor—have led me to a new exploration which the ethnologist of today can no longer avoid. Only twenty years ago it was still possible to consider these cities an aberration, a kind of foreign element in the body of civilizations which were antagonistic to large concentrations of people. How times have changed! The villagers are invading the cities with a determined persistence which is gradually sending them toward the most heavily populated areas. In a decade, the cities of Senegal and the Ivory Coast have doubled in volume, and the same increase has required only seven years in the largest of the African centers which make up Brazzaville. The cities are spreading by absorbing old farmlands and hastily assimilating villages adjacent to their fluid boundaries. Aerial photographs bear witness to this urban voracity.

The growth is so rapid that, at best, the native quarters look like villages which have suddenly contracted elephantiasis, and more commonly resemble camps with an endless steam of new

173

arrivals. A premature and restless urbanism occasionally produces the equivalent of our poor suburbs for the use of rich Africans. Real-estate agencies, assured of official support, are importing the "pay as you go" plan and trying to capitalize on advances to underpaid wage earners. Black and white speculation thrives on short-term investments; it plays upon this chessboard whose squares are separated by a pattern of eroded, sandy or muddy streets.

This accelerated growth of cities is occurring today over large sections of the earth's surface. Everywhere it is breeding the same temporary and precarious structures, the props of a poverty which itself threatens to be permanent: the outskirts of Calcutta, where the homeless sprawl sleeping, dazed by the heat of the earth; the shanty towns of North Africa, crowded with men living on anger instead of bread; the slums of the great Chinese cities, where newcomers are waiting to build the cities of the future with their still-bare hands. Everywhere cities appear, immediately attain the dimensions of ours, which had grown with a kind of organic thrust, and outstrip them, without having time to accumulate along the way the monuments of a too-brief past. Although it is not necessarily true that every civilization worthy of the name is urban, it can be said that in a sense every city presents the foreigner with an image of the civilization that produced it. The skyscrapers of Manhattan give the scale of New York from a distance, but they also represent the vertiginous dynamism of a society which as yet has discovered neither its limitations not its failures. And Soviet urbanism, if one credits the commentaries it provokes, reveals a society so intent on its future that is sacrifices the already outmoded obligations of the present.

But what of those African cities where, shielded from official buildings and residential areas, Negro quarters consisting of transplanted huts and hovels rather than livable bourgeois homes are expanding indefinitely? They bear witness less to a civilization than to its absence. In the confusion and uncertainty, ethmic groups collide and customs tend to erase each other like overlapping waves. Here Negro citizens camp in the hope of attaining wealth which the industrial powers distribute only sparingly, and many must be content to catch the crumbs and leftovers that fall their way. As Jean Dresch pungently observed, "The cities are built by whites and populated by Negroes." Indeed, this phenomenon must be regarded as the first of the African revolutions: a besieging of positions occupied by

174

the colonizers. The latter react in an ambivalent manner, for although they are pleased to have a large reserve of laborers at their disposal, they are nervous at finding themselves surrounded by large numbers of people who are all the more dangerous in that their energies are channeled neither by administrative organizations nor by traditional restrictions. In a real system of filtration, the South African authorities have very quickly demonstrated that they have placed fear ahead of their immediate gain: they have chosen to curb economic development rather than allow the pressure exerted upon the white neighborhoods to increase.

At the same time that emigration toward the urban centers of Africa is accelerating, the European implantation is also growing. Enclosed within their families and the narrow field of their social intercourse, their "circles" and "clubs," the whites are both more withdrawn into themselves and more vulnerable to the demands rising from the Negro quarters. They affirm their way of life without concessions to an exoticism which is watered down in any case. They protect themselves; they remain on their guard, unwilling to be contaminated by their African surroundings—except on those rare occasions when "good society" is permitted to escape its boredom.

This withdrawal has the statistical basis which always characterizes a foreign ruling minority, a phenomenon which was brought home to me by contrast after spending some time in Honolulu. With the quasi-disappearance of the Hawaiians (300,000 in 1778, 40,000 in 1884, and around 12,000 in 1950) and the substitution of populations which have turned the islands into a meeting place for the Far West and the Far East, it had become harmless to sing the praises of the indigenous civilization. Anyone was free to smack his lips over traditional flavors and bedeck himself with those garlands whose clinging and insidious fragrance airline stewardesses preserve to improve the luck of the traveler returning home to San Francisco. In front of official buildings the golden statue of King Kamehameha stands draped in splendor, his arms outstretched in a gesture of welcome. At the Bishop Museum the treasures of the dynasty are exhibited under scholarly lights and protected by an alarm apparatus so sensitive that it prevents any temptation on the part of the visitor to reach out and touch the purple plumed mantles. And, in an institution reminiscent of the French Maison de la Légion d'honneur, children of the survivors receive a refined education which no longer hesitates to

175

nourish them with vanished glories. This passion for the dominated civilization leads to curious academic sanctions, like those summer courses in the hula which send to the campus every morning knots of young girls carrying under their arms the bamboo sticks with which they regulate their movements. The passion grows all the more intense as the society that preserves it declines.

In Negro Africa the situation is in no way comparable; the opposite ratio leads to the defensive withdrawal of the "foreigners," and reinforces their refusal to comprehend indigenous realities. In this always precarious and dangerous state of inequality, there is no way of arriving at co-operation or even at a sincere acceptance of the "exotic" cultures. Such acceptance only occurs either after the fact, when the inequality no longer exists, or before the fact, when the weaker member has become virtually extinct, an alternative which nobody would knowingly choose.

Now, as I abandon myself to my impressions of African cities, it is Ibadan, the great Negro city of Nigeria, which rises first from the depths of memory. Lying some sixty miles inland between forest and savanna, as its name indicates (*Eba-Odan,* near the savanna) it contains over 400,000 Negroes. Ibadan was originally a den of thieves and outlaws. One of these, Lagelou, succeeded in imposing his authority and exploiting this strategic position sufficiently to build a town whose pride in its "sixteen gates and seventy blacksmith shops" was traditional. Tribal wars erased the original design, but the city was rebuilt and is now powerful and impressive, a Negro capital which does not owe its birth to the accident of colonization.

From the small airplane which I took from Lagos I suddenly caught sight of it, sprawling, amorphous but massive, in a fairly open plain dominated by Mapo Hill. Here the European residential quarter no longer determined the shape of the city; it appeared on the fringe, as if the better to be tolerated. I distinguished that tangle of cramped and crowded dwellings which announced the heart of the city: this was the quarter of the very ancient Yoruba clans, powerful because of their age and the number of their representatives. But it was from the terrace of Mapo Hill, the center of administrative life, that I was to feel most keenly the impression of disturbing power that Ibadan gives. A golden haze softened its forms and gave them color, and there rose a confused noise, strange because alien to my experience of city noises, which was insidious and exciting. I wondered by what sleight of hand Mapo Hall, that solemn monument with its tall classical columns, had found its way into this disconcerting urban landscape. And my question took on new force when I visited the assembly room of the city council: a gallery of portraits of the "Olubadans" who had been the leaders of the city dominated the somber and heavy furnishings of an English parliament. There was none of that flagrant incongruity, that bizarre effect. The British setting suited the Yoruba ritual. This reminds me of an official demonstration I attended at the University of Ibadan which was a harmonious encounter between the leaders of the city, proud and erect in their colorful robes, each followed by a man carrying the insignia of his authority, and the professors, dressed in the robes symbolic of their respective disciplines. More than an accidental conjunction, it was an expression of agreement on at least one point: reverence for tradition.

Impressions, some lasting, some less so, gather along the streets. One survives, persistent and imperious: more than the capital of Negro pride, Ibadan is a religious capital—but one that has been constructed under the sign of pluralism. Besides the ancient initiatory cult of "Ogboni," the inventories of secret societies reveal multiple forms of the Masonic fraternity which recall their homologues in the Liberian Republic. Islam, propagated by the Haussa—tradesmen, magicians and occultists—has built more than six hundred mosques without destroying ancient beliefs. Christianity, introduced over a century ago, has given rise to many deviant sects and has opened the way for prophets like Joseph Babalola, who have a reputation for working miracles upon the sick and the dead. Thousands of disciples come here in hope of healing or salavation by faith, prayer or unction. Religious life continues to leave its mark on the old Yoruba city, giving rise to a swarm of cults which coexist, albeit precariously, surviving bitter rivalries.

My memories remain vivid by virtue of the contrasts they reveal. A wide boulevard had been opened, cutting into and mutilating the temple built in honor of Shango, god of thunder, in the process. In the part that still stood—the remains of a modest elongated hut—a constantly milling crowd continued to worship fervently. But Shango has managed to hold out in the face of other vicissitudes: he continues to dominate the beliefs and religious fervor of Brazilians and Haitians descended from deported slaves. Elsewhere, before the temple of a secondary god, a young newsboy, shaking his rags, bawled the headlines of the *West African Pilot:* "Riots in Enugu. Troops fire on miners." Ibadan, Negro capital and holy city, is a center of Nigerian nationalism and of a revindication which has written some of the most glorious pages in African history: for instance, those offered at the time by an exhibit at the university. Books and brochures devoted to local history and to industrial or political problems were on display at the libraries for the examination of interested parties.

One evening, through relatives of my friend Paul Mercier, I tried to make contact with some of the leaders behind the national movement. It turned out to be another "voyage to the end of the night," which gave us the illusion that we were outwitting the surveillance of the British authorities. We hopped from one quarter to another in a maze of streets that all looked alike. Consistently, our supposed guide would elude us and leave us at the mercy of a few confederates. At a very late hour, we finally caught up with one of the political leaders. He received us in pajamas, already half asleep, in the drawing room of a comfortable bourgeois home filled with flowered cretonne. In all the doorways there appeared the heads of women,

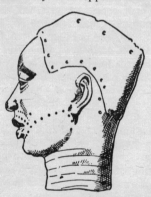

Fig. 46 An Ife bronze head

relatives, and servants—curiosity, suspicion, or a habit of guardedness acquired during the underground activities? The man turned out to be evasive and cautious in the extreme, but there was no doubting either his passion for independence or his political maturity.

One last impression should not be dismissed as a mere study

in contrast. The old Ibadan appears in a confusion of mud houses with corrugated iron roofs facing crowded and congested courtyards teeming with shops and stalls where artisans repeat centuries-old gestures. It is a series of enormous villages inseparable from one another, in each of which the markets, busy and rich, serve to regulate an agricultural economy carried on by men who are as much peasants as townsmen. The new Ibadan deploys its isolated houses, with their painted façades, Venetian blinds, balconies and verandas, along the principal streets of the northern and western quarters. It brings together well-to-do tradesmen, most of the intelligentsia and, cheek by jowl with the Yoruba bourgeoisie whom they are trying to lure into borrowing against the immediate future, the Syrian traders. The division is not as neat as the topography implies. For citizens of the old school and the new bourgeoisie, there is a single brilliant cultural heritage which is an object of pride and strengthens their resistance to outside pressures. Many are the occasions for celebrating this common interest; it finds a commercial outlet in the advertising slogans adorning transport trucks as well as the buses serving the city and its suburbs.

Ibadan does not mislead by means of some insidious, mirage-like effect; the surrounding country gives the same impression of a population dense, vigorous and sure of its control, as one glance out the window of one of those jumpy little airplanes of West African Airways will reveal. I was struck by the complexity of the landscape that unfolded: roads and railroad tracks, and a succession of villages caught in their network. It is not only the modern economy that is leaving its mark, but also the activities of Yoruba villagers that are creating the familiar scene of a prosperous countryside. From the thirteenth to the seventeenth century this region of Nigeria was the home of powerful civilizations which produced at Ife and then, by contagion, at Benin, an artistic achievement which unquestionably constitutes one of the richest heritages of all times. Its disappearance does not mean death; as always, the future of Africa is being fashioned with that same sureness of hand and mind responsible for those magnificent bronzes on which our museums pride themselves.

Compared with the Yoruba capital, Lagos is a British city, at least if one stops with the image presented by Ikoyi. The residential quarter is separated from the commercial center and the streets occupied by the Africans by a kind of neutral territory consisting of the police headquarters and the golf course. The latter resembles the English countryside, as does each of those imposing stone villas surrounded by parks or lawns on which lawnmowers grind away. Every day a plane leaves for London, a link that is not without significance. England, with its insistence on organizing the landscape, can be felt everywhere. The city is an English creation, built to satisfy English needs and desires. Walk into a bank, and you find that by a veritable process of mimicry, the Nigerian tellers have acquired the calm and the sartorial elegance of their British superiors. The "Marina," the seaside boulevard, presents its formal façades. And monuments characteristic of Western activities dominate the city: official buildings, the sedate quarters of banks or businesses, hotels, the ostentatious offices of the Kingsway stores. In their shadow run the narrow and crowded streets containing the native shops: curios and phony exotica, cheap merchandise, the ear-splitting stores of music sellers, the colorful displays of small tradesmen. A traveling companion of mine once remarked, "I'm not sure why, but all this reminds me of Hong Kong." The comparison is justified: both cities are gateways to Asia and Africa opened by England, with the same type of men pursuing the same ends. At Lagos, this would-be international vocation of the British is epitomized by a signpost stationed outside the airport. Its arrows and numerals are aimed in all directions: London, Paris, New York, Vladivostok. Before this sudden invasion by the world, I found myself musing on the traces of English colonization in that Africa long defined by geographers as a "marginal continent."

In spite of the presence of administrative offices and consulates, Lagos does not look like the capital of one of the most powerful African nations now under development. It remains a port town, caught in the web of economic activity and political influence woven by England during the nineteenth century. The natives live wherever they can. Near the port the Appapa quarter with its variegated houses contains real citizens associated with the city and enjoying modest but regular incomes. Along the lagoon sprawls the inevitable shantytown: a jumble of flimsy huts covered with secondhand sheet iron skirt narrow alleys and tiny courtyards teeming with a humanity that is mixed, divided, transient and vegetative. Picturesqueness exists only for the traveler: hundreds of miniature stalls, women busy preparing food, groups combining the sheen of flowered fabrics with filthy cast-off clothing: a photographer's dream.

Even in Lagos, a Nigerian bourgeoisie has gained a foothold; some of its members have lost interest in that Africa devoid of material goods and cultural riches which camps on the fringes of "good" neighborhoods. They have acquired a taste for the English way of life which is symbolized by their provincial drawing rooms. They have become refined in imitation of their educators, having killed in themselves that precious Negro gift of spontaneity. They have become proficient in the genteel arts and games. They attend official demonstrations. Their political ambitions stop at a democracy which would have the innocuousness of their plush interiors.

I am quite aware that it is the bourgeoisie that furnishes the leaders of the national movement. The ordinary citizens are being mobilized to demand freedom. When I was in Lagos in 1949, petitions were circulating protesting the severe repression of the striking coal miners, and collections were being taken up to aid the families of the miners. A certain unity of opposition to British power could not be denied; but the word "freedom" did not have the same meaning for the bourgeois leaders as it did for the masses they controlled. One need only "feel" the city to discover a class structure which Ibadan does not reveal and to understand the urgent necessity for collaboration between the African and the European bourgeoisie, whereas the Yoruba capital reveals a coexistence heavy with distrust.

I must accelerate this procession of memories. The faces of the "colonial" cities of Africa have many common features. Since most of them are under construction, their topography is constantly changing. They all present striking discordances between the vitality of their good neighborhoods and the backwardness, more pronounced by comparison, of their "African towns;" between the outmoded, faded, ugly colonial style of buildings of the old era and the bold modernism of recent constructions; between the spaciousness that characterized them two decades ago and the verticality—Dakar, Abidjan, Leopoldville—of today. This upward thrust can be seen as the expression of a kind of pride in construction and the result of pressures exerted on the periphery of residential quarters by everincreasing numbers of Negro citizens. In its physical aspect as in its human aspect, the city is seeking its form in confusion.

I discovered Dakar in 1946 with an eye hungry for images of Africa. I arrived at the makeshift airport of Yof. The long trip into the city was marked by rural impressions and fleeing women scurrying off the road. A baobab was pointed out to me as the sacred tree of the Lebou villagers. In the *medina,* precarious houses stranded on the sand were crowded along sinister and anonymous streets. The Santiaga market with its crowds and displays, its stopped buses crammed with travelers and sagging under their loads—all this was invaded by the din of a public-address system broadcasting official information. Avenues along which African beauties strolled, powerful and solemn, hair artfully arranged, adorned with gold trinkets, clothed in expensive fabrics and in desire. The terraces of the cafés and restaurants were besieged by swarms of peddlers who, in their wide, deep-sleeved *boubous,* resembled jugglers; beggars droned; cripples dragged themselves along on little carts of salvaged wood, exhibiting their ravaged and misshapen limbs. Streets of Syrian practitioners, prudent in the display of their wealth, anxious to avoid a racism which turned them into scapegoats but which a journalist-blackmailer was nevertheless to revive shortly afterward by organizing an "operation quinacrine." (Quinacrine is a medicament used as a preventive against malaria. The play on words is based on its yellow color, and reveals a racism which stoops to the crudest possible means.) After that, several long monotonous streets framed by antiquated and dirty houses led to the "Plateau." Old middle-class Negroes lived here; they spent their time playing checkers on boards the size of tables. Half-breeds and their wives, luxuriant Portuguese women, suddenly recalled by their presence the ancient history of a Senegal which was very early open to Europe. The "Plateau" is a lofty place for extrageographical reasons. Power, the Church and Learning have their headquarters there, and European residences are spaced behind hibiscus and bougainvillea bushes in the interests of health and isolation. Abidjan, Douala and Brazzaville also have their plateau districts, which follow the same pattern for the same reasons.

But in my memory the Dakar of 1946 is above all the image of the home where the Senegalese writer Alioune Diop and his wife Christiane offered me their hospitality when the administration had sent me to some temporary lodgings. Everything about our meetings was simple, straightforward and cordial. A sense of kinship sprang up in spite of the hostile faces that surrounded us. We were rich in illusions and enthusiasm. Everything still seemed possible. We were trying to start a first-class magazine of the Negro world; it was born later in Paris as *Présence Africaine.*

I rediscovered Dakar during a brief stopover in the fall of 1954. All had not changed, but the transformation was such that I found meaning in the familiar comment, "Dakar is not Africa." All perspectives seemed rearranged. Certain prewar monuments, so obtrusive with their curiously ugly silhouettes, like the "lemon squeezer" housing the Chamber of Commerce, had disappeared.

I was surprised on my arrival by the modernity of the new airport, the same airport that is standardizing the great ports of call the world over. Was this really Dakar, or Casablanca, or San Francisco? Outside the airport a highway imposed its geometry; natives crossed on footbridges; the city was a few minutes away. Gone were those impressions of the African countryside. Plots of land had superimposed a checkerboard pattern: strange juxtapositions of hemispherical huts forming the so-called "Bosomville" quarter which, originally intended for Africans (to instill the taste and reverence for property), were bought up by lower-income whites; houses of civil servants, built in a zone referred to as "Point E," as if the old place names had been obliterated so as not to upset the urbanists' plans. New arteries had cut right through the *medina*, opening paths of progress and order. The administration had erected a "cathedral" to provide a center for its departments. Large hotels had multiplied, emphasizing the aspect of stopping place rather than capital city. As you left Dakar to go towards Rufisque, where I had once known a pretty road shaded by the dark and delicate foliage of filao trees, there ran a stretch of highway on which heavy automobile traffic competed for space.

But there is no point indulging in regrets. The metamorphosis is dazzling: a change in the direction of greater *whiteness.* The *urbs occidentalis* is increasing its horizontal and vertical extension, its material power, and its population. It includes more than 20,000 Europeans who are not very deeply rooted, more stratified as they become more numerous, isolated by their doubts and their obsession with "economy," confined within their coteries and anxious to control all the services necessary to their existence. The advertisements in the newspapers are full of revealing details: "Service for Europeans. Work done by European workers. . . ." The configuration of modern Dakar reveals the contraction of mixed neighborhoods and the expansion beyond the *medina* of developments in which whites are seeking privacy in an artificial setting of exotic suburbia—a last resort.

Despite the briefness of my visit, another transformation of a more humble variety struck me as I was taking an aimless stroll. In front of a dirty and dilapidated old building, a vestige of the early days of colonization, an excited crowd was gathering. This was the African labor exchange, and a demand for increased salaries was under discussion. A proletariat organized within large labor unions was discovering its strength; it was exerting pressure on political life and causing alarm. Its leaders were asking questions and constantly seeking a mode of action suited to the ever-changing situation presented by the African city of today. One of my former colleagues at the African Institute who was active in the C.F.T.C., curiously transplanted to this Moslem country as the *"Confédération française des travailleurs croyants,"** told me with a gravity that approached despair, "We must be informed of everything, always be on our guard. We cannot act like savages or children, and we do not have the right to make mistakes. I am studying sociology and political economy. All alone, it's hard. . . ."

Until 1958, each of my new visits to the cities of West Africa left me with an ambiguous impression: the cities were changing, but this forward growth was arousing as much anxiety as hope. On the one hand, there was the fear that in the last analysis the material improvement did not serve the conservative intention of the colonizer; on the other hand, the fear of being swept away by the explosion of masses of city dwellers. Racial relations originally founded on mistrust and dependent on delicate balances may be reconstructed once certain freedoms have been achieved. At Abidjan, where a new urban bourgeoisie is emerging, co-operation between whites and Negroes has been re-established. However, the Europeans are building their new quarters at a distance, on the Cocodi plateau overlooking the lagoon. There, in a checkerboard pattern of roughly laid out streets, rise the modern buildings of the college, a few villas, and an amazing water tower in the shape of a painted mushroom. At Douala, on the day that the Wouri Bridge, a work of art 6,000 feet long which spans the muddy estuary in a semicircular arch, was opened, nationalist demonstrations re-

*"French Federation of Believing Workers."
184

sulted in rioting which in turn was followed by repressive measures. There was no communion in the pride the Europeans took in this impressive technical success. Let us have no illusions about such seemingly spectacular effects. The Wouri Bridge is like the Vridi Canal that has connected Abidjan with the sea; one question, explicit or implicit, hounds us: "At what sacrifice, and of what profit to the Negro?" Our achievements have often been suspect.

Only Libreville remains languid among its coconut and palm trees, old-fashioned and so typically colonial that in the courtyard of the governmental palace one would not be surprised to see an administrator of the old school, rigid in his dolman jacket, his face haughty under his pith helmet. Even the natives in their quarters from which exoticism has been banished are savoring the overripe fruits of a French civilization of 1900. Whenever I have had to stay in that modest seaside hotel, the product of a sterile modernism which is soon dispelled by the nonchalance of its proprietor and the irritating indifference of its staff, I have been reminded of the sweet idleness of "the Islands." Faithful to an enduring custom, the passions remain those of the heart rather than those of the political arena. You still hear the slogan, "Libreville, capital of the free life." The mystery of slender and delicate half-breeds replaces that of the handsome Gabonese women, but one still observes that "marriage of colors" which inspired Maurice Bedel. The archives bear witness to this tradition: a report states that in 1918 out of "935 native women of marriageable age, more than 400 remain single" and that, of these single women, "65 cohabit with Europeans, while about a hundred actually live by prostitution." Remote administrative seat, unused sham port, the city seems to endure only to affirm its loyalty to a past full of still-glorious memories. The real natives, the Mpongwe, reduced to a few thousand and proud of an aristocracy with debonair names like Prince Felix or Prince Berre, are victims of the same mirages. They retain a nostalgia for their tiny lost kingships and indulge in dreams of glory. However, fabulous mineral wealth will rouse the capital to economic revival and modern illusions.

SOME OBSERVATIONS ON THE
NEGRO TOWNS OF BRAZZAVILLE

At Brazzaville I had my fullest experience of the African

city. At first I was more sensitive to the beauty of the setting than to the societies that lived there, more aware of the picturesqueness of the native masses than of their problems. In the early days of my visit, I liked to go to Stanley Pool to contemplate the river and distinguish in the distance on the other bank the capital of the Belgian Congo, so powerful and modern that I felt as if I were facing another frontier between the old world and the new. I have kept the notebook pages on which I recorded my observations as they occurred to me. Their only virtue is spontaneity. They demonstrate that a kind of surrender to impressionism, to the natural and sociological landscape, represents a prerequisite to all research. The phrase "testing the water," no pun intended, expresses this requirement rather well. Why not turn today to these first impressions?

December 1948: The river carries little islands of vegetation torn up by last night's tornado; weeds sailing madly toward the rapids in tangled masses. From time to time splendid papyruses with long mellow stalks appear, as if planted in the current.

A ship passes, steaming toward Bangui, blowing its whistle interminably, with the pretensions of a vessel on the high seas. It has the proportions of a miniature steamer, and is further elongated by a curious appendage, a sort of seagoing shed covered with sheet iron. Two paddle wheels churn the water, leaving darkish gushes in its wake; all the waters of the Congo must have gone into this brew. Emerging from a pile of cans and sacks is the upper deck, where a few passengers "float" in their wicker chairs as if in baskets. This scene is so old as to be ageless. With a slow, steady, monotonous glide, the boat disappears behind Mbamou Island accompanied by a flock of screaming parrots. Stanley Pool is forced to imitate Lake Geneva with inferior resources: bluish borders, narrows, streams of verdure; here, the pretense of a port, a custom-house, a frontier. The black and multicolored swarming of porters, men selling Belgian money, sightseers and dreamers. Many stand and watch the river, indifferent to the passage of time.

"Across the way," to use the stock phrase, is a real city. Leopoldville lies in a fine mist, lifting a single tall building. From a distance, the comparison with the French capital is still a harmless game. . . . Up close, the inferiority complex of certain Brazzavillians is easy to understand: concrete roads, numerous commerical buildings, modern hotels with noiseless servants and the latest mechanical gadgets; finally, the avenue congested with American cars. Impressions of opulence, speculation, of the bold persistence of a capitalism which is off to a new start, unlike French colonial capitalism, which has surrendered all risks to the public powers. The Congolese Belgians reveal a certain upstart's arrogance: optimism, a sense of superiority, and an unshakable confidence in the future of their system. . . . Signs are in the native language, but Negro citizens are kept at a distance. For the moment, their kingdom is not of this world. This does not mean that they have renounced it, as the underground durability of politico-religious movements demonstrates. . . .

Leopoldville lacks an animation which is not exclusively commercial; it has stifled any Negro spontaneity with which it has come in contact. It has the air of a wealthy provincial city with grassy traffic circles and one-way streets, commercial districts, and boulevards whose houses or villas are protected from the intrusion of strangers. Its social life is curtailed, confined within the narrow limits imposed by segregation, exclusive selection and coteries.

These first impressions have changed in favor of Brazzaville. Picking up the challenge, the French capital was in turn seized by the modernist passion and by a need for size which seemed unjustified by its precarious economic situation. Three-quarters of a century behind the times, the city was born: new airdrome, new hospital, two scientific institutes, two cultural societies, a prow-shaped cathedral for the largest of the native centers, a school, hotels, apartment houses, villas, a few homes for westernized Africans, the first factories, and finally, a central power plant. Suddenly, people had the feeling that what had existed before was only the illusion of a city—which is almost the case. But now everyone is demanding the reason for this urban explosion. The development of the backlands seems risky, since the native population is too small and scattered, and the resources of the federation are limited. This city with its new face seems the result of a bet; up to now it has been forced to "live beyond its means." From 1948 to 1950, with the confusion of projects under construction and the demand for manpower, villagers constantly invaded the two African centers in the hope of picking up a few crumbs in the form of wages. A hope that was soon to be extinguished: by 1952, the scenery of construction having been removed, unemployment made its appearance in the Negro sections of Brazzaville.

The present configuration has not erased the old contours. Spread out over more than six miles, first bordering, then overhanging the Congo, the city carries the two Negro quarters of Poto Poto and Bacongo at her extremities, as if at arm's length.

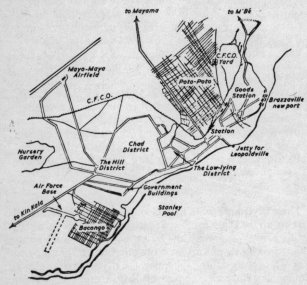

Fig. 47 European and African quarters of Brazzaville

Besides the fundamental principle of separation—everyone in his place—it illustrates a taste for simple compartmentalization. The region next to the river, the "Plain," contains houses of commerce and businesses. Overlooking this is one side of the plateau on which the Catholic mission settled very early, flanked by a village, since disappeared, with the touching name of "Marriage." In an intermediate zone, the "Chad," the military has taken up residence. Finally, the "Plateau" proper constitutes the administrative and residential quarter. This scheme reveals the incomplete quality of these urban colonial societies which have long resembled plays with four characters: the slaver, the civil servant, the soldier and the missionary. But within these rough divisions further partitions may be distinguished: the administrative departments and businesses have "concessions" where their personnel and their families live and where, for the most part, the network of social relations is exclusive and hierarchical.

In spite of physical appearances, the "white" city shows no more imagination than the African neighborhoods. Its compartmentalization, although less obvious in the social area than in the domain of urbanism, is not therefore less real. Its various elements seem unable to communicate among themselves except through the intermediary of the "hierarchical channel." Moreover, that urban development which has tended in certain European cities to create neighborhoods or suburbs coinciding with specific social classes has here a quality of caricature. It is also interesting to observe that human intercourse, which does not obey this formalism and tends to increase the number of individuals in contact, is concentrated within clubs of national origin, such as the Friends of Corsica and the Friends of Brittany. The African citizens follow this procedure themselves for different and in a sense opposite reasons: they are seeking a human frame of reference which the city does not provide, while the Europeans are trying to escape the social restrictions which confine them within oppressively narrow boundaries.

Poto Poto and Bacongo are checkerboards in which neither the houses nor the pawns themselves have any distinctive individuality. The physical similarity has not, however, favored the fusion of groups and individuals: incidents costing human lives in connection with certain electoral campaigns have demonstrated only too clearly the violence of racial antagonisms which are obscured by the apparent monotony. A crude geometry has carved these centers into sections devoid of personality, since official nomenclature has resorted to an alphabetical and numerical order—A/1, B/2, C/3, etc.—and these sections are in turn divided into numbered "blocks" and "lots." The imagination recovers its rights only in areas which are still sparsely populated, on the fringes of these Negro towns of 80,000 persons.

In these marginal areas one finds newcomers and individuals anxious to escape the conformity and bondage of a standardized existence. Magicians live here, on the pretext that they are near the "bush," home of the "spirits" which are their accomplices and instruments. I often wandered through these disorganized neighborhoods which are brightened by the whiteness of a clay in which Poto Poto seems slowly to be sinking. I was on the lookout for something unusual, some incident which would succeed in pulling me out of that depression which eventually results from frequent contact with native suburbs. I found Albert W., a man who had just moved there as the result of a dream which, he said, had "forced" him to take up the profession of healer. He was tired, having served the whites for some twenty years, first as a "boy," then as a cook. After taking orders from others, he had turned the tables and now told others what to do. It was more profitable and more impressive.

He received me on the threshold of his "concession." Thin, wrinkled and dirty, he seemed prematurely old; "The heat of the ovens has weakened me," he explained later. He had abandoned European clothing for the traditional loincloth knotted at the waist, for it was important that the ancestors and "spirits" be able to recognize him and be sure of his loyalty to the "true beliefs" and the "true rules of life." He avoided my eyes and hesitated some time before inviting me to come in.

In the courtyard of tamped sand were ficus and spurges which, since they are somehow associated with the elements, act as lightning rods. Two houses occupied most of the property: a straw one in the old style served as kitchen and quarters for Albert's wife; another, of clay, was divided into two overnight rooms reserved for patients, and two other rooms—but my host indicated that he was planning to build, to enlarge his "hospital." A girl fled at the sound of our voices, her face contorted and her arms trembling violently.

"What's the matter with her? Is she afraid of me?"

"Nothing . . . I am treating her. A jealous woman has sent a spirit to devour her brain."

The shabby reception room contained a wooden bed, four chairs, a table, and a wicker armchair piled with objects which were concealed under a filthy dishrag. A young boy brought beer and glasses. Albert flung a frothy spray onto the ground as an offering to his ancestors. We remained silent, doubtful of our ability to communicate. Through the partly open door a Negro soldier ventured timidly, saluted, then disappeared at the sight of me. I took the opportunity to ask a few questions.

"Is he leaving too?"

"He saw you."

"What did he want?"

"I am helping him to become a corporal. I am giving him a treatment."

"What kind of treatment?"

My host did not answer immediately. He walked over to the wicker chair and drew back the cloth that covered it. With a gesture he indicated all his working equipment: two statuettes of recent commercial workmanship which represented the masculine and feminine ancestors; a stump of dark wood with two hornlike appendages which symbolized the maternal and paternal lines and the fertilizing power of the figure 2; a husk stained with dried traces of ground cola; an old perfume bottle filled with a dubious-looking concoction. Albert handed me this bottle, saying:

"See, this is what I give to soldiers who want to be promoted. I rub their faces with it—it gives them the brains and intelligence of a leader. . . . The fellow you saw just now is a good man, so I add some smoke from Albert cigarettes to make it stronger."

I learned further that this mixture could be enriched whenever the ancestors expressed, through dreams or meditations, a desire for any given object. Albert looked me straight in the eye and added:

"The ancestors want a bicycle, but I am too poor."

I pretended not to understand. He smiled mischievously and led me to the courtyard.

"See, this is where I offer chickens and cola nuts." The altars were two replicas of straw huts, one quadrangular and the other circular. They were decorated with bunches of straw into which the feathers of sacrificial chickens had been stuck, and one of them had at its threshold a hole dug in the ground for libations. Kneeling or sitting on a goatskin, Albert would wait long hours for contact with the powers residing in these altars, for the revelations which would determine his treatment.

"What diseases do you treat?"

"All. Women who want children, and other female complaints. People devoured by violent spirits. . . . I am a fortune-teller. I give confidence to those who ask my advice. I help people find success."

Doctor, conscience, divine mediator: all these specialties had their fixed rates. The prices, which were written on a little slip of crumpled paper, were in line with those charged by the profession at the time (1950): first visit, 100 African francs; massage, 200 francs; serious illness, 500 francs, etc.; then the charges for boarding and obligatory sacrifices. Albert W. also made house calls.

"Will you give me a ride in your car? I must visit some patients."

My host prepared for his round of visits. He armed himself with a rusty old spear and a fancy dagger with a wide blade. He stowed his ritual instruments in a small raffia shoulder bag. In a flash he had become the typical villager of ancient Africa. As we were driving along, he suddenly asked me to let him out. He dashed over to a parked taxi and disappeared.

This example has a double interest. It shows how religious activities (in this case, the ancestor cult discernible in the background) are first degraded and then commercialized for magical purposes; but above all, it shows the importance in the lives of city dwellers of the therapeutic techniques of professional magicians. Albert and his colleagues are primarily "morale boosters." They operate falsely in the area of physical intervention, but they do have a psychological influence on citizens whose insecurity, new conflicts and comparative solitude have plunged them into confusion. It would be a mistake to accuse them of flagrant dishonesty. Besides, none of their clients complains of having been cheated: in studying the archives of the small claims court, I found only one trial resulting from the failure of a magician's treatment. The victims of this illusionism seldom resort to legal means; but even if they did, and assuming they were as numerous as our skepticism supposes, the magicians would find as many witnesses for their defense as our own quacks do in their quarrels with the Ordre des médecins. Subsequent encounters with Albert gave me a chance to observe to what degree he was subject to discipline and a kind of asceticism, in what sense he himself was both duper and duped, impressed by the few successes which had enhanced his reputation.

In a city which may be called improvised because most of it has been built in a hurry, the material and social conditions of existence can only be precarious. The majority of men are wage earners, but the wage is primarily that of the laborer. Having arrived with the illusion that they might save money, often against the price of a dowry, the young workers soon feel the weight of the cost of living and of usury, both of which are particularly heavy in a society in which everything costs money. The official definition of their salary, based on the "irreducible needs of the single individual," is tragically absurd. Here is a list of the household goods allotted in a typical annual budget: "1/3 storm lantern, 1/5 canteen, 2/5 stool or chair, 2/3 bowl or basin, 2/3 saucepan, 2/3 plate, 3/5 napkin and knife, 1/5 table." This list gives an index of the gap separating dreams from reality!

Since he is underpaid, the urban laborer is naturally exploited by his African landlords and tradesmen, who appropriate as much of his meager salary as they can. He lives in cheaply built rooms almost without furniture, often doubling up with friends in order to reduce the rental. He buys his food from shopkeepers who know how to lure him into debt by a kind of charge account system. And the rate of interest on loans runs from 25 to 35 per cent a month! Having brought a certain image of social relations from his village, where food and lodgings are not evaluated in terms of money and where relations of brotherhood and reciprocity still operate, he discovers at his own expense the law of supply and demand and the bondage of paid labor. He begins to feel resentment. He is trapped in the city by his debts and the shame of his failure.

But he suffers even more acutely from the uniformity and comparative solitude of the urban center. He has become an anonymous, uncommitted individual, although he still remains on his guard. He often lives as a bachelor, vaguely connected to some distant relative or group of comrades. He lives isolated among strangers, disoriented by the confusion of customs, the novelty of the practices and temptations. In the absence of a frame of reference he has only one infallible rule: to shift for himself. Indeed, this is what he is advised to do in more expressive language, by the Europeans to whom he confides his anxieties. He is lost, in most cases against his will.

A few energetic men have taken the initiative of forming ethnic associations whose purpose is to counteract this alienation by reviving "racial brotherhood" and by acting in time of death so as not to leave deceased persons in the hands of strangers. The attempt has not been entirely successful. The educated persons who controlled these new groups remained too remote from the uneducated mass of citizens, too formalistic in their approach. I attended an attempt to revive one of these associations, known as Mbongui after the village where the members of a single "scattered family" were gathered, which was addressed to the inhabitants of Bacongo. The opening session took place in the assembly room of the Cultural Circle before a sparse audience but in the presence of a representative of the administration. The leader of this undertaking, a post office clerk, was formal in his white suit and had the air of a professor who was more pleased with himself than he was with his audience. In a nervous, droning voice he read a prepared speech to the accompaniment of rattling papers. His auditors sat stiffly, like school children. This academic ritual was ill-calculated to arouse the enthusiasm of men who were disillusioned and who remembered the exciting ceremonies they had once known.

I have a copy of this inaugural speech and I shall quote a few passages which may explain its lack of success:

Ladies and gentlemen,

On behalf of the honorable chairman of the department of politics, and representative of the High Commissioner, I should like to make available to one and all the organization of our "Mbongui Association," based on its unwritten origins and in line with its tradition. [There follows a discussion of several aspects of Bacongo life.]

In conclusion, I should like to express my deep appreciation to our parents and grandparents who originated the aforementioned laws, statutes and rites which bred good qualities of intelligence and industry. . . .

I also want to thank the European, who has administered his laws, his statutes and his rites and who has taught us to read and write, and to follow careers which have created intellectuals and good workers. . . .

For although our parents and grandparents are all dead, their laws, statutes and rites still prevail. But the French proverb says, "When the snake dies, his venom dies too." To be worthy of such ancestors we must have qualified leaders.

Mindful of their responsibilities, the young people of the present generation have deemed it useful to return to their primeval source to reap the counsel of brotherhood in addition to the good customs of the Europeans, and dedicate themselves with sure confidence and conviction to collaboration with the French Union.

Thank you very much.

Aside from a deference to the official point of view which is partly strategic in nature, a speech of this kind, whose dullness and lack of spontaneity contrast with the colorful exuberance of the traditional style, has not the slightest chance of achieving the anticipated commitment. It fails to establish that powerful communication at which the old chiefs and village orators had been so skilful. Its rhetoric is barren and without resonance. This observation raises a problem involving our responsibility. This speech provides a mirror of our instruction; it shows how inadequate it has been until very recently. With makeshift schools we have turned out makeshift scholars who, deprived of their very ancient and very vivid means of expression, often sound like tape recorders playing to themselves.

The passion for learning, however, is undeniable. Every year in October the schools turn away lines of children who are waiting to be admitted. My inquiries in Poto Poto showed that many dedicated self-taught persons live there. They become the victims of undisciplined reading: books fall into their hands at random either through inadequate information or through the pressures exerted from Paris and elsewhere by the dealers in quick learning and the purveyors of occultism, who see every Negro as an easy customer. The conditions for intellectual development are disastrous. There exists no great body of literature which is the product of traditional African genius, to which to refer. And where is one to acquire a background for the reading of representative works of foreign civilizations? The sacred works which are vulgarized by missionary activity have long provided the chief sources of inspiration. An analysis of the texts published by educated Africans reveals the formal influence of these models.

There is more to it than this inadequate intellectual apprenticeship. Nobody can adopt a foreign language and a foreign way of thinking as if they were borrowed clothing. The lack of fit is obvious; it takes time and favorable conditions for the transformation to occur. If it does not succeed, the result is that species of intellectual vacuum which amuses certain small-minded colonials, who collect picturesque writings to give themselves an illusion of superiority. I cannot help thinking of Alfred Jarry's song about brainwashing. This is what comes of uprooting an individual who, rejected by a civilization which has become "backward" and "primitive" in his own eyes, can only arrive at Civilization through the back door.

The allusion to Jarry and the literary school of which he was

195

the inspiration is appropriate here. Some of the political texts I have come across give the impression of mere verbal exercises. They are particularly rich in stereotyped versions of the movements founded by the Congolese leaders and prophets Simon Kimbangu and André Matswa. In a curious style which betrays a freely assimilated missionary education, they express the first antagonistic reactions to religious and administrative domination. Before turning to these, I shall quote a document which illustrates this style of expression and these liberating intentions; it is a leaflet which circulated in the Negro sections of Brazzaville in 1946.

To the High Commissioner of French Equatorial Africa:

Many thanks to the Governor of Brazzaville!

I was deeply moved by the great joy I encountered in Brazzaville, for you have surely left the way open to my children, who pray to the all-powerful God.

When I arrived in Brazzaville, nobody knew me, either among the whites or among the Negroes. I shall invade Brazzaville with a great fire. I shall embalm it with tears of fire.

Hearty congratulations and cordial salutations to the Balali who, with a steadfast resolve, praise God, the true God, and who have bowed completely before the orders of the Eternal, the God of goodness. . . . Governor of Brazzaville, if you were so powerful, intelligent, and learned, why was my arrival unknown to you? Why did you not know me?

When I return, I no longer want to see all the missions of all your nations: Protestant, Catholic and Salvation Army. The only religion that reigns will be mine, which will spread its wings over all. Know that the land belonged to us, Simon Kimbangu and André Matswa.

Expressions of this sort are explained by the lack of leaders prepared to plan their action in a modern manner and by the cultural, economic and social level of the urban centers and the backlands. In 1949 and 1950 political parties and labor unions were still regarded by many young men as frauds imported by the colonizer; the word for labor union—"*sinedikate,*" from the French *syndicat*—had become synonymous with "collaboration" and "collaborator." On the other hand, the politico-religious movements I just mentioned found many followers among the Bakongo.

One day when my investigations in Poto Poto had continued into the small hours of the night, I suddenly became aware of an uproar rising over the city. As I listened, I distinguished something that sounded like a lamentation, a strange and solemn hymn being sung by a crowd whom I imagined to be moving. All at once I remembered a little broken-down shack overlooking the Flea Market near the Porte des Lilas, where every Sunday a band of poor people came to sing their vast misery and their imminent hope; some of them would emerge from this ramshackle chapel and, mingling with the crowd of indifferent strollers, would continue the song that had just helped them to forget their condition. I began to follow this African procession which had transformed the atmosphere of the city in an instant. More than a thousand persons, men, women and children, were advancing with lighted torches, singing of the suffering of the Congolese "prophets" and pledging a loyalty which was proof against any ordeal. At the head of the procession several young men carried a large wooden cross. Near by a man draped in white, his breast covered with emblems, was gesticulating in the throes of a genuine sacred possession: this was the new leader of the church. A little behind him and imitating the spasmodic step of the pontiff, a young boy was flourishing one of those posters showing a Christ figure being assailed by German bombs which were once used to denounce Nazi cruelty. This crowd, inspired by a faith created to its measure and to the measure of its needs, and utilizing certain Christian symbols which it had transformed into instruments for opposing the established order, gave an amazing impression of power. But where was it bound? Toward illusions which would provide only an apparent liberation, or toward a progress which could be realized beyond these disturbing rituals? It was, however, toward a new Congo, a kind of promised land, that these people dimly aspired. From time to time one of the marchers would fall to the ground, his torch flung aimlessly like a spark, and flounder in the dust of the road, overcome by that sacred frenzy which assures a freedom of expression several thousand years old.

In a society in which human relations are variable and therefore dangerous, as they are in every new Negro city, the illusion makers and morale boosters enjoy an unquestionable influence. They provide short-term satisfactions by familiar means.

This phenomenon is becoming more and more noticeable. Its counterpart is the reticence shown toward an educated minority which is in any case unable to penetrate its isolation. One of my informants never spoke of the members of this social category except as "the gentlemen." Popular terminology refers to them as *moundele ndoumbe*—the "white man's creatures." And yet for the most part these men have a sense of their responsibilities; but trapped by a comparative material and intellectual comfort, they have lost that communicative warmth which is the African's sole test for distinguishing his real friends from his false ones. They are often taken in by that *petit-bourgeois* morality imported by certain cautious, timid and thrifty colonials of recent vintage whose whole purpose is to justify their own barrenness of heart and mind. I have had occasion to study this kind of thinking in conversations with citizens who felt they had achieved "an intellectual and moral evolution above the average." Their arguments combined to form an image of the man of the people which was pure caricature: "He cannot hold onto property. He is overly influenced by bad movies. He does not want to belong to a civilized religion. He does not educate his children, but lets them dominate him. He encourages prostitution for his own profit. He is interested only in enjoying himself," and so on. It was like the monotonous refrain of a critic.

The problem of the enlightened young woman is the least debatable of those I encountered. Too few and freed from the tasks which tradition had imposed in the village environment, women living in the cities enjoy an advantage and a state of detachment for which they are ill—or all too well—prepared. Although many of them, generally the older ones, have become less fearful and submissive, they are content to perform domestic chores. A few seek relative economic independence by carrying on small businesses which, in addition to personal income, provide those chance relationships which they crave. Others, of whom there is an increasing number, "shift for themselves:" they gamble on their coquetry while they can. And in an incredible legal jumble in which traditional demands for indemnity are mingled with demands for alimony borrowed from our laws, conflicts arising from adultery monopolize the activities of the petty claims court. An unmistakable antifeminism is betrayed by the African press. For example, this quotation from a local newspaper: "The badly educated, so-called 'enlightened' woman, accustomed to a life of sexual license, has become a plague on society. Jealous of her 'new freedom,' she does nothing but shuttle between the houses of white men and the fetisher's hut, the market and the dance hall." The moralist speaks without mercy.

Sometimes I would meet my informant in a Poto Poto bar. Here we could speak more freely, and the place, with its mixed crowd, was an excellent observation post.

A few tables and chairs of the kind you see in lower-class bars, beer and wine, and on the walls, advertisements for the movie house next door created an unexpected decor: *Tarzan the Invincible, The Black Demon, The Wonderful Cavalier, Avengers of the Far West, Apache Horse of Death, Terror at the Ranch.* All over the world a whole new mythology within visual reach is attracting the same public hungry for the impossible and for new heroes. A public-address system broadcast the recordings of a local star; the most popular one recounted with shameless plagiarism the feats of Tino Rossi and the inconstant and unhappy loves of a girl named Marie-Louise.

In one corner some young women seated around a table formed a noisy group; they were drinking beer, munching roasted peanuts and smoking. They wore long dresses of printed cotton and scarves of the same material on their heads. Their toenails were painted with a dark red polish, as were their fingernails, on hands which opened occasionally like that sinister flower, the black tulip. They were surrounded by some men of too studied an elegance who were disdainful, seemingly indifferent to their chatter. In their conversation the phrase "shining star" recurred frequently. I asked Apollinaire, a young Mbochi who had become my assistant for the occasion, the meaning of these words.

"Oh, that's the name of a woman's club. There are many organizations like it in the city: 'The Rose,' 'Violette,' 'Lolita,' 'Dollar,' 'Elegance' . . . Right now, the women are discussing plans for their annual party."

"What is the purpose of these clubs? As I understand it, men cannot belong."

Apollinaire hesitated. He observed me with a smile full of implications, as if he found me naïve, or shrewd in a clumsy way.

"Oh, these are women who join together to help each other out in emergencies. But they also like to give nice parties with dancing and singing. They are all beautiful on those days, because they wear the same new clothes and jewelry as well. . . .

199

Their president is a man. You see that tall guy in the blue suit? He runs the 'Shining Star'."

He paused; he seemed to be censoring a thought which I could easily guess.

"Are there other titles which belong to women in the association?"

"Well, they elect a president who must already be rich and make an impressive appearance. This is the *mama mokonzi*. They choose a treasurer, and a commissioner whose job is to accept or reject new members. They also have a 'first singer,' the prettiest and the one with the best voice, who composes or selects the songs. . . . These women know how to charm, and many men desire them. But they are too expensive!"

"Do the parents push their daughters into these organizations of high-class prostitutes?"

"Oh! You know, they no longer have any authority. And then, they are only too glad to receive the profits. Some of them get four to five thousand francs a month. They think their children must love them very much since they are so generous. That's enough for them."

This argument attributed to the parents who are accomplices of this prostitution with its respectable facade does not correspond to reality. The young girls do no violence to their feelings when they become these courtesans concerned solely with coquetry and amusement, but they resent the speculative pressure of which they are the object. One of their songs, a lament heard in the streets on evenings when the moonlight makes it possible to play *kebo,* expresses this resentment:

> Hear me, my friends!
> God gave us mothers.
> Mothers who kill us,
> For money.
> Some day, how will we stand
> Before God,
> The All-Powerful?

This surrender to commercial love is not, therefore, devoid of bitterness. But the young women do not linger over these anxieties. They dress in costly fabrics and vie with one another in buying jewelry. They dance. They sing. The provocativeness of their movements gives commercial eroticism a glamour in which our societies are no longer even interested:

Come: Whom do you fear?
I no longer have a husband.
I married very young,
Thinking there were no other men.
If only I had known!
Let me love you. You're just my type!

In Africa, once *par excellence* the land of generosity and giving, to the point where this trait seemed a surrender to idle and sensual ease, such a commercialization of sex constitutes a revolution in itself. It shows what extreme limits of freedom these young women, who are just as numerous in Leopoldville and other cities as they are in Brazzaville, have reached, only to fall immediately into the bondage of social relations governed by the lure of gain. It is difficult to imagine from a distance the consequences for the individual of a situation which involves not only the confusion of a society in transition, but the competitiveness of a crude and primitive mercantilism.

This urban society is waiting to be built. It is in need of new leaders, new values, freedom of expression and creation. As long as these conditions are unfulfilled, the Negro city remains a place where a great many people struggle in poverty and obedience to the harsh law of joyless labor or the futility of illusions. The social fabric is too taut for the urbanite to find that human warmth to which his past had accustomed him. He continues to seek it, less within himself than without, for he is totally unprepared for a detachment which would presuppose greater egoism on his part and a certain minimum of comfort.

The cafés, which resemble other houses except for a few wooden benches and tables set up on the ground, are becoming the new meeting places for friends and co-workers, replacing those social centers that dominated the life of the village. The bottle of beer and the glass of red wine have replaced the gourd of palm wine, but the same need for the security of human fellowship may be observed. On Saturday night and Sunday, however, all restrictions forgotten, Negro citizens give free rein to their craving for joy, physical relaxation, communication with others. In all neighborhoods, around tomtoms beating out traditional motifs or makeshift orchestras, dancing is uninterrupted. The sound of drumbeats rises over the city, occasionally accompanied by snatches of song. Beyond, in the European quarters, the Sunday boredom settles in.

I have tried to present only a few images and impressions. I shall add a final scene, because it remains clear in my memory. Along the road leading to the native cemetery a sparse, straggling crowd is moving at a brisk pace. At its head a man is pushing a bicycle on which a child's coffin is precariously balanced. Near by, an adolescent boy is holding a wooden cross which he flourishes with a jerky motion because of the rapidity of the march. Those who follow, awkward in their starched garments and clumsily dressed hair, pant, occasionally singing fragments of hymns. Their haste is still a mystery to me, but I like to see it as a symbol of the precipitation with which a small band of Africans will soon seek to rid themselves of another corpse: that of a modern civilization which is unwelcome in their country, because it is patterned too much after our example and to suit our convenience.

7
Opposing Movements

▼▼▼

AFTER leaving Brazzaville to study religious and political dissent in a rural setting, I spent some time in the nearby district of Mayama. Some twenty-five miles beyond the administrative post, the road divides. One branch disappears toward regions which the European has overlooked; the other, after passing the Catholic mission at Kindamba, joins the great highway that spans the Congo together with the railroad. This modest crossroads, which includes an inn where I took up residence, offers two alternatives: flight to a haven which old Africa used for escape, or access to a region aspiring to a modernism which is still precarious and timid and which the villagers conceive in their own way. The distinction is not clear cut, and there is a common trait: in both regions, our supervision is considered too expensive to justify its inadequate or dangerous results.

A "commanding village," to use the Bakongo expression, has grown up around this fork: Loukouo is a mixed community, composed of dissimilar elements and dominating a territory which does not belong to its present occupants. Built to order, it served as a base for a now deserted market and a school. The groups represented have not been able to live together for long, for lack of understanding and fertile land. There remain only a few handfuls of peasants, traders without customers, and

203

curiously, a small group of ex-riflemen associated with a retired corporal. In Loukouo there are no streets, no common centers where clansmen gather; only dispersion in an ill-defined communal space, as if these people were waiting for a real village to appear. This temporary settlement, where individuals no longer bound together by the old social ties are encamped, presents a kind of image of the construction of Africa: where is one to find the principle or unity?

This is the question I asked myself as I wandered from house to house. Political authority had declined: the chief of Loukouo had lost all influence and his rival, the corporal, a stranger to the region, was without prestige. Economic interests, once effective, had disappeared. My impromptu guide, Gabriel Mayéla, complained of the difficulty of living in this place. In a disturbingly melodious voice and with an amazing fluidity of gesture, he described his frustrations as a former schoolteacher returned to the soil and his failures as a tradesman who had barely managed to pay for his license. This man, who must have been about forty, had a charming distinction and endured considerable difficulties without being overwhelmed. Without self-pity, simply in order to help me understand local problems, he played back the film of his latest misadventures:

"I taught in the Catholic mission schools, first in the bush, then in Poto Poto and Bacongo. Since I was educated at the Petit Séminaire in Brazzaville, I found work easily. It's a difficult, underpaid profession. Above all, I do not like the ways of city people. They have no warmth, and it's a bad place for old people. . . . I decided to settle in the village of my relative, the 'crowned' chief Bwango. I told myself that a man without land is like a tree without roots. But the soil is not good; one must be content with little, like our forefathers. I tried to be a retail tradesman. The market no longer exists and I could not afford to buy a truck. Now, I am forced to give up. I will try again later, if my relatives will help me. Everything is difficult here. You heard what your guide said: "This country is finished." The villagers believe it's a matter of religion, and keep saying that the whites have created confusion everywhere . . . there are too many new churches. Bwango thinks we should return to the cult of the ancestors. But the people say this is not progress."

"Has the mission had a great deal of influence in the country?"

204

"It did once, but things changed a long time ago. The peasants think the Fathers have not taught them all they know about God. They feel that the religion of the Europeans leaves the wealth in their own hands and hides a secret which nobody is willing to reveal. So they have decided to search for themselves, to put their confidence in their own prophets. As you know, they tried to burn Kindamba."

"You have remained a Catholic. Don't they mistrust you?"

"I am often unhappy. I no longer know where to turn myself. Bwango criticizes me. Others accuse me of not helping to build the new religion of our people. The Fathers accuse me of being too cautious. . . . What can I do? What would be right for us is what would divide us least."

"Do you see a solution?"

"Oh! I haven't even thought about it. Anyway, I am not respected enough to do anything. We had a man who wanted to work for our future—André Matswa. He suffered, and he ended up dying in prison. . . . The villagers still call him our Savior. They vote for him in the elections. They look upon him as the Negro Christ. . . . I cannot find a truth that satisfies me. I do not trust men who want to build new churches only for Negroes. But I am sure they are trying to find the only solution: to give us power, *ngolo* as we say, by uniting us better."

"But what if they were simply taking advantage of the circumstances to mislead you?"

Mayéla avoided the question. He amused himself by stroking his young boy, who had just joined us. I did not insist, amazed that he had confided as much as he had. I made a point of showing renewed interest in the humbler but more personal problems of my interlocutor. In the end he confided his plan with a simplicity that was free of any cynicism we might read into it.

"I would like to be elected to the Representative Council. If I succeed, then perhaps I can get a new start in life. . . ."

Mayéla did not think for a moment that this body would help to answer the questions he had raised so incisively. It operated on an altogether different level in his mind, the level of areas invaded by the European, that is the world of goods and material realities. The serious problems of the region had to be considered *in situ,* without outside interference, by men who had not only the ability but the right to do so. Between these two domains there was no communication.

Mayéla accompanied me on my visits to the heads of families. In front of most of the houses stood a long pole which gleamed with tallow from the candles it supported.

"What are those?"

"Those are places of prayer for followers of the new religion. When people want to make fun of them, they say they worship

Fig. 48 Tunic, cap and badges of an initiate of the messianic movement

the 'God of candles.' They reply that the Catholics do the same thing *inside* their chapels."

As I extended my research beyond Loukouo, I discovered how widespread the phenomenon was. In some villages the candles were arranged on a kind of private altar strewn with wildflowers. My guides explained that the flame indicated to God (Nzambi Poungou) that the believer was turning toward him to seek counsel and assistance. The debt to the Catholic ritual is obvious, but it would be a mistake to see it as no more than a crude imitation. Undoubtedly there is more or less conscious and direct reference to the meanings once associated with fire, as if the flickering flame embodied all that remains of those ancient fire rituals I was able to attend in various regions of the Congo and Gabon. In excluding sacrifices, offerings or material symbols, the new cult eliminates that sacred manipulation which once assured communication between man and his gods. It is hard for the villager to believe that he need only turn toward them wholeheartedly in order to be heard. He needs a material intermediary to establish contact. As he sees it, to light the candle is to create a symbol which not only permits this communication but proves the power of the Negro church.

We were finishing our first round of visits. Mayéla left me suddenly, then returned and said in a low voice, "Go and see the tailor; he is an interesting man, but he is a fanatic."

I found the man at work in a kind of shed formed by the overhanging roof of his house. He was running his machine, an old Singer, at top speed, making it tremble beneath his feet. He was rushing to complete a long black cotton robe whose cut suggested either a dressing gown or the Moslem *boubou*. He did not look up, as if he were unaware of my presence. After watching him for a moment, I tried to question him, feigning amazement.

"Who is it for? Robes like this aren't worn around here."

"It is a costume peculiar to our church."

He had not stopped working. He toiled over the garment with a kind of rage from which the machine suffered, working in white thread a breast emblem consisting of the Christian cross enclosed between the arms of a V.

A young man appeared. He was wearing a strange cap something like the ones worn by French pastry cooks, embroidered with the same motif alternating with a four-pointed star. On his chemise, fastened with safety pins, he wore a mourning band and emblems with the same cross and V-for-victory motifs. He greeted me and leaned against a supporting post, smoking a cigarette and striking a nonchalant and possibly provocative pose. I decided he was testing my reactions.

"As you see, our tailor receives many orders."

"That's fine—it shows the people can afford to buy new clothes."

"On the contrary, we are all children of poverty."

"What do you mean?"

"We are poor because the white man's God does not help us become rich. He does not love us. . . . Now, we have learned to act. We go without, and give our savings to the church. This way we shall find strength."

"For what? To live better?"

"Yes, to obtain the good things of civilization. For another reason too: we are tired of always obeying the Europeans. We want to rebuild our country according to our own desires. You cannot know what we want; you are accustomed to giving the orders without paying attention to our ideas."

"That is no longer true. Why, I am here in Loukouo to learn and to help. . . . You know that I have learned Bakongo ways here and in Boko."

"The Fathers learned our customs too, and they deceived us just the same. We only trust men like Nganga Emmanuel. He is the leader of our church. He will show us the way."

"He will not show you how to make roads, how to build schools and dispensaries, how to enrich the villages with new crops. These things have nothing to do with religion. Nganga Emmanuel is only interested in teaching sacred songs and threatening those who do not follow him. . . ."

By presenting my objections in such a direct and rudimentary form, I was trying to force the young man to explain himself further. He seemed to have reached the point where the habitual Bakongo reserve no longer operates and real conversation is possible. I was overstating my case to this end. He hesitated, absent-mindedly fingering the cloth emblems at his breast; he started to answer:

"You do not understand what we want. Anyway. . . ."

He walked away. I called him back.

"Have a cigarette."

"Thank you, I don't smoke."

"Come now, you're making fun of me. You just threw away a butt."

"But I don't smoke that brand."

It was a polite refusal. All at once I found myself at that impasse so familiar to administrators. A whole people, in their desire for greater independence from the European, has avoided the gifts they have offered. It has accepted neither the free distributions of seed nor the services of native provident societies. It has rejected official presents. It has rejected the help of missionaries, and at one time even the women used to flee during distributions of holy medals. Through the intermediary of the chiefs, it has scorned financial offerings which it could have enjoyed. Repeatedly over the past few decades, these gestures, sometimes accompanied by less peaceful demonstrations, have revealed a desire to alter the social relations imposed by colonization. By refusing gifts, the Bakongo has maintained his distance and expressed his protest. Ingenious enough to preserve his economic positions, he has broken contact to avoid being trapped at an inferior level. Such a withdrawal has attested to his impatience to become responsible for his own destiny, even for the worse.

Perhaps this is what my young companion was thinking; but he had disappeared. The tailor was still running his machine with the same violence; he was just as reticent, and refused to answer any but the most routine questions. With all others, he feigned ignorance.

A few days after my arrival I decided to pay a visit to the Catholic missionaries at Kindamba, out of courtesy and curiosity to hear their ideas. Mayéla had asked to accompany me. He arrived with his whole family, as if for a picnic. We drove through several villages in which only the children were excited to see us; they ran behind the truck, lost in a cloud of dust, yelling *"Moundele! Moundele!"* (The white man! The white man!)

"What is the name of this village?"

"Moagangouba . . . there were more people once."

"What does the name mean?"

"Oh, that's easy; something like 'throw away the peanuts.' The people destroyed the seeds which the administration gave them. You know the story. . . ."

The mission was a red brick building near a chapel, raised slightly above the road and overlooking a very orderly garden. It formed a separate universe of its own. It looked like some enclave of farmer-monks interested in pacifying and teaching by example. It made one feel calm and relaxed as well as surprised by the persistence which had succeeded in creating a familiar peasant economy. The herd, maintained at the price of a constant struggle, the hutch, and the kitchen garden provided familiar landmarks and suggested that a real countryside could grow across the monotonous bush. One escaped from that sense of fragility and instability created by Bakongo civilization, which is so indifferent to settling down or leaving monuments. But these first impressions were quickly altered.

I discovered that the mission was besieged by forces that were all the more insidious and powerful because they were not immediately apparent. It aroused outside opposition; the villagers accused it of being a pitfall for the African. It no longer maintained the unwavering confidence of the founders of the Congolese church. It was withdrawing, cutting itself off. The Christian peace seemed to be slipping through the fingers of the monks and their disciples. A few months later, a band of believers in the 'new faith' camped near its buildings, waited for the right moment to set them on fire, and dispersed at dawn, having renounced its sinister plan.

The antagonisms arising from colonization and from the opposition of two not only different but unequal civilizations have therefore the quality of a religious war. An underground conflict is developing. The villagers deny the universality of the Church, because they see it as associated with the privileges of the white race. The missionaries deny the Negro's capacity to have an independent religious life which is not a reversion to "savagery;" they refuse to converse with adversaries who, in their eyes, can arrive at truth only by total submission.

Outside of a small female community established separately and a lay brother, there are only two missionaries in Kindamba. The "brother" is of Alsatian origin. He likes order and authority; he has a peasant tenacity and ingenuity; he builds, plants, gives orders and allows the Negro peasants no other loyalties or concerns besides his own. The older Father is a heavy, powerful-looking man, warm and direct. I soon learned that he was physically hampered by a serious cardiac condition. I found him to be anxious and capable of sudden violence. A sense of failure had led him to a solitude which had aroused the hatred of his former Bakongo disciples and, he said, given rise to a new "fetishism?" He expressed his helplessness by anger—and was almost tempted to leave the intractable side of the Negro to the devil. He expressed his resentments bluntly, in a long monologue:

> "The people here are liars and have no character. They pretend to submit to you, then they deceive you. . . . They are living on the illusion that they have recovered their freedom through their prophets of disaster. They accept nothing that comes from us for fear we will take advantage of our gifts. . . . False cults have never been so numerous; they come to the very doors of the mission. I tried to get rid of them and destroy their altars. I barely escaped physical violence. My bitterest antagonist was a former catechist. All our troubles come chiefly from men who once had our confidence and are using our teachings to supplant us. . . . They combine everything in their ceremonies; fetishes, fits of possession, prayers they have stolen from us, gestures copied from the priest's, proces-

sions that imitate ours. It's disgraceful! They no longer want us as interpreters of God. They say that we alone enjoy the benefits of our intercession. . . . You know this country, there is anarchy in the villages. The only unanimity is in opposition to the whites. A few scoundrels give orders not to supply the mission, and soon we are unable to procure a thing. You can feel the desire to isolate us, to weaken us. These fanatics still hesitate to destroy us, but only through lack of courage. One can do nothing for them. I have secured a prohibition on collective demonstrations, but the meetings take place in small groups around altars set up in the houses. . . . God alone can recognize them as his own. In my opinion, not one of them is worth much."

I have quoted this monologue to show the degree of intensity this religious war had reached by 1949 and 1950. Because of fatigue and discouragement, the attitude is exclusively negative. My investigations of neighboring districts did not corroborate this profound pessimism, but it remains highly understandable as a reaction to the failure of a long missionary career and as an expression of fear in the face of a movement directed primarily against Christianity. Its error consisted in seeing nothing beyond these discouraging impressions. Although the religious aspect of the Bakongo movement is the most obvious one, there are others. What the villagers want is not only to recover control of those sacred techniques indispensable in their eyes to the health and wealth of every society, but also to regain their former freedom of action. They want to reconstruct their civilization, to restore its strength and unity. They can do so only by opposing all the outside restraints they have endured and by strengthening those "alliances" which re-establish their self-confidence.

The second of the Kindamba missionaries, a young man whose gentleness was combined with an evangelical zeal and who was active in the villages in a quiet way, revealed a subtler understanding of the Bakongo problem. He did not subscribe to the indictment I just quoted.

"There is something to this besides fetishism. The villagers are making a mistake, but the needs they feel are very powerful."

When this man entered a temple of the "new" religion during a ceremony, he had the self-control not to lose his temper.

He observed and meditated on the causes of a heresy which had an undeniable magnetism. He decided to give up the old methods of Christianization by force. His tolerance seemed suspect to the missionary authorities, but he did not abandon his policy of silent attendance.

When we left the mission at the end of the day, Mayéla said nothing for a long time. I did not even have the curiosity to ask him how he had spent his time waiting for me. I abandoned myself to the enjoyment of the coolness, the quiet, the darkness—and the opportunity to forget for one moment all human cares and all thought by becoming one with the peace of nature. Mayéla broke this spell when we drew near the encampment.

"Here you are. . . . You have seen what different men the two Fathers are. But they will both have the same problems. The Bakongo are tired of sharing God with the white man."

A few days later, as I was preparing to leave for the outlying villages, Mayéla came to announce the arrival of Nganga Emmanuel, one of the priests and founders of the new cult. I had not anticipated such a simplification of my task, and I hoped to learn a great deal from this encounter. I began looking through my notes for what information I already had. A few vital statistics were inadequate to place this amazing personality. Nganga was decended from slaves; he was not born into the "clan." This social inferiority, which had not inclined him to tolerate any form of domination passively, made his present reputation even more unusual. The Catholic missionaries had educated him, and for eight years he had played the role of head catechist of his village. During this time he enriched his knowledge of Christianity and of the most popular sacred writings. But the determining factor in his development was the friendship of the leader André Matswa. From this contact he learned to reject inequality; he participated in the first antiwhite demonstrations and was deported to Chad. He left the Catholic mission when he realized that the servants of Christ did not side with the Bakongo. After his discovery that the God worshipped within those walls was first of all French, his claims took on political overtones as well.

Without my hearing him enter, Nganga Emmanuel was standing in front of me, accompanied by a young boy. He was about fifty years old, short, thin and badly dressed. His clothing—trousers and a kind of flowing blouse covered with symbols and braid—was of a dubious white. He wore a boy scout

212

hat with the sign of the Christian cross between the arms of the V. His restless eyes avoided mine. He leaned on a stick, reluctant to enter. Was this really the rival of the Kindamba Fathers?

Accepting my invitation to sit down, he presented me with a small plucked chicken and an egg which his young companion solemnly proffered. I tried to reply with a gift of my own, but he refused.

"Why?"

"Impossible! I brought you this to show you my confidence. I do not wish to make a profitable exchange, but to honor you as a stranger welcomed with pleasure, without evil intentions."

His voice was harsh and loud. His uneven, nervous delivery betrayed an ill-contained anxiety. He fidgeted constantly in his chair, having lost that placidity and infinite patience which had so impressed me in most of my African acquaintances. I watched him, wondering how to start a conversation in which we might express ourselves openly. I told myself that we were beginning badly, since he had just lied and tried to trap me. In forcing his gift on me, he was forcing my loyalty and friendship; at the very least, he was neutralizing me. In refusing mine, he retained all his freedom of maneuver; he had made no commitment in my behalf, he had not compromised himself. So runs Bakongo logic, which in this case was accompanied by a determination not to receive anything from the hand of a white man. Never until that moment had I realized how irrevocably my race and my membership in a particular social system could classify me automatically, apart from my intentions or desires. In Nganga Emmanuel's eyes I was unquestionably on the side of the enemy. But I seemed more vulnerable to him because I was new to the region and in a sense naïve regarding its problems. That I was merely the least of all the evils, and my ethnological curiosity, explained why he had taken the trouble to see me. Actually, as I learned later, an entirely political reason also motivated his visit: he was trying to obtain official recognition for the "Negro Church." The Congolese Progressive Party had demanded "the right to freedom of worship," but its actions had lacked conviction and sincerity. Anyway, the most diverse support had become necessary to attain this end—or at any rate, to obtain a real tolerance.

Our conversation remained cautious; it consisted of banalities which enabled us to avoid the issue and which followed the African custom; for in these civilizations where rhetorical art is

213

rich in effects and devices, a long prelude precedes important discussions. I decided to ask a question inconsistent with this tiresome game. It was the type of attack which in traditional oratorical contests forces the debaters either to broach the subject of the argument or stop talking.

"Would you tell me what reasons motivated you to found this church at Galamboma?"

Nganga Emmanuel answered with a rapidity that surprised me; I could hardly manage to follow him. He had decided to begin talking freely.

"I followed my heart. Nzambi Poungou spoke to me, it was my duty to listen. Nobody prepared me for this task; at the mission I learned how to speak to God. On the road to Vindza, Baloula initiated a former magician after making him burn all his fetishes. But this man remains ignorant. How could he know how to worship God?"

"Who is this Baloula? They say he is mad."

"Oh! He is like one who has lost his head. He never stays in the same place; he runs in all directions. He wandered in the bush for several weeks and was believed to be lost. This is where he had the revelations. Since then, he has never worked. He travels through the country educating the villagers, as the prophets used to do."

I too had lied; I could still picture this Baloula, whom I had seen once leading a candlelight procession through the urban center of Bacongo, and again with a retinue of disciples, trying to hide in the savanna. A man of about thirty whose body never stopped moving and whose face was constantly contorted, he seemed drugged with hymns and revelations: a primitive mystic, an object of disgust to the rich and enthusiasm to the poor, of the type that appears when civilizations are in flux. Nganga Emmanuel lacked this disturbing grandeur. A product of his Christian past, he sought primarily to give form to the new cult, to rationalize it by performing a veritable feat of plagiarism upon Catholicism. I urged him to explain and justify his experiment. He seemed anxious to provide an answer that would be satisfactory on the level of reason rather than passion. I challenged him:

"Why do you not choose between Christianity and the cults practiced by your ancestors? That would be clear cut."

"Fetishes cause too much trouble; they divide and weaken us. Anyway, they are things of the past. Only the old chiefs keep them in the hope of some day recovering the authority

214

they have lost through lack of courage. It is the missionaries who have killed our religion. It is important that we make a new one. . . . Every race has its language, its customs, its ways of understanding life. The Catholic religion is not right for us. It forces us to give up all our customs. We no longer know whether we are Bakongo, Basoundi, Balari. . . ."

"Are there no other reasons?"

"No, that's all. We have saviors who can speak for us because they are close to God: André Matswa and Simon Kimbangu. They have suffered for the Negroes. Jesus Christ suffered only for the whites. . . . With their help, the way of Nzambi Poungou will be open to me."

From the Congo to the Cape, founders of new churches very much like Nganga Emmanuel are heralding the ultimate triumph of Negro saviors over the "pale Christ of the white men." They are predicting a combined subversion of man and elements which will put an end to colonial domination and cultural oppression. Nganga Emmanuel himself has threatened "storm and flood." He has sustained the illusion that a new Africa can rise from an apocalyptic chaos that will have erased all traces of the white man's hand. He has promised access to the "road to heaven"—*nzila ia zoulou*—for those who know how to fight.

I said nothing for a moment, and he returned indirectly to my question.

"There are men who do not belong to any religion. I hate them—they are dangerous people. If you do not see them practicing a cult, it is because they are secretly engaging in sorcery. They should be destroyed. The sorcerers have sown too much disorder in the country since we have been unable to combat them. . . . Only Negroes can fight these dangers. We must build a great religion for ourselves."

"But you are adding to the disorder! The villagers do not all follow you, and some are as afraid of you as they are of the sorcerers."

"Ah! Who told you that? The missionaries, no doubt? They spread lies. They hate us because we tell the truth to the Bakongo people. . . . When I preach in my chapel, I give only good advice. I tell my followers to love and help one another, not to steal, and not to commit adultery. I explain how we must organize to live well. They will serve as an example for other tribes in the Congo."

"They say you are putting the peasants on the wrong path.

215

You make them pray and sing when they should be working in the fields and in the villages."

"The people who live near by come on Sunday and Thursday, for that is the day we pray to André Matswa to help us. The others go up to Galamboma on feast days to learn the songs and prayers. There are many converts on those occasions. They cannot all get into the chapel. . . . They are right to leave their work. If God is not with them, they will remain in poverty in any case. Wealth will not be theirs."

"Everything is not as simple as you pretend. There are other Negro churches in the country which do not seem to be in accord with yours. There are too many prophets and not enough leaders."

"We need a miracle to recover our strength and freedom. Who will provide it? The priests of our religion are established as far as Dolisie and Pointe-Noire. . . . I know that the people of Boko mistrust us, that they believe only in Simon Kimbangu as Savior, and have taken the model for their cult from the Protestants . . . but eventually we must come to an agreement and unite. And when that happens. . . ."

He did not finish his sentence. The young man with the strange cap covered with emblems had just appeared out of nowhere. He greeted me absent-mindedly and started talking to Nganga Emmanuel so rapidly that I could not follow him. The two men walked toward the door. My visitor disappeared silently, just as he had come, but before leaving he insisted that I come and visit his "missionary post."

The religious settlement of Galamboma is very much isolated from the road on a kind of small, barren plateau. I found it after a rapid and exhausting march, so impatient were my guides, Mayéla and the young man in the cap, to show me this new place of pilgrimage. The surrounding bush was dry, sparse and uninhabited. A few undistinguished plantations preceded a large clearing in which a huge building, the chapel, sprawled and some residential houses were scattered. Nganga Emmanuel came forward alone to meet us. A man with a red scarf around his neck—the distinctive mark of a certain category of believers—crossed the yard, then disappeared. I was sure that the people had fled on hearing of my arrival; there was an emptiness which attested to their mistrust and fear. I felt momentarily discouraged. In my naïveté I felt like some imperial official, curious and peace-loving, who had involuntarily aroused fear by invading a Christian community of ancient

216

Rome. The comparison was not so inaccurate: there is in this undertaking an unconscious return to the beginnings of Christianity.

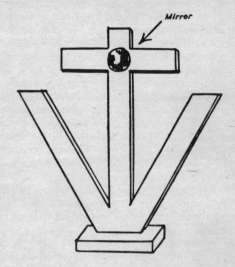

Fig. 49 The cult object on the altar

When we walked into the chapel, all three of my companions made the sign of the cross. I was amazed at the gesture.

"But what do you mean by making the Catholic sign of the cross?"

To my astonishment it was Mayéla, who still had the confidence of the Kindamba Fathers, who answered.

"We have changed the wording to: 'In the name of the Father and of André Matswa and of Simon Kimbangu'."

The building was made of clay in imitation of bush missionary chapels. It was open at one end, but had no windows, admitting only a subdued light. Rows of benches, simple boards set on posts driven into the hard dirt floor, flanked a central aisle. At the back a small wooden railing, broken at the center to allow the priest to pass, separated the congregation from the altar. During services, which were regarded as corresponding to the Mass, the priest leaned on the railing to give his *nlongui* (sermon). The raised altar was reached by a few steps and was

217

covered with those red blankets which were used for barter at the time of the first colonial expeditions. On this altar, beside the symbol of the church, were a photograph of André Matswa, a dagger of ancestral workmanship and an oil lamp which burned constantly, like the flame of the Holy Sacrament. In the background loomed an enormous V carved of wood and holding between its arms the cross of Lorraine. The motif, painted this time, was also repeated on the partition supporting the altar, together with symbols for the star and the cock. This was the main part of the symbolic equipment.

No one can deny that there has been an attempt at purification with respect to ancient rituals requiring numerous instruments, material representations, and manipulations. Indeed, Nganga Emmanuel has led recent campaigns for the destruction of "fetishes" and related objects. Drawing his inspiration from the unadorned Christianity of the Protestants who unwittingly initiated the Congolese movements, he has tried to found a cult divested of any appearance of "savagery." But this impoverished symbolism nevertheless constitutes a language which reveals the founders' intentions and suggests the reasons for their success.

The V anticipates reality by celebrating the victory to be won over poverty and suffering by the believers, who are known among themselves as *bana-bansana* (orphan children). They have adopted Churchill's wartime sign, turning it against us to predict the end of our domination. The cross of Lorraine carries the idea of material power and the ability to conquer in the face of defeat. The star, according to Nganga Emmanuel, represents "God illuminating the world;" it affirms the divine omnipresence and stands for the protection of which the true believer is at every moment assured. The cock refers to Peter, founder of the Church of Christ, and reminds the faithful of the necessity of resisting any force that might betray the Negro Savior. The antique dagger stands for the loyalty sworn to the ancestors, as well as the piety due to these allies who are forever indispensable to the welfare of the living; it expresses the promise to restore to the Congolese tribes their former glory. The symbolism of the color red, represented by the old barter blankets covering the altar and by certain scarves with pointed ends, is one of the most powerful; formerly associated with blood and fecundity, prestige and authority, it is now linked with the idea of the martyrdom of the Congolese Saviors and their disciples, the idea of revolt.

These last themes occur frequently in the "messages" and songs composed from the early days of messianism. Beyond expressions of suffering endured and complaints of the state of isolation and weakness of the Congolese people, courage and hope are found in the refusal to submit. In general, these sacred texts constitute a literature of resistance whose themes are borrowed from Christianity. They announce the "good news," the ultimate victory of native messiahs and the Negro church. The joy of this expectation erases the sadness expressed so repeatedly over the theme of miserable solitude.

Some of the prophecies that circulated around 1930, a period of tension between Europeans and Congolese, formulated very definite intentions; but as events later showed, they carried a kind of verbal satisfaction rather than a provocation to open an immediate revolt. Still, their tone alarmed and occasioned a reinforcement of police supervision.

War is imminent. By the beginning of the rainy season, perhaps. . . . We hereby announce Gods' glad tidings to the whole world. Those who belong to our church are forbidden to speak to those connected with the Government or the Missions or those who have remained in the shadows. The time of red blood is come. . . . Those who rise up shall enter into the glory of the victorious kingdom. . . .

The whites do not know that they shall find death and destruction in a foreign land. The buffalo and the elephant are powerful animals which can do any labor because of the size of their bodies. They are as strong as Goliath. But they lack the intelligence to make ready the paths and roads of their departure. The death of the elephant and the buffalo is at hand. The liberation will be final.

And again: "The lizard has laid her eggs, but she has been killed and her eggs have been kept by others who will bring forth the young."

Although these allusions employ a traditional mode of expression, they need no commentary. Messages comparable in their wording and content have circulated in the last few years. They express a truth which is still alive, and to which we must attend. The allegories are intended as much for us as they are for the members of the Congolese church.

I asked Nganga Emmanuel to show me the most recent of these writings. He declined, explaining that they were only to be found around Boko. Instead, he transcribed one of the religious songs which had become so popular that it was hummed even in the Negro sections of Brazzaville. It was a disturbing and painful cry for help.

We others who have no support,
We others who have no defender:
God, all-powerful father, watch over us!
Father Congo, father, who will remember us!
We others, who will remember us?
Matswa, all-powerful father, watch over us.
Matswa, all-powerful father, send us a defender. . . .

The young man in the cap left suddenly; Nganga Emmanuel continued to conduct my visit. He showed me the white, red and black robes that he wore for different services; each had a meaning—joy, glorious martyrdom, mourning—which harmonized with the tone of each ceremony. An outer garment corresponding to the chasuble of the Catholic priest and embroidered with the motif of the V and the cross, was worn over these sacerdotal vestments. Nganga Emmanuel put them on and as if suddenly inspired, he described the "beauty" of the Sunday Mass:

"The people enter the chapel silently. The women are veiled in the manner of nuns. We light all the candles . . . the congregation kneels and the prayers begin. The *bitanguis,* the choirboys, recite the opening words and the congregation responds. . . . I give a sermon to remind them of the rules of conduct. I ask our Saviors to protect us and give us strength to resist evil. . . . I lead the hymns. . . ."

The young man had returned with a crudely carved straight flute in his hand. At a nod of approval from Nganga Emmanuel he began to play a sad melody composed around a short theme which was repeated interminably. He stopped and said:

"That is the hymn of our church. Do you want to hear the words?"

And he took up this lament, which affected me in a completely physical way:

We are the orphan children.
Brothers, weep!

Our father Matswa came to die for us,
For love of us!

Nganga Emmanuel took me to his house, a modest dwelling in no way differentiated from the others. He showed me into the central room, a kind of parlor containing a few rudimentary pieces of furniture, whose walls were covered with symbols of the new religion. In the end he revealed the principles governing the organization of his church. At the top was the leader of the communities (*mfoumou boundou*). He was paired with a leader of the women who corresponded to the old "heads" of lineages in the traditional social system. Each of the villages under the authority of the church had a head, curiously referred to as the "help," who was responsible for religious education, collective ceremonies and assistance to "brothers" in trouble. It also had a feminine counterpart, the "head mother" (*mamma mfoumou*), complete with a traditional title of respectful attention, who guided the women and saw to the material welfare of young initiates. The latter, referred to as "guardian children," were assembled into groups patterned after scout troops and also recalling the old initiatory fraternities. The young members, in groups of a dozen, underwent a periodic instruction at the Galamboma mission which served as an elementary political education as well as a preparation for religious activities.

Thus all the elements of Bakongo society tend to be incorporated into this system, which was similarly conceived by its various founders. The traditional principles governing social relations have been utilized to ensure the exclusive predominance of the church over and above differences of clan, generation and social status. The church tends to enforce a kind of "unique clan" based on the martyrdom of the two Congolese "saviors:" like the single party in certain modern societies, it seeks to impose unity. In the literature which has evolved in the past few decades, André Matswa and Simon Kimbangu are referred to as "Kings of the Congo." They are becoming symbols of unity. They serve as pretexts for the establishment of a religious administration which aspires to political power.

In much of Central Africa, which includes large sections of the two Congos and Angola, Christianity has played a role of unintentional collective emancipation. In monotheism it has contributed a principle of unification. It has provided the example of a Messiah who, sacrificed by the public powers as a

221

common criminal, triumphs over the authorities to the infinite joy of the believers. It has brought all the revolutionary force it possessed at the time of its origins, together with the expectation inherited from Jewish messianism.

The mind stands amazed before this case of history repeating itself after two thousand years. Despite the great distance in time, similar social positions endured by peoples at a comparable level of civilization are producing very similar reactions. The analogy becomes even more apparent when one rereads Max Weber's *Ancient Judaism*. Here we find the same insurrection of prophets against the established powers, the same desire to unify and build a nation, and finally, the same messianic hope rising in the face of a domination that has become intolerable. The comparison can be carried further. Because of this uplifting experience, the Bakongo people regard themselves as a chosen race favored of the gods. They find in it a reason for confidence and new strength, a determination to impose their will upon other Congolese tribes. Their passion for unity overflows their boundaries and arouses the mistrust of their neighbors, a mistrust which sometimes develops into violent opposition, as has occurred during several electoral campaigns.

After my visit to Galamboma, I did not see Nganga Emmanuel until I was leaving the area, having concluded the first phase of my research. He was wearing the same costume decorated with symbols indicating his eminent position in the church. He was accompanied by several young disciples all sporting the distinctive scarf—red, and embroidered with symbolic motifs—around their necks. As the truck started, he waved goodbye and charged me with a mission which was later to cause me trouble:

"Tell what you have seen. The truth is enough. Tell them in Brazzaville that we want a place to build our cathedral. . . ."

In the three districts around Brazzaville, I was able to contact the heads of the "centers" founded by the prophets. The phenomenon, although it took different forms, was similar everywhere. In the more modernized regions, which partly coincided with the zones of Protestant influence, the movement was better organized, better prepared to operate on the level of political opposition and therefore more anxious to stay underground in order to survive. In other areas, the reaction it channeled retained a primarily religious flavor. It was above all a liberation from Christianity, in which case it sometimes gave

222

rise to a spiritual adventure characterized by difficult retreats.

I had the good fortune to come across an account written by a believer who, exhausted, had renounced his faith after "receiving religion" at a center located some thirty-five miles from the capital. Here is the text as it is:

Before being admitted to the order, I was taken and placed between two posts which marked the site of purification. My arms were held by two catechumens while a third beat me on the back with a stick. The place where this correction occurred was called "Calvary." When this operation was over, and we had returned to the center, the leader of the group promised to baptize me at the end of my stay. The baptism was performed in a pond located some distance away. All the believers had given up bathing for several months as a sacrifice. An enormous layer of filth coated their skin and gave off a suffocating odor. Their hair and nails had not been cut.

Morning and evening, prayers were recited communally. The leader gave a sermon every day, using the text of the Gospels. Then, with hands raised to heaven, he invoked the names of André Matswa and Simon Kimbangu. For long hours the initiates sang religious songs. All the candles were lit. From time to time one of the initiates would run off. He was possessed and guided by the invisible Spirit of God and his two Saviors. This running would continue for from thirty to forty-five minutes; when the man returned, he would come and tell the leader what he had "caught" during his hunt.

This accurate account of a genuine "spiritual hunt," which seems to be a variant of sacred possession, reveals the persistence of an old initiatory theme along with obvious Christian contributions. All the techniques of psychological influence including mortification of the flesh are thus added to reinforce the effects of these contributions. In many centers the rituals use a ceremonial copied from the missionary churches together with spectacular procedures peculiar to the traditional religions. I have already described the first aspect. To give an idea of the second, I shall describe a meeting held by one of the groups in the vicinity of Boko which I was permitted to attend.

The gathering took place near some old tombs scattered in the bush. Only candles and storm lanterns illuminated the place and the assembly of believers. In spite of my presence, the priest did not hesitate to deliver a sermon of unmistakable violence in which he predicted the imminent disappearance of "imported" religions, asked the people to pray for the elimination of the missions, and foretold the end of white domination and the coming to power of the leaders of the Negro church. Next, he led some religious songs very similar to those already discussed. These preliminaries, which seemed interminable, were followed by a communal practice intended to inflict a real psychological shock, an ordeal well suited to cause the revolt of the entire organism. The priest went over to the tombs, carrying some long rods of a very soft wood which he drove into the damp earth "far enough to touch the dead;" after each of these soundings, he broke and pressed the stalks to extract a bit of sap and water. One at a time, the believers were summoned to drink a few drops of this liquid in which the mud had been diluted. I can still see them, tense, contracted in their struggle against the disgust and fear aroused by this direct contact with their ancestors. Christian communion had been changed into this formidable test which represented not only a way of communicating with the dead and therefore obtaining strength, but also a pledge of loyalty to the dead. The believers were obligated to remain in the church by the most powerful and binding of oaths.

After renewing this bond and leading the congregation to the verge of exaltation, the priest gave the signal for the sacred dance. Men and women formed two facing rows as in the ancient choreography. But the imaginary sexual act no longer determined the advance of the sexes toward one another: the partners sought only that state of grace which is surrender to the embrace of the Spirit. The dancers began to tremble from head to foot, to move convulsively, and to stare into space. The order of the dance had been broken. Men and women ran in all directions, yielding to an outside force which overpowered them and seized control of their movements. A young girl fell suddenly, struggled and crawled on the ground, howling. The priest calmed her by a simple laying on of hands, demonstrating his impressive power.

A hold so complete cannot fail to mystify and disturb. The Negro church has brought about what three-quarters of a century of colonization has failed to achieve. It has pursued modern goals—for it desires the progress of Bakongo country and wants to control the means of obtaining it—while at the same time respecting the most African ways of living, thinking and feeling. It has spoken a language suited to the cultural level of Congolese peoples and has made innovations without upsetting the familiar sociological landscape. It has aroused enthusiasm by strongly opposing colonial domination and by trying to reconstruct a society torn apart by conflicting civilizations and by its chaotic history of the past two centuries. The founders of the movement have helped to bring about a recovery of confidence and a reorganization of Bakongo society.

The rod which is sanctified in the cemetery and which the believers retain throughout the dance is, curiously enough, regarded as a defense against the atomic bomb. It is said that waving it in the air can cause the fall of an attacking plane. We must see this as something other than "primitive" naïveté or a surrender to the illusion of magical thinking. Nobody is deceived by such a statement. It is not to be taken literally; the believers are trying to show that they are not as impressed by our material power as they once were. They are aware that it is possible to resist our domination in spite of our equipment and technology. Promises of liberation are often accompanied by statements announcing the impending arrival of industrial civilization and praising the ability of the Congolese to produce the objects they now possess "only with their eyes." The Negro church is not content to show its "elect" the way to a remote Kingdom of God; it wants to found a new society in which Negroes will have greater wealth and independence. It believes that the Kingdom of God may also be of this world.

The ambiguity which characterizes such a movement is apparent. The most responsible leaders have a clear awareness of the modern objectives which condition the progress of the Congo, and do not lose sight of them. To obtain a large following, however, they are forced into a compromise which accords too much importance to traditional attitudes and practices. This accounts for a success which the leaders of political parties do not, therefore, enjoy. It also entails an undeniable weakness; the exaggeration of the religious aspect threatens to lead to a kind of collective mysticism, a contemplative passivity which several leaders are beginning to mistrust. The respect for ancient practices threatens to favor the most conservative elements, which advocate a return to the past as the only way to recover lost happiness and security. At every moment unanimity is born of ambiguity, an ambiguity which is favored by the fact that every Bakongo is living in the expectation of a change and becoming increasingly impatient to reject foreign tutelage. Future reactions might lead to the primitive violence of men who end by preferring disorder to an "immobilism" which has become intolerable by aggravating their material and cultural deprivation, men who find compensation for inferiority only in xenophobia.

On the eve of my departure from Brazzaville, after I had written up the results of my research, I was to add a final document to my notes. It was a prayer with a theme of lamentation which I heard while strolling beside the Congo, seeking a final image for the splendor of its waters:

"The Negro is bound, but the white man is not. The invaders bind the Negroes and bring them endless suffering. They have bound Kimbangu and Matswa. But they can do nothing against them. Oh! Jesus Matswa, our Savior, come and defend our people."

I have not played up an exceptional case; my stay in Gabon enabled me to study comparable phenomena in connection with the Bwiti cult, which is most widespread in the south but extends to the frontiers of Cameroon. In discussing the reactions of the Fang, I have repeatedly alluded to this belief which has modernized an ancient Gabonese ritual.

On a borrowed foundation—the originators being the Mitshogo, a tribe whose traditional institutions are still preserved—the Fang have built a composite religion which revives lore and myths in process of disappearing. This religion serves as a sort of cultural conservatory and tries to provide the answers to several urgent questions, beginning with those raised by Christianity. The Bwiti is emerging as a rival faith, adapted to the needs of the Negroes in their relations with the sacred and opposed to missionary control. It competes with Catholicism and Protestantism, even though it is patterned after them in part. In the myth of foundation, Christ appears, then the Virgin Mary, who becomes identified with the First Woman and mother of mankind, then certain saints or angels, who replace the old individual guardians. The idea of salvation is adopted. It offers not only the hope of a reward after death, but also the certainty of acquiring the knowledge that assures control of material riches. Thus we recognize the twofold ambition already expressed by the Congolese movement: the desire to escape hardship and alienation in this world as in the next. But missionary Christianity also provides a model of church organization to which the founders of the Bwiti have referred in estab-

226

lishing a network of parishes, a hierarchy and a sacerdotal officialdom which enable them to emphasize the "civilized" character of their undertaking, and to influence villagers who have become detached as a result of the relaxation of ancient social ties. So that in one sense the cult reveals a concern to combine the need for religious innovation with incitements to reconstruct Fang society and civilization. Insofar as it represents a renewal of initiative, the Bwiti is opposed to colonial domination. It expresses the Africans' right to plan their future as they wish. It figures in the area of modern political struggles. During the elections to the French Assembly, the opponent of the official candidate was a man who owed part of his prestige to his eminent position in the Bwiti church.

This new faith exerts an undesirable attraction in several districts. It creates outlets for intense energies and demands those extreme psychological experiences which the Negro likes periodically to undergo. It demands a complete transformation of the self, a liberation from a standardized and difficult existence. It restores order and confidence where the forces of disorganization—and hence of insecurity—have flourished.

I attended an exhilarating all-night ceremony in one of the largest temples in southern Gabon. The rectangular building, built in imitation of the guardhouse that defended the old Fang village, was decorated with wreaths of braided palm leaves and oriflammes. The pole painted with esoteric motifs which supported the building near the doorway, and the altar in the back leaning against a room which served as a "sacristy," had been renovated. A large central fire lent its glow and its play of shadows. These three elements constituted the sacred poles around which the whole ceremony was organized. A few storm lanterns hung on the walls. The temple was full: on one side were the women, each of whom was dressed in a simple white garment that fitted tightly across the breast, and on the other the men, who had abandoned their European clothing for the short loincloth which was better suited to the dance. All were waiting with an amazing tranquillity which seemed akin to meditation. The women held in their hands the rattles which they used to beat time to the songs and movements of the peculiar choreography. I was consumed by an impatience I could hardly contain. Anxiety seized me, for I feared that once again I should have to restrain myself to resist this contagious release, this sacred frenzy which must be about to erupt.

The priest and his assistants had made their preparations in a

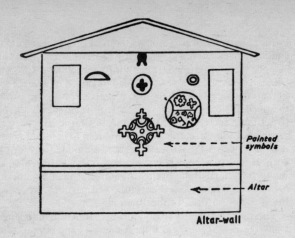

Painted symbols

Altar

Altar-wall

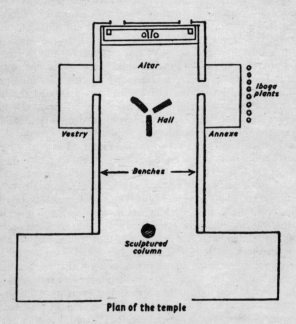

Altar

Iboga plants

Hall

Vestry

Annexe

Benches

Sculptured column

Plan of the temple

Fig. 50 Plan of an old Bwiti temple and elevation of end wall

private place. They had shared a concoction made from the grated rind of a plant named *ibo'a (Tabernanthe iboga)*, a hallucinogen and aphrodisiac. Their interminable dancing would reinforce these effects and carry them all, so they said, to the frontiers of true understanding and to the sources of power.

A confused uproar was heard from outside. Voices rose, drowning out all sounds of the village. The priest appeared, surrounded by his servants. I hardly recognized these men whom I had visited in the course of their everyday lives. They were wearing garments of tiger-cat and monkey skin over their *cache-sexes* or raffia loincloths. Their faces, which had been smeared with dye and covered with symbolic marks, were framed by headdresses of brightly colored feathers. They leaped and ran in all directions, holding lighted torches in their hands. They were performing a purification by fire before opening the ceremony.

Then the dance began around each of the poles dominating the architecture of the temple—a series of jumps, stamps, leaps and movements which might be described as compulsive. The torsos of the men streamed with sweat and their muscles stood out under the play of the lights. From time to time one of them rushed over to a pail of water, drank great draughts, and then resumed his intoxication motion. The congregation sang and accompanied the priest by dancing in place. The women shook their rattles, the only instruments which provided an occasional musical accompaniment. The rhythm accelerated. The group had become a single creature, tensed for an impossible victory. I felt profoundly foreign, separate, trapped by my human dignity, encumbered by a body which had lost even the memory of its glorious potentialities. I felt like a kind of cripple to whom no one could pay the slightest attention.

There was a lull. Two of the priest's servants walked to either side of the fire and sat down upon carved wooden footstools whose crossed spiral supports had a religious significance as well as an aesthetic value; both were motionless and massive. The faithful ceased their movements. One of the initiates went and stood beside the altar. He was holding an eight-stringed harp gleaming with sacrificial blood, a symbol of the First Woman.

The master of the cult walked alone to the center of the temple. He advanced cautiously, reciting a prayer in a very low voice to the rustling accompaniment of the lightly shaken rattles. Suddenly, becoming bolder, he began to move and his

229

voice rang out. He invoked Bwiti, creator of all things, holder of all the secrets man can hope to possess. He sang. The harp added its shrill voice to his chant. Again and again he demanded the revelation. His arms yearned toward the invisible presence. He seemed exhausted. And then he fell back, as if drunk with love, repeating the name of his god in a moan of sexual fulfilment:

"Bwiti . . . Bwiti . . . Bwiti . . ."

With a start, he recovered himself. The dance began again with all the faithful joining in; it was wild and violent, a mad pursuit of new visions.

Late that night I slipped away. The singing and the noise carried to my house. They invaded me, banishing sleep, stopping only when the village cocks announced the break of day.

What does our civilization offer that is capable of arousing a fervor of this kind, an involvement spelling adventure for the body as well as for the mind? Our churches put inner life and moral principle ahead of that exaltation which leads to the threshold of unconsciousness. They seem cold, devoid of supernatural presence, ill-suited to impassioned communion. In the eyes of the villagers the missionaries are so many "wet blankets" in the celebration of the fulfilment of man and the glory of the gods.

There is a point we have overlooked in our dealings with Africa. Civilizations which have little or no recourse to writing and books have produced intellectual activities and lyrical expressions which we are ill-equipped to understand. The word and the gesture take on an importance which we underestimate, a seriousness which is almost sacred. A few schools and missions have not changed this state of things. When we deprive the Negro of those means of expression which really belong to him, we are imposing the heaviest of penalties, such as the French would have known if the occupying forces had refused all permission to write, sing or paint, and transformed us into mere machines of production. But this is not all. At the same moment that the African found himself culturally dispossessed, he was placed in an economic system for which he was in no way prepared; he was projected into enterprises in which he became an anonymous working force. This obliteration of the personal touch in everyday life and in dealings with things reinforced our attack on Negro civilizations.

Such observations help to explain the intensity of the reactions I am describing. I can still remember one of my young

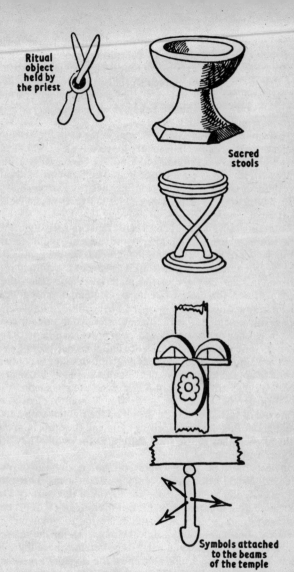

Ritual object held by the priest

Sacred stools

Symbols attached to the beams of the temple

Fig. 51 Objects from a Bwiti temple

Fang informants—the man who introduced me to the Bwiti cult—expressing his anger with a disturbing violence. He was under the stress of an extreme agitation. His eyes glowed with a fire that nothing could extinguish. This scene took place as I was leaving. He was wondering all of a sudden whether I had simply been playing with this belief which was his *raison d'être*. He was almost shouting:

"You must help us become as strong as the Catholics. Do not forget that Bwiti knows how to take his revenge. . . . They cannot stop us from worshipping our God. We have a religion like other people; why are we persecuted? The Spaniards kill our members in Guinea. The missionaries destroy our relics. . . . Who has the right to deny us the chance to live as we choose? It must be stopped."

Opposing movements. Terrifying storms are brewing in Africa, storms which threaten to have the suddenness and devastating power of the convulsions that are shaking the continent. The Negroes are even more painfully aware of the cultural dispossession than they are of the material dispossession they have suffered for the past century. Contemporary political leaders cannot ignore this "slow and irresistible, humble and savage movement" toward a life not fashioned to suit our convenience. They depend on this force to provide an impetus for their demand for real independence and their need for power. They are adjusting their methods of action in order to confuse us and to appeal to the most traditionalist among the Africans. The "enlightened" leaders of Kenya who are channeling the anti-British rebellion known as the Mau Mau movement have made use of such procedures: they bind the fighters with a traditional but singularly compelling oath, and they proclaim the right of the tribes to use their culture as they will. They are playing with fire.

In his book on the young Ghana, the American Negro writer Richard Wright offers some very significant ideas. The man who is currently responsible for the destiny of this country, Dr. Nkrumah, told him that only three or four members of his entourage were capable of understanding what is "going on" in the area of economic and political change. As for the masses who gave the governmental party its power, they have literally been seduced. They drunkenly repeat the slogan, "Freedom! Freedom! Freedom!" whose immediate significance to them is the freedom to be African without shame. They are bound by oaths which have all the force of the old pledges. They idealize their leader, attributing to him all the qualities of a Messiah and a worker of miracles and seeing him as the "Redeemer," the "African Mahatma," the "gateway to the future of Africa." The intellectuals educated in English universities remain aloof, but they form only a meager opposition.

Old Africa carries all its weight in spite of obvious modernizations, in those countries marked by our influence as in the others. In Mali the political parties have had to come to terms with a powerful initiatory society known as Komo. In Guinea and the Ivory Coast, in the highlands, the "African Democratic Assembly" has consolidated its hold through a comparable association, the Poro. Prophets are appearing and their passion is stronger than the tailor-made elites and the other traces of a civilization which has exported the idea of tolerance without knowing how to be tolerated.

▼▼▼▼▼▼▼▼▼▼▼▼▼▼▼▼▼▼▼▼▼▼▼▼▼▼▼▼▼▼▼▼▼▼▼

TODAY, with the perspective of the intervening years, what images come to mind at those moments when an inner necessity makes me long for Africa? Images of places I love, places that reveal the magnificence of the sea or the rivers. Above all, images of faces. In Africa there are no monuments and few works of art capable of making a lasting impression on the mind of a foreigner. Negro civilizations present a certain style of life rather than a certain style of art. They have not built for posterity; they have preserved a perpetual present. It has taken the upheavals caused by colonization, the need for freedom, and the discovery of the possibilities of a better life to make them decide to rush toward the future.

It is the faces themselves that clearly reveal the riches, the hopes and the vicissitudes of these civilizations. The African crowd is the only book where these are described with all the illustrations one could desire.

Going backward in time a great distance, I find the image of Masamba Sek, an old Lebou chief whose guest I was in the village of Grand Mbao. It would be difficult to guess his age, but he himself claimed to be close to eighty. A tiny man who still dressed in magnificent *boubous,* he impressed me with his upright bearing and natural dignity. He was so amazingly alert

234

that one forgot his extreme age and fragility. When he appeared in the little streets on his way to the *pinetye,* the social center, the villagers kept their distance and showed him an absolute deference. His fine, elongated face, surprisingly free of wrinkles, with its dark eyes which could be both inquisitive and mysterious, had a real distinction. A white beard, worn short, completed the picture. I could not help but be impressed and respectful.

Masamba was grateful to me, or so I thought, for not taking a condescending attitude toward him. He visited me often at my headquarters in the village school. A few weeks after my arrival, he expressed a desire to spend an evening with me in the presence of a few notables. I looked forward to this meeting with some apprehension: I was sure it would be another of those stilted and artificial social occasions. I had arranged a few floor mats so that we could sit down in the traditional manner. I had bought cola nuts and prepared coffee and tea.

I can still see those men arriving, lined up behind their chief, all decked out as if for some solemn event, silent and ill at ease. I was careful to greet Masamba with the appropriate gesture, clasping his right hand in both mine throughout the exchange of civilities. I saw in his eyes a pleasure he could hardly contain: the pleasure of no longer finding himself stripped of his prestige before a white man. He began to explore my room, marveling over my things and uttering those repeated exclamations with which I had become so familiar: *o ah, o ah, o ah.* . . . I realized suddenly that these villagers, who lived a few miles from Dakar, were probably encountering for the first time what might be called the intimacy of European life. Our houses had never been open to their eyes as theirs had been to our curiosity. Seldom if ever had they enjoyed those disinterested contacts, free of any professional demands or desire to impress, which permit a friendly encounter and a mutual understanding.

My guests sat down on the mats and munched the cola nuts, after breaking them into small pieces; we made a scene that was startling in its unreality. None of us found the necessary spontaneity, because our effort was too atypical of customary intercourse between Negroes and whites. I was afraid of showing that exaggerated solicitude which does not deceive the Negro; they were afraid of becoming involved in some plan designed to take them in. Masamba expressed renewed concern over the purpose of my research. He tended to see it as a

235

subtler—because more indirect—form of the administrative inquisition. Then he questioned me about France, asking how fishing was done, what species of fish were caught, and what the herds were like. He revealed the daily preoccupations of the Lebou villager, but he was skeptical of the indications I gave him of our greater efficiency. He reacted by expressing polite surprise. When I explained the technical reasons for this comparative success, he replied that equipment and knowledge are not enough to ensure success; one also needs the approval of God and the genies. We had reached an impasse. A century of artificial relations, maintained for fear of jeopardizing our domination, had done little to bring about a meeting of the minds.

As he was about to leave, Masamba cast a final glance over my furnishings. He was intrigued by my army cot and by the Sudanese blanket that covered it. He immediately made a veiled request that surprised me:

"I like that. It would be good for a chief like me."

The remark did not conceal the intention that motivated it. Several times already the old man had solicited monetary gifts. How was one to reconcile his undeniable dignity with the reactions of the experienced con-man? I know that even in the case of such an ordinary event, our points of view were radically different. Masamba had no passion for material wealth. His home was modest, more barren than our poorest interiors. He had all the property—heads of cattle—and wives necessary to maintain his prestige. He was able to satisfy his taste for the clothing that constituted his social facade. Was his demand for gifts then merely the whim of a chief accustomed to an absolute claim upon the property of his dependents? Was he a victim of that illusion that sees every European as a rich man and therefore bound to generosity toward everyone he meets? Did he imagine that an exchange of gifts was the only guarantee of relations that were friendly, or merely free of evil intentions? I do not know, but I do not believe that in the present case greed is a good explanation.

Masamba Sek baffled me further with other ambiguous aspects of his personality. Besides being a political leader, he was the head of the Moslem religion. He seemed enthusiastic about this, trying to sustain the fervor of the faithful and encouraging parents to send their children to the Koranic school. He had built a modern mosque which was an eloquent monument to his piety. But he had neglected to deepen his understanding of Islam, so that certain notables were able to accuse him publicly of not making the rituals conform to the Law's requirements. He derived a profit from neighboring palm plantations by supervising the sale of palm wine, and at the same time he proscribed the consumption of alcoholic beverages. He tolerated the marginal cults preserved by the women and did not hesitate to turn to them when circumstances required unusual measures. Hence his apparent rigorism in the area of religion was in fact softened by numerous indulgences.

The old chief, whom I encountered in the early days of my ethnological career, remains for me a symbol of the enigmas which Africa eternally presents to the inquisitive foreigner. Behavior which he believes to be simple conceals motives and justifications which transcend his familiar frame of reference. Behind the indifference of ordinary people or the imperturbable dignity of notables lurk uncertainties and anxieties, tricks by means of which delicate balances may be preserved. All of which begins to become clear when one realizes the contradictory influences that have been endured and the vicissitudes of a history which does not have the honor of appearing in books.

I can still see Masamba Sek as he was when he came to see me off, standing proudly beside the small square facing the mosque and the schools. He was wearing a *boubou* of a heavy embroidered fabric and a black fez. He made an almost imperceptible gesture of farewell. Beside him and a little further back Diop Maguette, my former guide, was the image of the new generation in his battered felt hat, badly patched shorts, and T shirt hanging over his belt. An enormous pair of worn-out shoes hung like two millstones below his skinny legs; an image of poverty as well. My memory has preserved this study in contrast along with the picture of a band of children racing after the disappearing car.

I remember Madera, my assistant at Conakry, with a vividness that he cannot possible imagine. He met me at the port in 1947 when I had left Dakar after a difficult convalescence in an indescribable battleship which had been converted into a sort of floating caravanserai. The minute I laid my eyes on him I knew we would be friends. His relaxed manner of the young modern African appealed to me. I liked his glance, which was direct and free of servility, and the efficiency with which he handled the red tape presented by a large administration with complicated and discouraging demands. I fondly recall the features of his finely chiseled candid face, which was illuminated

237

by an intelligence I later came to respect. He was always beside me, quiet, efficient and friendly, whenever my role of pioneer in colonial scientific research led me to despair of success.

I have already said that our offices occupied part of a quarantine station that was still inhabited by incurable or dangerously contagious invalids. It was a gallery of physical degradation: madmen screamed in their cells while others covered the walls with incredible graffiti; lepers dragged themselves along in their filthy and bloodstained bandages; smallpox victims with their thick and crackled skin waited, shivering in the sun, to die. A few days after I moved in, Madera came to tell me that a man had died right under our windows. We watched for the arrival of the "detail" of prisoners who removed the body, wrapping it in a mat, and walked casually to the adjacent cemetery. It was simple, too simple. I was shocked and disgusted. Madera seemed indifferent. I tried to question him. The tragic and pitiful quality of this scene hardly affected him; he was quicker to condemn, with restrained severity, the absurdity of our interventions in the face of the calamities that befall the Negro.

At this moment I was keenly aware of the immoderate and exaggerated quality of our reactions to death when compared with those of peoples who are considered less civilized. Christianity has done little to help us accept more serenely this transition to final dissolution. When Madera lost his eldest daughter to a disease as fatal as it was mysterious, I tried to express my sympathy and grief. He replied, "It is mainly for the mother that this death is terrible." I decided to attend the little girl's burial. I joined the procession, a long line of men following the corpse which had been wrapped in a blanket and a mat, as it approached the cemetery. A few minutes later the body was lowered into a shallow ditch and covered with earth, while the spectators droned prayers from the Koran; then the crowd disappeared. We are shocked by such rapidity in dealing with death, such apparent inability to feel. We are baffled by this division of labor which leaves tears to the women and entrusts to the men the duty of conducting a short and hurried ceremony. One must remember, of course, that Islam has been responsible for an impoverishment of ritual. But this has only reinforced the impression of greater impassiveness made by the African confronting death. He accepts death, while we struggle against it, as we do against every challenge that nature presents. Also, his expression of grief lacks that spontaneity and devastating quality we know. It is codified and ordered in accordance with collective concerns rather than individual "cases." However, this does not give us the right to accuse the Negro of insensibility. The crises of existence and the expression of emotion vary from one civilization to another as much as the restrictions imposed by the prevailing morality. The observation is commonplace, but we are all too inclined to forget it.

The same honesty that he demonstrated in his work and his personal relations Madera brought to his duties as a man who was educated and therefore more aware of current African problems. I never saw him behave in an arbitrary manner toward the personnel under him. He was neither tyrannical nor capable of corruption. He had a highly developed sense of duty and justice.

He did not take advantage of circumstances to carve a rapid and compromising political career. He joined the ranks of the opposition because he did not want to dissociate his interests from those of the masses. The pleasant home which he shared with his wife, a young schoolteacher, was open to everyone. Through them I met some of the Guinean partisans—enthusiastic, noble, confused and eloquent men reminiscent of nineteenth-century French Republicans. I never won their complete confidence—after all, I was still the white man, the *Toubab*— but I received the maximum possible sympathy in a situation not altogether favorable to spontaneous cordiality. I still remember those picturesque meetings held in front of Madera's home, when a colorful and joyous crowd would honor recently elected political leaders with singing and dancing. Mamba Sano was just beginning his parliamentary career. He was full of plans, promises and ideals. He reminded me of those popular representatives who came to power in the early days of the French Republic. His admirers would deafen him with their songs; they wore pictures of their spokesman pinned on their clothing.

Madera could be very hard on the old aristocracies and administrative leaders. From my notebook I quote a passage from his indictment: "These men can be more cruel to the Negroes than any of your whites of the old school. They impose their will through force. They take advantage of their power to increase their wealth. They are bought and they buy in turn. They corrupt. . . ."

These remarks are far from unique. I have heard them else-

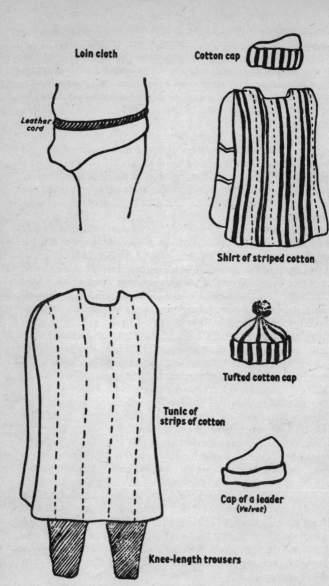

Loin cloth

Cotton cap

Leather cord

Shirt of striped cotton

Tufted cotton cap

Tunic of strips of cotton

Cap of a leader (Velvet)

Knee-length trousers

Fig. 52 Male dress of the Kono area

where. I encountered them again a few years later when I was studying Ghana and the popular subversion organized by Dr. Nkrumah, leader of the Convention People's Party and now prime minister of Ghana.

But I remember Madera above all for a few simple images. A man who revealed himself for the first time and quietly as a friend, sitting at my bedside when I had been taken to the hospital after an automobile accident. The only person who came to see me off when I left: Madera was standing helpless in the

Fig. 53 Decoration of a Kono hut: a masked figure

rain as I took a last look at that primitive and sinister Conakry airport. One day I learned that he had tried to locate me during a short trip to Paris. He left without succeeding, but later, although our respective circumstances had changed, we re-established the bond of friendship.

Old Africa is symbolized in my mind by a Negro peasant, Foroumo, who was my informal host in a small Kono village in that forest region which I have described at the juncture of Guinea, Liberia and the Ivory Coast. He was difficult to approach because of his suspicion and mistrust of language, by which one always runs the risk of being trapped. He recoiled before my indiscretions.

He was a man of about forty, short, thickset and muscular. His rather coarse, prematurely wrinkled face was modeled on a powerful bone structure which seemed about to protrude everywhere. Over his tight-fitting undergarments he wore the *bawi,* a kind of long robe made of strips of cotton woven in the

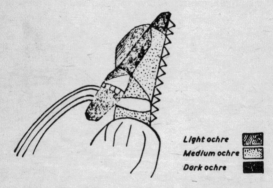

Light ochre	
Medium ochre	
Dark ochre	

Fig. 54 Detail of the head in figure 53

—village and open at the sides. On his head he wore a Phrygian-style cap of cotton, or velvet when the solemnity of the occasion required. His step was slow and heavy. He never seemed in a hurry, because the course of his days had been planned once and forever. He felt secure when he was enmeshed in the web of his habits.

I surprised him at dawn by gently raising the palm-leaf-vein door of his house. He groaned, stirred on his bed of dried earth, unwound his cocoon of covers and sat up rubbing his eyes. He recognized me and motioned me to enter. We exchanged the conventional morning greetings:

"*Bahou nya.*"

"*On e i bwa.*"

He shook himself for a moment. He squatted beside the hearth in the center of the single room, blew on the embers and waited, grumbling about his first wife: "Even the white man gets up before her!" He called out. In all the adjoining houses, I heard conversations being resumed, the sound of life struggling to recover its rhythm. Foroumo seized a jar of water, took several long swallows, and put it back with other pottery on a platform of dried earth which served as a sideboard.

Then came the slow procession of the members of the family, a litany of salutations to which Foroumo responded with an ill grace, for he was hungry. His youngest wife wanted to tell him about the dream she had just had, but he was not interested in her chatter. We took our places around a little enamel bowl containing the warmed-up left-overs of last night's meal. The peanut sauce was still excellent; my host expressed his approval by clicking his tongue.

He filled a pipe with some of his homegrown tobacco. He cursed himself: on his way out of the house, he had just bumped against the amulet which guarded the threshold. Was it a sign? Everyone was attentive. Did he want hot water for his toilet? No, he would bathe in the river, on the way. He decided to supervise the distribution of provisions. Certain nonbulky products were arranged on a shelf suspended from the ceiling of the house. Grain and vegetables were kept in an attic which the women reached by means of a thick notched branch which served as a stairway.

The children played in the "yard;" raised on makeshift stilts, they were happily engaged in imitating the antics of the "long" masker. Some young men arrived carrying a hoe; Foroumo had hired them to prepare his rather extensive fields in time. He demanded his implement. All walked off, talking loudly.

When I joined them for the midday meal a large strip of land had already been plowed and some girls had just brought the food. One of the young men was roasting yams in the coals. Foroumo was silent; he ate slowly, taking time to roll each morsel of food into a pellet. Someone volunteered a few news items. The village of Keoulenta was looking for drummers for the feast of excision. It was time to collect the gifts. It was a good thing the girls were going back to the old school; it would make them less arrogant and more serious. . . . Foroumo ordered his men back to work. The heat was oppressive. The men's bodies gleamed with sweat.

On the way back in the late afternoon, Foroumo complained of fatigue. "I am getting old," he said. But he felt that age brought respect, as well as restricting one's labors. As soon as we arrived he demanded two lounge chairs of braided raffia. He stretched out, asking for palm wine. Foroumo was a generous man: he had given a handsome *bangui*, highly appreciated in the region. Everyone savored this moment of silent relaxation. One of the young laborers, sitting cross-legged on the ground, mended his shirt, which he had torn in the underbrush. He lighted a cigarette, and passed it around after talking a puff. In the shadow of a house two girls were grinding grain in a mortar. They knew we were watching them; they threw themselves into the game of coquetry even as they were making fun of the men and uttering long shrill cries: *yi-i, yi-i. . . .*

When evening came, all the women busied themselves with the preparation of dinner. Foroumo had asked them to have plenty of food and not to spare the meat, for working in the fields made a man hungry. Once again, he ate in silence.

After dinner small groups formed. Voices became softer. Sounds were muffled. I tried to question Foroumo about the clan which made up a neighboring village, but he avoided the question.

"I cannot answer you. It would not be right. There is a chief and his followers down there. You should go and talk to them. . . ."

I tried to resume a line of questioning I had abandoned a few days earlier. It had to do with some unmanageable genies who interfered in human affairs, always with evil intentions. The *manllio hinega* knew how to change their shape, they were both bald and amazingly hairy, they attacked late travelers, beat them, robbed them and spit in their faces. But once again Foroumo refused.

"There are things one should not talk about at night."

Indeed, the darkness was all around us; it had invaded us, soothing and disquieting at the same time. Foroumo's young wife approached; she wanted to talk about the dream which he had refused to hear this morning and which had haunted her all day. They disappeared into the house; the door fell with a soft thud. I realized that behind this daily routine, this rural monotony, this surface calm in harmony with nature, lurked fears and anxieties from which the Negro freed himself with difficulty.

I am not trying to pick a face for each of the countries in which I have had occasion to pursue my studies; but for me Gabon, with its Herculean problems and its uncertainties, will always be symbolized by the features of M. To tell the truth, I had very little contact with this man; the local administration took a dim view of socializing with the principal leader of the opposition. I knew him primarily through his ethnographic studies on the Fang group to which he belonged and through the influence he exerted on a large part of the territory.

I went to see him in Libreville in the offices of a commerical company where he was employed. On first sight he impressed me as the typical businessman: European clothing, studied gestures, affected diction. A pronounced baldness, rare in Negroes, reinforced this impression by giving him the air of a benign and impoverished scholar. But the depression and anxiety which seemed to dominate him soon struck me. Slightly stoop-shouldered, he kept looking around as if he sensed danger. He avoided all specific questions. We decided to meet the next day in a bar.

An ugly, dubious-looking place overrun with flies, it had the advantage of being relatively empty at that time of the afternoon. M. was just as tense and suspicious as he had been the day before. He watched me, pretending to sip his drink slowly.

So this was the man who had been a source of official anxiety for the past ten years! I drew up the list of facts I had gleaned on various occasions. His education and his profound understanding of Fang culture had caused him to be chosen chief of a southern canton at the age of twenty. But he was not satisfied with this authority, which had been conferred on him by foreign hands. He took part in the introduction of the new cult, the Bwiti; he reached an eminent position in the "church" by trying to adapt it to contemporary needs. He was dismissed by the administration over a case of ritual murder; this was the beginning of an unequal battle which was still being waged. A bizarre idea came into my head: I tried to picture this anxious, unobtrusive, cautious man dressed in skins, with painted face, ready to spring to start the sacred dance. Which was his real face? The complexity of his personality has increased still further in recent years. There is an M. who is the modernist leader of the "Fang Congress" organized in 1947 by the local authorities. There is an M. who is the founder of a political party opposing the candidate enjoying official support. The two rivals confront one another less through controversy and debate than in a game of competing magics and "religions" which is far more dangerous. I found this amazing statement in an account of a former electoral campaign: "The rally was called off; the friends of M. had thrown too many magic obstacles in the path of his rival."

The bar in which we were sitting suddenly seemed not so much sordid as strange. We had made little progress. The conversation was dwelling on some problems of unwritten law which my companion had raised in two scholarly articles. I decided to come straight to the point:

"Can't we talk about something else?"

"That is difficult! I am afraid of word getting to the police; there is always someone listening. . . . You know my reputation. It is based largely on gossip."

"At least I'd like to know why you went into politics."

"You have been through Gabon, so you have seen what drives me to despair. The poverty of the Fang in the Ndjolé region cannot be ignored. And what about Coco Beach? Such misery leads to the degradation of not caring whether one lives or dies."

I hesitated before asking a question to which I wanted a clear answer.

"Why is your behavior so ambivalent? You're the one behind the Bwiti, behind the clannic movement, behind the 'Interracial Gabonese Committee'. . . ."

M. began to laugh. It was the first time I had seen him lose his solemnity. But I knew this African laugh; it was a way of getting out of a tight spot, part of the strategy of evasion. I was sure my hopes would be frustrated.

"Let's just say that one should use the appropriate terminology . . . I would rather talk about the Bwiti from the ethnological point of view. This would be closer to your professional interests."

Disappointed, I let myself get involved in a learned controversy. However, his explanation of the purpose of the cult provided a partial answer.

"It is in the realm of religion that our civilizations must for the moment resist. Christianity robs us of our originality. . . . For the old ancestral cults, which did not unite us, we have substituted this movement from Libreville to the frontier of Cameroon. We must band together; from this, progress will come. The familial religions of yesterday divided us. They were destroyed by the missionaries; there is no point in reviving them."

As I watched my companion walk off, his weary step took on a new meaning. I saw him as a man weighed down by the task he had undertaken, a solitary rebel, discouraged by the deceptions it obliged him to practice. In glorifying "race," in stirring up religious passions and the desire for illusory revelations, in permitting a return to religious rigors, did he realize that he was playing with fire? Wasn't he bothered by the different roles he was playing, roles which together represented the various ages of Africa? Such problems ought to have overwhelmed him. On the other hand, I felt that our Western psychological structure is infinitely more vulnerable, so accustomed are we to think and act in only one register. In the course of my inquiries in the interior of Gabon, I came to realize the prestige this man enjoyed with the old as well as the new generations. His very ambiguity was responsible for this twofold and contradictory success.

Psychological tensions of this kind are not without their risks, as the case of Victor-Blaise revealed during my visit to Brazzaville. Lewis Carroll might have invented this "mad clerk," who combined astonishing truths with the most extraordinary verbal ravings. I saw him for the first time after he had just brought his "message" to the office of a high official who had recently arrived in the capital. Calm but insistent, he tried to justify the importance of his interruption. He claimed that he had been chosen to perform a great work, for on November 11, 1947, a shower of falling stars had formed a halo around his head. He was contemptuous of the orderly who, by all appearances, would never have been honored by such a "coronation." On the corner of an old newspaper he made a pencil sketch of the constellation which had given him the right to call himself "Saint Victor-Blaise." He insisted that he be received, giving his titles as "Emissary of an Oppressed People" and "Official Saint of the Country."

Born outside Brazzaville, he was early subjected to the most varied influences. He received an unorthodox education which he later supplemented with haphazard reading. He was converted to Christianity, retaining from his contact with the Catholics a taste for a powerful church capable of providing a model of social organization, and from his dealings with the Protestants the possibility of drawing freely on the sacred book. All his utopian writings contain references to the Bible. He managed to find employment as a clerk. During this time he lived in the urban center of Bacongo. He took part in the movement of revindication organized by André Matswa. After Matswa's death he became the propagandist for a movement which operated more and more on the religious level. He claimed to be a prophet, announcing his revelations *urbi et orbi*. He patterned his behavior after that of the priests. He renounced all worldly activities, placing responsibility for his existence in the hands of God and his followers.

The local administration regards him less as a "subversive" element than as a visionary. It is nevertheless harassed with letters and proclamations. In one of these, Victor-Blaise compares the "elect" who have understood Matswa's teaching with the "damned" who, he says, "have voted against God and are endangering the country, including the European colonists, those pessimistic capitalists." Surprisingly, and in contradiction to certain of his suggestions, he demands that the role accorded to "enlightened Africans" be limited. Either by their skepticism or by their sincere belief in Christianity, he feels that they compromise the task of religious renovation which he is trying to undertake.

ECHO OF THE WORLD

HALO OF ST. VICTOR BLAISE WAMBA

THE CONSTELLATION OF STARS AT
11 a.m.   11.11.1947

Fig. 55 Motif used by Victor-Blaise on his writing

I tried to meet this prophet, who was frenzied in his ideas but subdued in his behavior and still looked like a petty clerk. Each time he eluded me with an extraordinary talent for escape. In the end, he left only a handwritten manuscript setting forth a kind of political and religious doctrine. The writing is elegant and flowing, the calligraphy that of a clerk trained by the old method. But the words are often irrelevant and create an effect of redundance or sheer nonsense reminiscent of the productions of the surrealist writers. In the midst of coherent arguments there occur unexpected questions like, "What is a mystic body? What is a monitory?" or aphorisms equally unusual and out of context: "For peace, monarchy" or "Communism means common men." At one point, a single word—dualism—provokes a chain of associations that sounds like a schoolboy's game: "These are the elect, the damned, God and the Devil, Good and Evil, comprehension, incomprehension, let's call it prehension, metaphysics and metempsychosis, vision, cognition, monition, premonition, induction, intuition, etc. . . ."

In spite of this surrender to the stream of words, this difficulty in controlling his thoughts, Victor-Blaise's "messages" do have meanings which we cannot overlook. In any case, they are convincing enough for the prophet to be surrounded by believers. The document to which I just referred is a synthesis of the most frequently encountered ideas, expressed in a chaotic French, but with a certain rhetorical talent in the native tongue.

In the first part, Victor-Blaise tries to define patriotism: "passionate love of one's native soil and the determination to defend it against the enemy." He attacks those *"arrivistes"* who lose sight of this ideal in order to "obtain what they regard as a good position." He demands the coming to power of "literate and conscientious specialists." Particularly sensitive to social degradation and inequality, he conceives a political system based on our institutions and demands respect for the Declaration of Human Rights. He conceives a "legislative assembly" governing along with a "sovereign," thus trying to combine the principles of modern democracy with the principles underlying the Kingdom of the Kongo of yesterday and the dissident Congolese church of today. He violently opposes the "oppression that breeds rebellion and disorder:" "What will happen if a few monopolize the means of achieving happiness and leave the others only poverty and despair? . . . We shall have a greater chance of being happy if those around us are happier." With a kind of boomerang effect, he adopts our own morality to accuse us. This is further complicated by nostalgia for an idealized former Congolese society in which social relations did not have the inequalitarian character they present today.

In the second part of the text Victor-Blaise deals primarily with the religious problems created by the propagation of missionary Christianity. He begins with an affirmation: "God is our life." This is followed by an echo calculated to awaken the spirit of sacrifice: "Temporal goods are false; the true good is to be one with God." It is along these lines that the "Watchtower" Congregation has organized a subversive movement in southern and eastern Africa and elaborated myths with an apocalyptic meaning. Victor-Blaise must have seen this literature, which circulated for a time in the African sections of

249

Brazzaville and the nearby villages. He declares that "God will make a new alliance." He writes, "I proclaim, and we proclaim, the truth that was announced by Christ, the true presence." He denounces a certain religion which is "the heart of the coalition against the fatherland." He demands everyone's right to "practice the religion dictated by his conscience." The protest is registered on the religious level, and it is on this level that "autonomy" is desired.

It is apparent that this unusual text, whose style is frequently obscure, nevertheless contains a point of view which parallels popular sentiment. It predicts a new age and the return of a "Messiah" who will establish the reign of justice. Victor-Blaise expresses his confusion and owes his influence solely to the anxiety of a large portion of the Congolese population. He combines, not altogether successfully, the ancient revolt of the prophets with democratic demands that clash with modernism.

It is under the sign of uncertainty that I choose to place the last of these portraits. I met A. at the government information service in Brazzaville. Although our relationship had an official basis, I was immediately charmed by the natural dignity and the intellectual and moral preoccupations of this man of robust appearance who was an enemy of excess in language and gesture. He was born in Gabon and had the stocky build and generous, open face of the men of that country. He belonged to a tribe which had a long history of friendly relations with Europeans; from this he had acquired not only a curiosity about things foreign, but also a sense of the fragility of the small Negro societies that cover a whole section of Gabon. A. received an extensive education in Libreville; he was one of the best students in philosophy at the Grand Séminaire. I was unable to discover his reasons for renouncing the priesthood, but he remained a devout Catholic and exerted a real influence at the mission in Brazzaville. He held an important administrative position which had kept him in the city some fifteen years, and he seemed perfectly adjusted to this life. He had the good fortune to have made a long trip to France from which he had been able to derive maximum advantage—learning all that he could from the discovery of a different world.

These preliminary remarks are necessary, for they show a man devoted to our beliefs, our customs and perhaps even to our interests. Is this not a case of total success, a proof that our methods of colonization do not lead inevitably to personal failure? From our first interview, I was astonished at the excessive attention A. gave to his clothing. This was not a case of an awkward imitation of our style of dress, but of that elegance, as rare as it is understated, which betrays an ingrained habit and a refined taste. In an essay published a dozen years ago and which I came across by chance, A. expressed his views on this subject. He wrote in an admiring tone, "European dress represents the most perfect form of beauty ever achieved by the aesthetic sense of man." A conformity of this kind goes much further; a little further on, the author stated unequivocally, "We advocate the expansion of Western civilization throughout Africa."

This wholehearted conviction conceals fundamental and surprising anxiety. It reveals a profound doubt as to the intrinsic value of African civilizations. Assessing these civilizations in terms of institutions, beliefs, languages and arts, he concludes that they reveal "nothing but potentialities." He asks the colonizer to "create *ex nihilo* the institutions which characterize civilized countries." He is totally intolerant toward traditional societies, which he sees as both crippled and paralyzed by the power of "native fetishism." Such a categorical denial is not without its dangers. He shows a refusal to accepts himself as a Negro, with his individual and irreducible characteristics, his cultural riches to defend. He reveals a fear of being identified with those who symbolize the state of "savagery." He advocates headlong flight toward a foreign civilization.

This does not mean that A. was unaware of his responsibilities and duties. He was the leader of the *Education africaine* movement, with which he tried to win over other Congolese. He threw himself into the project, but without great success.

"We were unable to influence the people we needed to reach. The undertaking remained suspect. We were accused of being under the thumb of the Europeans, of having only our own interests in mind. . . . Some of my opponents objected to my Gabonese origin or my association with the mission. I was discouraged by the mediocrity of the results. And then, politics came along to complicate my job!"

An attempt of this kind is like a factory worker trying to get a promotion by going to night school; it simply brought home the sense of his own isolation. But did he find refuge in this "white" society which so fascinated him? He never advanced beyond its periphery. I still remember those official functions at which he would take care of the African representation, a role which, in spite of his apparent poise, made him feel as if he were playing a kind of game in which he was merely a straw partner.

He had a very keen sense of the problems created by the modernization of Negro societies. But he could not endure the confusion of the present period of transition, which he saw as a provocation to weakness and immorality. In the essay I just mentioned, he questions the religious policy of the colonizer. Because of its lack of unity and because it allows the presence of rival churches, this policy has robbed the Negro of his "rudiment of religion" and has transformed him into a man "without an axis." A. favors an authoritarian intervention in behalf of an exclusive faith. He dreams of a unitarian Christianity capable of making "spiritual brothers" of all men and of establishing a rigorous social system which would free old Africa of the divisions that weaken her and the myths that delude her.

Although it is more rationalized and therefore more accessible to our understanding, is not this hope just as fantastic as that of the prophets who predict the Golden Age?

Today this noble man is disillusioned: he no longer underestimates the obstacles to progress, to the advent of a society both less divided and more modern. He is disabused. I remember the remark he made shortly before my return to France: "I have been too concerned with other people. In vain! Now I must think about myself."

This statment contains a confession of loneliness, an admission of defeat. For A., this loneliness and defeat provide an occasion to enrich his inner life. He is tempted by the peace which attends a piety detached from all worldly cares. He no longer knows which of all the paths that lie open leads most surely to an African future that might restore his lost enthusiasm.

9

Where To?

vvvvvvvvvvvvvvvvvvvvvvvvvvvvvvvvvvvvvvvvvv

DOES not the ambiguity of modern Africa reflect the ambiguity we carry within ourselves? In Africa we see magnified to an extraordinary degree the image of our own uncertainties: this uneasiness before the onslaught of a progress which must destroy before it can improve; this obliteration of outmoded civilizations which accompanies the radical transformation of societies heretofore well protected within their narrow boundaries; this anguished rootlessness of men who, confronted by a landslide of these proportions, no longer know "what saint to worship." In Africa as in Europe, all is called into doubt with equal violence. In one sense their destinies seem interdependent, not because colonization has bound them together, but because both must abandon categories of thought and behavior which are out of tune with the world under construction. Both are too old, in their most "civilized" aspect, even though this oldness has very different origins.

Both civilizations reveal symptoms, illusions and hopes of the same kind. One finds a parallel decline of religions which once supported creative civilizations; the violent uprooting of the individual from a security which could continue only in a sheltered world; the conflict between a social order which resists change and the first stages of a material transformation whose consequences are irrevocable. On different levels, the phenomena are as analogous as the reactions they provoke. The face of conservatism is everywhere the same. The need for a "savior," a "leader," takes an African as well as a European form. And in both cases the most realistic minds are turning to the American and Russian examples for the techniques of manufacturing modern societies. Africa, following in the footsteps of Europe, is beginning to feel this magnetic pull.

Without wishing to force the analogy, there is no denying that modern Africa, which is partly the work of our hands, offers, if you will, the distorted image of our own inadequacies. The frustrations we experience there have the same roots as our difficulties in remodeling the society and civilization in which we live. Certain material successes do not justify our inability to establish in Africa social relations and creative activities that surpass those we have destroyed by our domination. Meanwhile, we have chosen to advertise this feat as a "civilizing mission." It is not enough to have taken Africa out of the age where history had forgotten her, as it were, and brought her to the first decades of our nineteenth century. Many young Negroes are no longer satisfied with such a rate of progress. Soviet Russia has accomplished a swifter and more substantial "enlightenment" in Asia; this, in spite of the example of China, explains her growing influence and the fact that Marxist socialism is regarded as an effective technique for developing "backward" countries.

But the ambiguity we find in Africa is also one made inevitable by our role as colonizers. Our pride and our interests make it impossible for us to evaluate the range of our influence or of its effects objectively. We are reluctant to add up our deceptions and disappointments for fear of providing arguments that could be used against us. We refuse to recognize our weaknesses or the profound changes responsible for the presence, albeit in the last row, of an African delegation at the anticolonialist conference at Bandung. We continue to place the blame for our own deficiencies or miscalculations on the Negro. Since there must be a scapegoat, we say that the pupil has deceived the master and repays him only with ingratitude. The crude trick we have played has backfired. The Negro is using it to ignore the inadequacies of the societies he has built and to accuse our domination of singlehandedly opposing the progress of the African world. Bad faith breeds bad faith, just as racism breeds a racism that is first defensive, then aggressive.

Is it possible to evaluate the complex position of the Negro nations of today objectively? Is there anyone who could do this without incurring the opposition of both sides? In a polemical brochure published during the time he was leading the opposition, Dr. Nkrumah impugned various white witnesses more or less involved in the colonial game. He put them all in the same category. First of all, the administrator and the businessman, authors of the political and economic domination; close behind them the missionary, guilty of bringing a Christianity which was intolerant of the Negro and too tolerant of the colonial system, and the ethnologist, held responsible for a control which, by occasionally conforming to scientific conclusions, became more restrictive. But reactions of the same kind are attributable to whites anxious to maintain a certain form of European presence. To reject conformism and received ideas (received how recently?) immediately brings on the accusation of subversion. Apparently in such a context the mere fact of thinking independently constitutes not only a contribution to the independence of the African peoples but even an "antinational" activity.

To discover Africa is to lose the possibility of remaining neutral or merely receptive, not only because of the contradictory influences I just listed, but also because repeated contact with the Negro civilizations has the force of a challenge which carries one far from one's familiar boundaries. When I arrived in Dakar in 1946 I was motivated primarily by a desire for escape and expatriation. The ethnological experience I was anticipating had the value of a retreat in the original sense of the word: I was looking for a withdrawal which would enable me to recover from a period during which I had scarcely enough time to think; I felt the need for a radically different form of existence. I approached Africa less for her own sake than for mine.

I was soon to realize the naïveté of these expectations. In the course of everyday life Negro societies present a peasant monotony which quickly manages to kill their exoticism. I had not lost my taste for activity or movement to the point where I could easily adjust to these rhythms. The adventures which the Negro peasant agrees to pursue are adventures of the mind, but he pursues them by paths which I was incapable of finding. The passion for seeking revelation through ordeals requiring a total renunciation of mind and body could not replace my passion for precision and lucidity. This distance which was always maintained, and not by design, accentuated my position of professional observer, whereas originally I had entertained the hope of a genuine conversion.

Besides, I found that the forms of civilization to which I had aspired had, at least in some cases, taken on an aspect of anachronism. Was I to study old Africa just when the new Negro generations were setting themselves the task of unlearning a portion of their past? There is always something absurd about being more of a royalist than the king. And in the last analysis, I found that the vital lesson to be learned lay in this effort on the part of Negro peoples to recover their dignity, to become less unequal partners, and to demand a certain universality of their culture. Under the circumstances the ambiguity of my approach can be imagined. Having longed for Africa in order to achieve a certain distance from my own civilization, I found myself confronting those transformations by which Negro societies were becoming "westernized." I struggled to maintain an equal balance between these two tendencies; as it happened, I found that this situation made for a strict objectivity.

During my occasional returns to Africa after absences of several years, I have tried to sum up my impressions without losing myself in details, so as to form a general picture. After Emmanuel Mounier had completed his tour of the Negro world, he was left with the impression of an "awakening." This is saying too little, and saying it in a way that allows us a role which we are losing more and more rapidly. It is much better to speak of a waiting, a passionate desire for change. The Congolese, who for the last thirty years have lived for the moment when the miracle will come to pass, symbolize this attitude. Nobody knows exactly what such a victory can bring, if not an overthrow of the present conditions of existence.

For an ever-increasing number of Negro peasants colonization has made the traditionalist Africa, as well as the expansionist Europe which was built during the nineteenth century, unbearable. By means of an insidious warfare, these two cultures have destroyed one another as ideas. Is not Nganga Emmanuel, founder of one of the Negro churches of the Congo, the most obvious example of this double rejection? Before his strange and delicate chapel he is burning the last "fetishes" attesting to old African loyalties, but he also exhorts his followers to believe in a Messiah who is no longer identified with the white world he condemns. All the prophets who have advocated this absolute rejection of the former gods and of the "imported" God cherish the hope of building a better society out of the wreckage of the two opposing civilizations. Let us not dismiss this as a crude utopia. The most publicized experiment, that of Ghana, conducted by the first African government, illustrates this battle on two fronts in a less abstract way. The Convention People's Party on which the experiment rests has the wholehearted support of the traditional order and its long-range goal is the construction of a socialist state, which shows its independence, at least theoretically, from the Western example.

Some thirty years ago Gertrude Stein wrote of the Negroes: "They did not suffer from being persecuted, they suffered from being nothing." Only the second of these statements is true. After enduring a control which has denied the value of his cultures as well as his capacity for initiative, the Negro is experiencing a powerful need for self-expression. He wants to call himself to our attention and to the attention of a world which has become more curious about his destiny. He is testing the limits of our weaknesses. He is trying to gain recognition as a subject of history after having long been an object of exchange or an instrument in the hands of foreigners.

The initiative of which he has suddenly proved capable demonstrates his desire to compel our attention as well as his determination to construct a society adapted to modern needs. Hence the amazing theoretical passion with which the young Negro intellectuals are fired. I remember the first attempts, which date from early in 1946. Public meetings had been organized in Paris at the Maison des Lettres and elsewhere at the instigation of the essayist Alioune Diop. Jean-Paul Sartre, Albert Camus, Michel Leiris, Léopold Senghor and Jacques Rabemananjara, the Malagasy poet who was imprisoned at the time of the Madagascar Revolt, participated in these discussions. At this point the idea was simply to prove to a cultivated audience the importance of the Negro contribution to world civilization. After praising Negro art, which became the banner in the war against the unimaginativeness of our aesthetic and the dullness of our sensibility, the young champions of Negro culture presented our cultural poverty with literary and dramatic works and new categories of thought. They came to offer us their riches, hoping to start a flow of exchange which would establish relations on a more equal basis. Their fervent proselytism disturbed a conservatism which was comfortably retired into its shell and had little interest in the gifts of men it has assigned itself the mission of educating.

The theory of negritude represents both an exaggeration and a transformation of this generosity. It follows it very closely, but changes its meaning by introducing a militant purpose. This time the Negro no longer asks us to "consider" the values cultivated by the civilizations of which he is the author; he thrusts these values upon us and opposes them to ours. By making them the instruments of his pride, he escapes the damnation to which his race seemed to doom him. In this way he fortifies himself against a sense of hopeless inferiority which has found expression in oral literature since the beginnings of colonization. My research among the Gabonese Fang enabled me to catch an echo of this absolute despair. In one of the modern legends, the Creator is shown distributing the goods of this world: he grants "wealth, authority and knowledge" to the white man and leaves only poverty and the task of "populating the earth" to the Negro.

The first enemy of the glorification of negritude is the acceptance of this inferiority. The glorification of negritude shows that pride and dignity have been recovered in the face of the European claim to "lay down the law." But it does more, and this explains its generosity. It wants to offer a truth which has been forgotten by modern societies, mechanized and encumbered with artifice as they are. The achievements it inspires glorify a harmony with nature that is almost sexual. It is an invitation to find, beyond the walls of our cities and factories, an incentive for being, in Sartre's phrase, "in love with all the forms of life." That Negro spontaneity which I have referred to so often is the everyday expression of this enjoyment. At the same time and by way of contradiction, the Negro writers who invented negritude have presented it as a long cry of affliction. Their songs, which recall the misfortunes of peoples who had been victims until then, are as frightening as a racial explosion. And yet they are merely the testimony of a race that has suffered more than another and has thereby become responsible for a revolt which concerns not only itself but all the oppressed. Sartre has written that negritude might justly be called a passion. It is the literary answer to that messianic and popular hope which inspires Christianized Africa. Both movements are characterized by the same refusal to submit and the same expectation of a new start in existing relations between civilizations and between men. Both embody a revolutionary hope, a hope that the world will change its face. But do they represent anything more than another myth added to the mythic capital in which Negro civilizations are rich? They idealize race or assume an illusory unity of the Negro world. They reject the past as associated with slavery and alienation, but they appeal to it in order to place the rebel Negro opposite the white master. They contain contradictions. They contribute to a kind of conceptual revolution, but do little to define methods of action. They are impaired by that lack of realism which Malek Bennabi accused of invalidating a certain Moslem renaissance.

In recent years young Negro intellectuals have gone beyond these affirmations. No longer content to show the Negro as the creator of undisputed civilizations, they are transforming him into a civilizing hero. They criticize our science and present our scholars as unconscious plagiarists. Cheikh Anta Diop, in a book as congested as the equatorial forest which is becoming the bible of African students, posits the Negro origin of Egypt and therefore of all civilizations. He even goes so far as to transform the "Par-isians" into descendants of the first occupants of the Temple of Isis. And Cheikh Anta Diop's disciples carry his demonstration even further.

Few great human achievements manage to escape their insatiable claim of paternity. Dike Akwa, in an essay entitled, "Itinerary of Negro Thought," demonstrates this in a way that is even more apparent since his approach is schematic. His momentum carries everything with it: Moses and Buddha, both Egyptian Negroes; Christianity, which "seems" to have been based upon a body of beliefs of which the Sudanese Dogon are the modern preservers; Nietzsche, Bergson, Marx and the existentialist philosophers, who have elucidated doctrines implicit in the practical philosophy of the Bantu tribes. Thus the evolution is nearing its completion: after raising Negro culture to the level of the greatest civilizations, the young African essayists are giving it priority and presenting it as bearing all others in its womb. Their scholarship chooses to be a scholarship of racial militancy, just as Soviet science once chose to be a tool in the hands of all proletariats.

But disconcerting as these movements are to the Western mind, we must not dismiss them. They express truths that owe far more to passionate intuition and revelation than they do to objective and careful analysis. While we struggle to arrive at truths one at a time, the Negro hopes to encompass everything at once by means of vital illuminations. Our methods of understanding remain very different. Whatever the ability of the African intellectual to enter into our systems of thought, he cannot erase the imprint of his native culture. He cannot, and he does not wish to, with good reason.

Now, this civilization in which sacred preoccupations continue to dominate or influence all human activities has left few permanent traces of its past vicissitudes. It endures through the medium of tradition, that is, of oral instruction. It rests primarily on speech, and the beliefs it transmits assign a creative power to the "word." These entirely physical conditions under which African thought has expressed and enriched itself have a determining influence. They prevent the accumulation of knowledge; they do not impose that discipline necessitated by writing; they inhibit that critical attention and that possibility of achieving perspective on one's ideas which enable one to escape conformism and refresh one's understanding. The more difficult it was to fix and record such ideas, the more likely they were to resemble one another.

Intellectual habits maintained for a thousand years or more continue to exercise an inevitable influence, even upon those minds most receptive to outside contributions. That this past has a distorting effect is demonstrated by the reactions of African students to Marxism. This doctrine enjoys considerable prestige as an instrument of resistance and a symbol of Soviet success in Asia, but as a social philosophy it is unconsciously altered. It's assimilation cannot proceed without an effect of distortion caused by the orientations of traditional thought. The phenomenon seems to be as common among initiators as it is among initiates. African Marxism will undoubtedly take its own forms, a specific brand of heresy.

These remarks should not be taken as derogatory to the Negro peoples. They are merely the product of a sincere reflection which scorns polemical devices. As a matter of fact, they indicate the vitality of unquestionably Negro ways of living. To open the discussion with the true representatives of the Negro world is to recognize them as partners, which makes it necessary to treat them neither as pupils with lessons to learn nor as listeners too delicate to endure the whole truth. In this sense the ethnologist has a responsibility to express his thought without reservations; he does not set himself up as a hired flatterer or faultfinder.

Most African societies no longer tolerate European domination. They want to regain a creative autonomy. They hope to modernize themselves without losing any of their originality. But it is proving easier to mobilize sentiment for the first than for the second of these tasks. Dr. Nkrumah is proving this today in Ghana, where the difficulties are such that the Negro writer Richard Wright has suggested nothing less than a total "militarization" of the population. Must freedom, then, be no sooner won than lost? With this difference, essential in the eyes of the Africans, that the control is no longer in the hands of foreigners.

The work awaiting the young Negro generations is calculated to discourage those most impatient for constructive action. Everything remains to be done. Nations or confederations with some cohesion must be built, transcending ethnic particularisms. These wholes must be given a material and economic foundation. New civilizations must be guided into being. And working against these crushing obligations, we must enter a double liability: that of colonization, which has always had the force of an evolution prevented from reaching its end. It has encouraged the development of education and economic progress, but it has also limited them. It has favored social change, but it has also restricted it. On all occasions the colonizer had made an effort to remain sole master of the game. Furthermore, the majority of the African states resemble embryos which have been "frozen" before they have had a chance to arrive at the end of their cycle, before they have acquired the form that would make them viable. And precisely because the Africans have had so little control over the various sectors of modern activity, they are ill-prepared for this resumption of responsibilities for which they are fighting or have fought. One might apply to the former Negro elites what the sociologist Franklin Frazier says of the colored bourgeoisie in the United States: by virtue of the impossibility of using their talents, they have often been led to live in an unreal world.

However, Negro societies have another liability for which they are solely responsible. The cultures they have created present unmistakable weaknesses. They are primarily effective on the level of human groups of limited extent and living in relative isolation; on this scale, they excel. They have lacked those techniques for the handling of space which are favorable to unification. They have also lacked the "literary" apparatus indispensable to the administration of large concentrations of people. Important attempts to form states revealed by African

261

history have generally miscarried because of this twofold incapacity; they have not left standing those structures which in Asia, for instance, have survived all vicissitudes.

The failure of unitarian efforts has brought about a reinforcement of "tribalism" and of that extreme diversity which causes the map of Africa to resemble a mosaic of cultural or linguistic zones. It has not favored the fusion of tribes which, in certain parts of the continent, represent very different ages of civilization and perpetuate "gaps" which oppose the construction of a modern nation. The withdrawn isolation of traditional societies also has important consequences. It has enclosed social groups within the limits of a microhistory and has done little to provide a historical preparation favorable to present-day experiences. It has sharpened a sense of clannic or tribal membership which continues to determine the actions of chiefs or leaders of the modern school, whereas the spirit of "public service" should prevail. I do not intend to weigh the pros and cons, but one further observation should be made. If an agreement to fight white domination exists, this unanimity covers a multitude of differences as to the goals to be reached, as well as conflicting interests. Some want an accelerated advance transforming the face of the Negro world; others dream of an Africa which would recover its former countenance. Some are trying to construct Negro nations within which particularisms would be abolished; others plan an ethnic majority that would re-establish inequalities that have been erased. Some foresee a collective action bringing greater prosperity to all; others imagine an assumption of power limited to a bourgeoisie which would reap the rewards with the responsibilities.

The new makers of the African future will overcome the obstacles by resorting to exceptional measures. But the risks attending such measures seem enormous: they are as great as the stakes. In this connection the case of the young nation of Ghana offers a wealth of instruction. Contrary to the bourgeois, cautious nationalism which is anxious to preserve its foreign relations, Dr. Nkrumah has mobilized popular forces. In order to maintain this large following, he has adapted the language of politics by simplifying it and giving it an emotional quality; he has attacked traditional powers, but has had to appeal to the dynamism that tradition still contains: he has undertaken to act like a modern statesman, but he has been obliged to appear in the guise of a sacred personage capable of performing miracles, a Messiah transforming the population of Ghana into a chosen people. It is difficult to foresee what tendency will prevail, should this delicate balance of contradictory influences be broken. Dr. Nkrumah has a profound understanding of African realities, and he knows how to apply it to meet the needs of his policy.

Within the limits of the typical Negro society, the individual is subject to a kind of "directionism" that governs his opinions and his loves, his beliefs and his fears, his leisure time as well as his various activities. He belongs to a social system in which everything is connected. And Nkrumah, ingenious organizer that he is, realized that the political party could not retain in Africa the characteristics it has in the liberal democracies. He has made it into a modern framework enclosing and unifying tribal societies. He has conceived it as a complete social system which operates not only on the level of administrative divisions, but also within specialized groups—from the labor unions and co-operatives to the women's and young people's organizations—and which regulates the details of daily life. The Negro peasant has been prepared for this total commitment which can replace his former clannic allegiance. He can imagine no effective loyalty which would not be exclusive and capable of influencing the whole of his behavior. The whole secret of Kwame Nkrumah's power is in having achieved such a conversion—but at the now apparent risk of a fierce intolerance.

The dangers of such a course are obvious. The African peoples, anxious to regain their autonomy, particularly in the cultural domain, are opposing imperialist Europe with movements characterized by xenophobia and militant racism. These are not weapons which can be wielded with impunity: they often do more damage than was originally intended. At the same time the reconstruction of Negro societies requires a "totalitarian"-type intervention without which it can only be illusory. What will be the outcome for the Negroes themselves if these two forces are combined in a permanent way?

Africa is beginning to move forward. Where is she bound? She sometimes presents the spectacle of a *renaissance manquée,* and yet she also provides an example of that glorious nobility which always characterizes men who are dedicating themselves to new beginnings. One is endlessly tempted to ask questions which the land continues to evade. Her dark face remains mysterious: she betrays almost as few clues to the future as a Fang burial statue offers to the mysteries of the beyond.

10
Landmarks

THESE Negro societies which in our intellectual smugness we assumed to be outside of time have, then, been catapulted into the present. All at once the news of the day has been Africanized. It arouses our passions; when in 1958 Guinea stated its socialist choice nationally and its active neutralism internationally, it aroused the fervor of some and the fury of others, and it disturbs or discourages us when it enumerates its uncertainties in these early days of 1962. Everybody forms his own image of Africa in accordance with his preferences or his illusions rather than the realities.

Africa is believed to be available and there for the taking, or bungled from the start, or an eternal mystery. And logically enough, she is besieged by seducers whose arms are loaded with marvelous technical gifts, redressers of wrongs, and interpreters of civilization of all kinds. Counselors too, closely resembling those officious advisers who, according to the popular saying, "run no risks."

But Africa today is also the dark face of our common anxiety. The old Belgian Congo collapsed suddenly with the force of an explosion in the summer of 1960. Violence pitched its camps there. International competitions took over through intermediary persons and "provinces." Now, the unexpected is the rule. In Leopoldville, the arms and technicians of several nations maintain order, run the social and economic machine, and support a precarious government. On the outskirts of the city, the Congolese have put up makeshift encampments and are rediscovering the security of the old economy of subsistence; a few miles away, Lovanium University looms with its new buildings and scientific installations protected by an international police force and presents the image of a future city. When I spent a few weeks in the Congo in the spring of 1961, I heard a significant anecdote. A young Mukongo turned to one of the Tunisian soldiers who was on sentry duty near the university and had the following exchange: "Is your country independent?" "Yes." "Since when?" "Five years ago." "Only five years and you're white already?" Thus the whole measure of disillusionment and anxiety in the face of the conversion to be accomplished is expressed by the symbolism of color.

However, this is only the first act of a drama the rest of which will be played on other scenes. In Angola a popular insurrection is contesting the oldest European implantation in Africa, the one Diogo Cão started when he and his men reached the mouth of the Zaire-Congo in 1482. Despite the rivalries of nationalist leaders and the extent of tribal particularism, this constant pressure has put Portugal in a state of alarm; the passion for freedom smolders under the ashes of plantations destroyed and villages burned. Nearby, the Rhodesias, especially the Rhodesia rich in copper, are experiencing the same violence. A twofold antagonism is growing there, one racial and one cultural. In massive demonstrations in 1961, some of the Bantus gave up their European clothing, their glasses and their watches as "symbols of oppression." They expressed their determination to destroy the industries if they presented an obstacle to their nationalism. They have recovered the passion of those Negro prophets who for decades have foretold the Apocalypse and the reversal of roles which would put an end to their dependence. From the Congo to the tip of the Cape a similar agitation is unsettling societies which might euphemistically be called multiracial. Ironically enough, the first Nobel Prize awarded to an African was in the name of peace: Albert Luthuli, leader of the African National Congress, often harassed by South African authorities, received this honor which was a tribute to his national fervor as well as his nonviolent policies.

On this side of the Congo, West Africa possesses "laboratories" of decolonization where the changes are rapid and the experiments diversified. For the traveler who reaches the Negro world by way of its western gates, modernism seems to have banished folklore. Dakar is still a port, but it has become a capital that has overreached itself: its administrative buildings, its university seem to be bursting out of their clothes; its new squares and avenues, its peripheral expansions create the impression of a city hoping for a destiny appropriate to its size. And the people are working to this end, for no African country is richer in political groups—in or out of power—ideas, or initiative. The workshops of the new Negro humanism are close to those where a certain socialism is being constructed; where my friend Cheikh Kane is pursuing his "ambiguous adventure," and assuming his technical responsibilities in spite of his fear that a mechanized chaos may replace the architecture of true civilization.

From Dakar to Conakry there is the distance of contrast; from Conakry to Abidjan, the disparity between poverty and bourgeois comfort. This was already my impression when I flew from one to the other of these cities in 1958. Their separate evolutions have scarcely altered the order of things. Abidjan is subject to competing influences, as its Palace testifies. The modernist passion expressed by the work of its architects is combined with a passion for business: the day of the triumphant bourgeoisie is at hand. In little islands of progress where new businesses and buildings are springing up and roads have been "refurbished," a new country is slowly taking shape; but in the intervening spaces, the old Ivory Coast survives everything by pricing its cacao and coffee or dreaming of paying transactions. I had been certain of this while preparing a scientific mission in the Banaflé region of Gouro country. The planter and the soldier, the administrator and the schoolteacher are agents of transformation, but the villages still harbor their dreaded "elders" and maskers who defend the social order or vested interests. It is the same everywhere: the new class is seeking rules for its cohabitation with the notables of the old school. It has the advantage of controlling political life and business, but it has not always succeeded in becoming a part of the real country. It is trying to make modern techniques available to a national expansion which is the condition of its own expansion. It is learning the profession of the leading classes, occasionally inviting professors of political science and economics to open temporary schools for ministers, deputies and high officials. A challenge has been made and taken seri-

266

ously, the challenge of showing that economic liberalism can be Africanized and succeed. But on the eastern frontier Ghana is preparing an opposite demonstration.

As I worked my way south along the Gulf of Guinea, the ambiguities became more marked. I made a brief stopover at Douala in the spring of 1961, a time when the city was oppressed by heat and humidity. The climate seemed heavier than it had at the time of my first visits, and the people more despondent, as if the leadenness of the sky had settled upon them once and for all. The revolts in southern Cameroon had almost ceased, but a transformation of the violence into constructive enthusiasm had not yet taken effect. It was a time of rest and waiting, although two salutary changes had occurred: a surge of unitarian passion with the reunification with a British part of Cameroon, and the promotion of qualified persons with the entry into government of young ministers with university educations. Intuition rather than judgment on my part, and possibly distorted by my impatience to reach Brazzaville, which I had not revisited for ten years.

I immediately felt at home in the Congolese capital—I recognized it. A new avenue had been opened at the opportune moment to symbolize the path of independence, and there were new buildings in the business and administrative district, but the main outlines had not changed. The flags of the Congo and of the embassies, the transformation of the old departments into ministries, a parliament located out of the main stream: these were physical signs which immediately revealed the new political regime. In a way, Brazzaville is evening its score with Leopoldville: after a few upheavals, order now reigns. The people of the north and the people of the south are no longer mortal enemies. The prophets no longer mobilize spirits and sorcery against those in power; they have city churches or cathedrals, as in the neighborhood of Boko. Only a few thousand diehards continue to cherish a dream which is shattered by the activities of the police, only to re-form immediately and sustain the old messianic hope. But the danger is that order may become the sole aim, and a kind of substitute religion. Insidious "counselors," who got their start in Europe and when times were bad, would be only too willing to encourage this conversion, forgetting the risk of explosion, which would be an answer to the one in the other Congo—as the majority of the foreigners held here by their possessions or their jobs are perfectly aware.

An ever-growing body of young people exerts an increasing pressure, not to mention those whom their education has estranged and who choose exile once their studies have been completed. In the course of a series of lectures I gave in sociology and economics, these young people questioned me, revealing their pride and patriotism as well as their anxieties. They hoped that achievement on a national scale would assure them of work and prevent them from joining the camp of unemployment and despair. They regarded the industrial project of Kwilu as an undertaking in the public welfare; they had transformed it into a positive legend. A minority, the seeds of a possible opposition, had passionately followed the adventure of Lumumba, been outraged by his assassination, and taken to wearing beards in the style of "Patrice" as a mark of loyalty. The young women in their turn had taken the initiative and wanted to contribute to the construction of a new Congo; with only a few members, they may activate a feminine population which has been a potentially rebellious force for centuries.

For the moment independence is still recent and the disorders of the country "across the way" inspire caution. The balance holds. It would be dangerous, however, if enjoyment of the fruits and wines of power were to cause the enormous and urgent tasks to be forgotten. The ruling class of accelerated bourgeois training will hold its own only if it can acquire the pioneering qualities of the nineteenth-century European bourgeoisie. Images of the "good old days" are suggested by the homes of the elite: the same furniture, the same decor, and the same fabrics or embroidery. And in this setting from out of our past, good manners preserve an unnatural quality. The affectation disappears, however, as soon as confidence permits freedom of expression and strips everyone of his assumed role. I treasure the memory of friendly evenings which I owe to the hospitality of my Congolese friends, evenings when my hosts did not censor their spontaneous irony and humor, and people and events of the day were subjected to devastating parodies. Privileged moments like these enabled me to put things back in their true perspective.

A swift foray into the surrounding countryside is sufficient to reveal the gap that has been established between the capital and villages whose peasants are still bound to their centuries-old tasks and miseries. As yet independence, far from changing this state of affairs, has made it less tolerable by Africanizing the masters. The marked inequality seemed a *donnée* of the colonial situation and the Europeans were accepted as the privileged beneficiaries of the techniques they had introduced and the businesses they had founded. But such inequality becomes totally unacceptable the moment it is the fellow Congolese who control the life of the nation. In a study trip to the Congo in May 1961, the agronomist René Dumont recorded the complaints of the peasants, and observed their disillusionment with the leaders living in Brazzaville. "Independence is for them, not for us," he was told, and indeed, there is reason to doubt the value of a freedom which does not alter the material conditions of existence. The problem is not restricted to the Congo. In most of the countries of Africa, the minorities now running the administration—and the civil servants or employees who constitute its clientele even in the political parties—are emerging as an upper, and in certain respects an isolated, class. The disappearance of the colonizer has destroyed the barrier which prevented wide differentiation in standards of living. The gap between the leader and chief beneficiary of progress and the ordinary man has widened to the point where it has crossed the threshold of security and a rupture is inevitable. The situation is aggravated by the fact that tensions between generations are being expressed and the impatience of young "radicals" graduated from foreign universities is mounting. The debate between the governments and the students has begun, from the eastern Sudan to Senegal, Guinea and beyond. In the eyes of the authorities the treason of the scholars seeems permanent.

These candid observations based on recent impressions and memories are not the result of disappointed love. They are offered simply to suggest the force of the movement that is inspiring Negro societies everywhere, and the immensity of the job to be done. Torn from her history in the late nineteenth century and forced to remain on the fringes of the great technical revolutions, Africa is recovering her autonomy at a time when all nations are undergoing upheavals. She must find the laws of her reconstruction, stabilize herself in an unstable world, and expand her role in international society. What symbols and landmarks will help us to interpret the work that has begun and gain some perspective on the events that are monopolizing our attention unduly?

A free Africa is looking to her distant past for the roots of her modern personality and sometimes for suggestions for her future boundaries—except where, contrariwise, she is learning to

269

know her past better the better to condemn it. It is a question of political strategy, and the role of strategy becomes greater in proportion as ignorance remains more widespread.

An African historical atlas published within the last few years amazes us with the white spaces on its maps, which resemble those that provided our geography of the continent before the nineteenth century, and with its lack of accurate information. A new period of exploration has begun whose goal this time is the discovery of a history most of which has been lost because it has left few traces. This backward march through time is passionately desired by Negro elites, for it permits the rediscovery of an authentic and free Africa, and provides a noncolonial background for modern initiatives. Its lesson concerns us too, for it reveals the existence of powerful and dynamic empires which originated works of civilization in the full sense of the word; and of political structures, often precarious ones, which underwent various vicissitudes, but some of which have survived from very remote beginnings to our time: for example, the Mossi Empire in Upper Volta, whose present boundaries were established in the thirteenth century. However, many of the old African states had disappeared or shrunk to the size of small royal provinces by the time the powers were established on the continent.

What are the modern consequences of this old order of things? The vanished kingdoms and empires have all left their marks. Sometimes surviving institutions still cover vast regions; a political and religious organization inherited from the Mali Empire, founded in the twelfth century, continues to absorb large sections of West African peasantry. More often than not there exists a nostalgia for the past and a desire for a renaissance. In the western Sudan certain guardians of the tradition of the Keita have tried to revive Mali, not within the confines of parliaments, but within religious centers and through the use of appropriate rituals. In the case of still-existing states, the situation is, however, reversed. It is no longer possible to idealize the past, and the problems resulting from modern developments are unavoidable: they have to do with the democratic pressure brought to bear on great sovereigns like the Mwami of Ruanda, and more modest chiefs like those in Bamileke country in Cameroon, who have been confronted by periodic peasant uprisings. Nevertheless, most of these kingdoms remain centers of force which future political boundaries cannot ignore; unlike the Peul of Fouta Djallon in Guinea, their traditional aristocracies will not all accept the institutional death inflicted by the first free governments in the interests of national unity.

Everywhere, precolonial history and its heroes provide symbols and themes calculated to liberate the emotions. Cheikh Anta Diop, the Senegalese scholar and essayist whom I have already mentioned, systematically contributed to the cultural revival by placing the African Negro at the source of the great civilizations which appeared in Egypt and those descended from them. In this way he founded a militant doctrine and predicted the unity of the Negro people. More recently, political leaders have referred with increasing frequency to glorious bygone eras. President Sékou Touré once compared the "harmonious civilization" of the Ghana Empire with the weaknesses of Capetian France. History is becoming an instrument of national glorification; but when it raises obstacles it must be erased. In a statement to the German journal *Der Spiegel* in 1959, Sékou Touré considered the immense political possibilities presented by an Africa without a past. He contrasted this freedom, so inspiring to the statesman, with the problem of reconstruction that Europe is experiencing because of the national bonds she has inherited from a long history. All the same, Negro Africa is far from being a blank page.

The events of the past and the varying evolutions may be deciphered from maps showing the distribution of ethnic groups, social types and cultures. More than India, the Negro world is a world of diversity. It has not been poured into the mold of permanent states; it has not been sufficiently bound by the cement of universalist religions; and colonial policies have served to accentuate the divisions and contrasts.

This situation is clearly apparent. A population map of West Africa, incorporating the former French Equatorial Africa and the Congo, shows more than 1,500 ethnic groups aware of their individuality and jealous of their identity. There are over six hundred African languages, exclusive of variants which often occur over short distances. And although the social systems present affinities, they are still numerous. Particularisms and the difficulties of intellectual communication impede unitarian efforts. The phenomenon is intensified by the fact that in many regions communication and commerce still operate at a slow pace.

Let us consider the example of Guinea, whose desire for national construction has been manifested by the enthusiasm of

271

her political leaders. Without indulging in a kind of smug and facile microsociology, it is easy to find two great pairs of conflicting ethnic groups. First there are the coastal populations and the Peul who drove them back and spread Islam during the eighteenth century; incidents at Conakry up to the eve of Independence attested to the old antagonism. On the other hand there is a partial opposition between Sudanese Guinea, historic seat of conquerors, the latest of whom is Samory Touré, glorious ancestor of the president, and forest Guinea which long endured the pressure of the peoples of the savanna. This explains some of the obstacles encountered by the Democratic Party of Guinea at the time of its introduction to this marginal region. The structure of the single party and the "mobilization of the people" proclaimed in October 1958 are becoming the instruments of a unifying action which is necessary to the consolidation of the nation and to economic progress.

This is not an unfair example. In several countries along the Gulf of Guinea, an antagonism between coastal populations who have long enjoyed a privileged economic position because they controlled the "banks" and the populations of the interior may still be observed. The vast area of Nigeria has known antagonisms which are all the more striking because of their scale: Ibo in the east and Yoruba in the west, sultanates to the north of these two great southern groups, "pagan" peoples confronting the Moslem groups which have surrounded them. Modern political life and the variations of Nigerian nationalism are conditioned by this network of relations between different ethnic groups and cultures.

It is only fair to point out that trade has played a decisive role in sharpening rivalry. This has been apparent in the Congolese zone. People of the Upper and Lower Congo have, in addition to their cultural differences, opposed one another as beneficiaries and victims of trade, and as competitors for control of the trading centers. This rivalry has long done more to influence the political activity of the Republic of the Congo than differences of doctrine or method, as the terrible Brazzaville riots of early 1959 so tragically proved.

These aspects of the African political problem should be neither overestimated nor underestimated. Large cultural wholes do exist which present a comparative homogeneity: West Africa is one world, if one refers to archaic contexts; the region corresponding to the Congo basin carries societies constructed on the same "model;" and East Africa, from the upper Nile to the

Zambezi, coincides with a single great zone of civilization. Similarly, it would be unfair to deny the kinship existing between religious systems, aesthetic conceptions and styles of behavior. But because of the physical and intellectual isolation, these common traits are seldom recognized as such by those who share them—not to mention the profound changes which have torn the common fabric in the last fifty years.

On the other hand, it is undeniable that ancient rivalries whose memory is preserved by oral tradition and by isolation within tribal boundaries explain the vigor of particularism. The nation and the abstract notion of citizenship do not always succeed in overcoming the influence of those "fraternities" which give the clans their cohesion but set tribes and ethnic groups against one another. Also certain traditional political units sometimes try to preserve their autonomy by appealing to the old colonizer. In Ivory Coast, the sovereign of the little kingdom of Sanwi, which has been reduced to less than 50,000 subjects, refuses to let his country be swallowed up by a unified state; he has demanded the establishment of direct ties between Paris and his capital. The problem is more serious in Ghana, where the Ashanti, who also control a large sector of the national economy with their cacao groves, are opposed to the integration of their country.

These lines of force which history has drawn have as much effect on efforts to draw up a new political map of Africa as the boundaries carved by the colonials and the recent reconciliations of related groups. One thing at least is certain: the national movements have a form which is immeasurably more distinct than the nations they are calling into existence. For that matter, the leaders have exalted freedom and independence, unitarian tendencies, and the need for African dignity and individuality far more than they have national values, which are materializing with difficulty in the case of territories whose contours remain provisional. The recovery of freedom in a given country is presented first of all as a good shared by all African peoples. This process of expansion is revealing; it shows the difficulty of defining an action occurring within the context of an unmistakable nation which is homogeneous with respect to economy, culture and language. In Negro Africa, the nations are in the process of formation and are still vulnerable in their current form. This does not mean that the movement should not be accelerated; but this—and not merely competing ambitions—explains why certain African leaders are tempted to curtail the national period and proceed immediately to the construction of regional wholes.

It is in West Africa that political developments have advanced the furthest, but the processes of transformation have not reached their limit. The new alliances remain unstable and competitive. The Mali Federation has collapsed. Their unions of a technical nature—such as the one resulting from the ties that have been formed between certain African states and Madagascar—seem less fragile than the reconciliations based on common ideology alone. One cannot underestimate the necessary stages: how is one to pass directly from traditional political units (often organized on the tribal or clannic level) to comprehensive federations without consolidating those intermediary units which are the nations? The acceleration of history produces telescoped effects by ignoring logical sequence.

For the outside world, which has long depended for its information on exotic chronicles and preconceived notions, Africa still belongs to the realm of mystery or legendary geography. Even now that it has invaded our daily lives its map is still unfamiliar and its civilizations are only beginning to find their way into school textbooks, almost behind our backs. Its well-known political leaders have, however, joined the ranks of those personalities who are harassed by cameras and magazines. It is through them that the Negro countries retain the attention of the outside world, and it is often because of them that we are able to understand movements involving peoples who are at the same time very old and very young.

During an official reception at the University of Dakar, Léopold Senghor told me, "I could give a course on your writings in which I would criticize your ideas." He could play the part of professor and theoretician as well as the role of the courteous host who represented Senegalese hospitality at its best. I saw him again shortly afterwards at his official reception by UNESCO in Paris. There he seemed to have found a milieu favorable to the revival of an old and challenging idea: "A civilization must be culture, that is, the transcendence of determinism."

This is a man who is not afraid to address the militant members of his party by speaking, according to his critics, "over their heads." His thought provides a frame of reference for the student of the ideologies and political doctrines which inspire modern Africa. It states a socialistic demand, but Marx's con-

274

tribution has been subordinated to religious values and "Africanized." It glorifies the colonial revolutions, which are primarily national, rather than the historic mission of the proletariat; it also places "national destiny" before the "destiny of the proletariat." And if internationalism is evoked, it is the kind that must unite underprivileged peoples rather than the kind that binds together dispossessed classes. These indications will suggest the distance separating the socialisms practiced today and the "models" on which they are based; radical critics claim that the African brand of socialism contains the seeds of its own destruction. And yet was it not one of the most brilliant left-wing opponents of the Senegalese political leader Abdoulaye Ly who praised the "indomitable dialectical abilities" of peoples long held in dependency? In practice, dialectics is used to preserve African values by transcending them, to avoid violence by jumping from traditional "communitarianism" straight to socialism. This practice may be unorthodox, but it has motives which cannot be ignored.

Above all else Africa is afraid of finding herself once again in the position of the schoolchild. She does not reject the lessons of the outside world, but she proposes to assimilate them in her own way and to draw from them her own conclusions. After a long period of compulsory passivity she is not resigned to the voluntary kind. She has suffered more profoundly from her political and cultural alienation than she has from her economic alienation. She is just as impatient to regain her creative vigor as she is to develop her productive capacity. Léopold Senghor put it bluntly and his words are worth attention: "What all these distinguished minds want, whether they are Westerners or Easterners, is to superimpose a European civilization upon us, to impregnate us with it in the name of universality. Hence exotic peoples such as ourselves would be eternally condemned to be not the producers but the consumers of civilization." The needs are great, but the realities have an inertia which necessitates an inexhaustible energy and devotion. There is the weight of traditional interests, whose preservation is assured by religious leaders and witch doctors, those effective critics or advocates according to the circumstances. There is the weight of interests recently acquired, to the detriment of the common good, whose corruption reinforces their power by hierarchically multiplying complicities. The conflict between those who are incorruptible and the greedy privileged members of the new class—those individuals whom Frantz Fanon

275

inveighed against before his death—has not spared Senegal. The same phenomenon obtains in various forms in all the countries which are in the throes of decolonization and development.

Silly so, Silly solé—The Elephant is here, the Elephant has arrived: the tireless throng repeats this song of welcome in honor of Sékou Touré at a gathering which for the women of Conakry is as much an act of love as it is a political demonstration. The Guinean president is a tribune who knows how to speak of poverty, labor and the dignity of the people in phrases that kindle collective emotions. He operates by means of the direct attack. He mistrusts words and ideas which do not have "the same meaning in Africa that they have elsewhere," although he himself manipulates them brilliantly. He has the vocabulary of the militant Marxist and a knowledge of revolutionary writings, but he refuses to "confine himself within the limits of an abstract philosophy." Indeed, the real Guinea of today—where capitalistic enterprises and socialistic efforts coexist and where the techniques of the East and the West compete—is just as syncretic in structure as the political thinking of its leaders.

The political doctrine of Guinea is hidden behind a realism characterized by both daring and timidity. It professes to be revolutionary, provided the principles that govern it are not imported ones. It rejects materialism because of the influence religion has had on all African societies. It rejects the class struggle, replacing it with the dynamism of a people newly aware of the tasks bequeathed by independence. It also glorifies the "communitarian" values of the traditional peasantries, the duty of rebuilding the African personality, and the obligation of solidarity with respect to all the Africas. This is the expression of a loyalty which Sékou Touré suggests by his official costume, the ample and impressive *boubou* and sandals. The symbolism becomes even more apparent when one remarks that outside of Guinea the Africanization of the ceremony is combined with radical choices—Modibo Keita in Mali and Kwame Nkrumah in Ghana. The Negro world readily translates its doctrines into the language of symbols; what I have been saying recalls this fundamental need.

The Guinean president is not a man to varnish the truth. As soon as the country had won its independence, he announced: "We will be the first African government to establish compulsory labor." And he insisted on presenting this mobilization of effort as a requirement of "honor," rather than the difficult condition of the improved living standards to come. To partisans who suffer from a guilt complex because of the "total democracy" established by the party, he replies, "We are and we must be the instruments of dictatorship." Here again, the justification is not of the common variety: "Not wanting to be neutral in the choice between freedom and slavery, between truth and falsehood, we reject any system of balances whose function is to find a middle term between that which serves the people and that which disserves them." Arbitration is excluded in favor of passionate commitment. The people are the crowning argument: the party is becoming the depository of their thought and the guardian of their will. This party which is everywhere present—in the cities and in the villages, in the ministries and in the offices, within the labor unions and youth movements and women's organizations—constitutes the sole national mainstay. It is the support of the modern society which is emerging from the multitude of traditional societies. It is trying to enforce unanimity and to preserve the universal momentum that was recovered with freedom. But this effort, which expresses the highest ambition for Guinea, is encountering obstacles, for divergent interests continue to exist, ambitions conspire against one another, and the transformation of the land itself carries its own contradictions. Episodic plots demonstrate the vigor of opposing factions, and are followed by incredible trials in which those who refuse to speak are consumed by the flames of revolutionary purity. These trials have their ritual element and are a transposition of those solemn practices which permitted the old communities to defend their customs and to restore order.

Sékou Touré and the party are fighting on all fronts, to employ an image which respects the letter of their language and their intentions. There is an impatience to be doing which has an unquestionable nobility as long as it weighs the risks. The first hurriedly elaborated plan for economic development which, by an optimistic arithmetic, converted the free labor into excessive capital and overestimated outside generosity, has been put to severe tests. Conversion of the currency alone, a symbolic art rather than an expedient economic decision, has led to monetary insularity. The state organization for internal commerce, which incorporated a multitude of intermediaries, did not prevent the scarcity of products and the secrecy of transactions. These mistakes have been cited frequently, and

277

with a varying degree of critical sincerity. They matter little as long as total devotion remains the first law of political ethics and austerity appears to be the common rule. In 1959 the hand of justice was cruel: the public execution in Conakry and Kindia of men convicted for theft had an exemplary value. But civic puritanism softens with time, and it is discovered that state capitalism may give some of the men who manage it a taste for private capital. From then on, doubt begins to spread. The difference between the standard of living of the leader and that of the ordinary citizen suddenly seems intolerable or challenging. And the young students, turned dissenters, demand "fewer foreign cars and more rice."

A legend of Sudanian Guinea declares that from the line of Samory Touré there will spring a new Mahdi, fighting with faith and justice, who will be victorious in his fortieth year. In 1962 Sékou Touré is forty. Is this the moment for the rendez-vous which destiny has arranged with a man who was described as a "conventional Marxist"? This man carries in him the passion of Africa. The force of his eloquence and his martial lyricism have succeeded in hiding his underlying motives. His aims—a socialism adjusted to the African personality, a certain unity of the Africas, an uncontestable and uncontested freedom and dignity for the Negro world—are, however, those also recognized and desired by several of the most respected African leaders.

The one who seems most dissident, President Houphouet-Boigny, is less remote than appearances would suggest. The comparative wealth of Ivory Coast accords him the leisure to experiment with the free-enterprise system, the opportunity to place state capitalism and private capitalism in competition. He has never concealed his choice behind a screen of fine phrases, since he is convinced that they never do much good. He has stated baldly and unambiguously, "In the light of our realities, the organization of the country must be accomplished by means of evolution rather than revolution." Here the difference becomes apparent: socialism is no longer the moving force of enthusiasm and material progress. The African way of economic liberalism is not, however, incompatible with contradictions. During the year 1961 certain radical measures were taken and the party tightened its control. Enlightened paternalism governs political life, and the model of the enterprising "planter" might well symbolize the present economic orientation.

I think it is necessary to have traveled in Baulé country to understand this way of doing things. These people know authority and admire thrift. Small fortunes are hidden in buried pots called "canaries": when the village of Kétiokro burned in 1953, more than seven million African francs were extracted from the rubble. And the inhabitants of Yamoussoukro contributed financially to the modernization of their "city," with Félix Houphouet-Boigny making up the difference, for this is the place where he has his roots, where he retires from his political responsibilities. When I passed through, enthusiastic guides showed me his house, his hotel and his cacao groves, which extended for miles. The president is seen in the role of a traditional chief whose authority is based on blood and ancestry and whose plantations guarantee power and generosity. The old African school of politics formed his style and explains his refusal to overturn the order of things suddenly; revolution was abandoned as soon as independence was in sight.

Félix Houphouet-Boigny joins his former partners when it comes to the rehabilitation of the Negro continent. He employs their vocabulary even while he is denouncing the antagonisms based on national experiments whose results are not yet decisive. He maintains that African freedom will remain conditional as long as a single tribe is still under foreign domination. He recognizes the common goal: the acceptance of a progressively unified Africa on an equal basis with other nations. But out of caution he approaches this goal gradually.

It was not my original intention to present a gallery of portraits, but to suggest the style of the architects of modern Africa. Everywhere that independence is freeing initiative, in the East as in the West, the same disagreements are found. They arise from similar tasks and are expressed by the same imported formulas: unity, socialism, neutralism and so forth. Everywhere too we find the same desire for loyalty to what remains of the African heritage. The oldest of the nationalist chiefs, Jomo Kenyatta, the "flaming spear of Kenya," has carried his determination to retain the forces, ideas and symbols of peasant Africa like an obsession. An old and still current anxiety is how to prevent the modernization of the Negro world from being purchased at the cost of a monstrous betrayal. It is with his own riches that the African Negro will rebuild his civilizations and make his contribution to humanism, as we see from the Mali flag bearing in its center the ideograph of Man.

Index

DISCUS BOOKS
DISTINGUISHED NON-FICTION